SEMEIA 88

A VANISHING MEDIATOR?
THE PRESENCE/ABSENCE OF THE BIBLE IN POSTCOLONIALISM

Guest Editor: Roland Boer
Board Editor: Gerald West

© 2001
by the Society of Biblical Literature

Published Quarterly by
THE SOCIETY OF BIBLICAL LITERATURE
825 Houston Mill Road
Atlanta, GA 30329

Printed in the United States of America
on acid-free paper

Contents

Contributors to This Issue v

Introduction: Vanishing Mediators?
    Roland Boer 1

ESSAYS

1. The Book Eaters: Textuality, Modernity, and the London Missionary Society
    Anna Johnston 13

2. Before the Second Reformation: Nineteenth-Century Aboriginal Meditations of the Bible in Van Diemen's Land
    Penny van Toorn 41

3. Explorer Hermeneutics, or Fat Damper and Sweetened Tea
    Roland Boer 71

4. Surveying the Promised Land: Elizabeth Jolley's *Milk and Honey*
    Dorothy Jones 97

5. Which Good Book? Missionary Education and Conversion in Colonial India
    Sanjay Seth 113

6. A Pisgah Sight of Ireland: Religious Embodiment and Colonialism in *Ulysses*
    Amardeep Singh 129

7. In Praise of Polytheism
    John Docker 149

8. The Word Set in Blood and Stone: The Book of God from Tribes to Kingdoms and Nations
    Paul James 173

RESPONSE

9. A Real Presence, Subsumed by Others: The Bible in
   Colonial and Postcolonial Contexts
     Gerald West 199

CONTRIBUTORS TO THIS ISSUE

Roland Boer
Centre for Studies in Religion and
    Theology
Box 11a, Monash University
Victoria 3800
Australia
Roland.Boer@arts.monash.edu.au

John Docker
Humanities Research Centre
Australian National University
Canberra ACT 0200
Australia
John.Docker@anu.edu.au

Paul James
Department of Politics
School of Politics and Social Inquiry
Box 11a, Monash University
Victoria 3800
Australia
Paul.James@arts.monash.edu.au

Anna Johnston
School of English, Journalism, and
    European Languages
University of Tasmania
GPO 252-82
Hobart, Tasmania 7001
Australia
Anna.Johnston@utas.edu.au

Dorothy Jones
English Studies Program
Faculty of Arts
University of Wollongong
Wollongong NSW 2522
Australia
Dorothy_Jones@uow.edu.au

Sanjay Seth
Department of Politics
School of Social Sciences
La Trobe University
Victoria 3086
Australia
S.Seth@latrobe.edu.au

Amardeep Singh
Department of English
Drown Hall, Lehigh University
35 Sayre Drive
Bethlehem, PA 18015-3116
USA
as1@duke.edu

Penny van Toorn
Department of English
A20, University of Sydney
NSW 2006
penny.van.toorn@english.usyd.edu.au

Gerald West
School of Theology
University of Natal
Private Bag X01
Scottsville 3209
South Africa
west@nu.ac.za

Introduction: Vanishing Mediators?

Roland Boer
Monash University

The promise of postcolonial theory seems to operate in a direct ratio to its limits. For it is remarkable how "postcolonial theory," the breakthrough enabled by Gayatri Spivak, Edward Said, and Homi Bhabha, has spread through the disciplines like a bush fire—philosophy, literary criticism, cultural studies, anthropology, political science, history, geography, and … biblical studies. To many, postcolonial criticism offered a method that is unavoidably political, especially a politics that is progressive. It also offered a way for certain voices, particularly those in the former colonial spaces, to throw off the gags and untie the cords that restrained our voices and writing hands. In other words, there was the possibility that the work of those inside the major metropolitan centres, focused on the Atlantic, would not set the agenda any longer for writing and criticism.

All of this rode on the back of postmodernism itself: the suspicion of master narratives (based on a spurious connection between theoretical totalization and political totalitarianism); the fragmented subject; the loss of historical depth and of affect; the break between signifier and signified, or rather the realization that signifiers merely referred to other signifiers, and so on. In particular, the end of master narratives seemed to both enable and recognize a host of suppressed voices in political theory and action, such as those of gays and lesbians, indigenous people and colonial subjects. It became possible not only to be heard but also to speak, and to look back over colonial periods and find continuous acts of speech, writing, and political opposition.

This still seems to me to be the major promise of postcolonial theory. However, it also produces the first of a series of vanishing mediators: the critics themselves. But let me bring Max Weber in for a moment, for in the pre-life of this volume, "vanishing mediator" has been understood in a number of ways. Weber's notion, especially in *The Protestant Ethic and the Spirit of Capitalism*, appears in the well-known discussion of religion, specifically Calvinist Protestantism, in the emergence of capitalism. For Weber, a crucial factor in the possibility of capitalism's emergence lay in the ideological framework, or theology, of Calvinism—doctrines such as the calling to a religious life, predestination, election, the dependence on God's grace by human beings who were utterly incapable of any good themselves yet were constantly impelled to good works in response to that grace, the discipline of Protestant asceticism and delayed satisfaction. Weber's argument is that with Luther the first step in the breakdown of medieval monasticism began: the end of a separate category for religious men and women meant that everyone had to become monks or nuns. Without institutions to pursue other-worldly ends, there takes place a thoroughgoing Christianization of everyday life. But this is precisely Calvin's contribution: in separating an unknowable other world beyond human experience from human life, this world can only be a place of testing and preparation for that other life. One's daily life then became the scene for an unprecedented rationalization, whereby every moment was subject to ordering, scrutiny, and accountability. The paradox here is that Calvin did not make human life less religious; rather, the whole of human life became a monastery. Yet, it was exactly this comprehensive religionization that produced both the possibilities for capitalism and the demise of Calvinist Protestantism as such. For, by sacralizing the whole of life, Calvinism also rationalizes it (a rationalizing inherent in the monasteries first abolished by Luther). Having enabled such a worldy asceticism, there is no longer any need for the religious content to remain. A purely secular ascetism becomes the logical outcome of Calvin's theology and practice, which is a means that can be discarded. Calvinist Protestantism thereby functions as a catalytic agent, a mediator that vanishes once its immediate task is over. Of course, the traces of the mediator remain in the shape of what follows, and Weber was too quick to predict the end of mediators such as Calvinism. This is precisely what I want to trace in the various mediators I will mention in a moment, for they do not vanish as readily as all that.

Returning to the first vanishing mediator—the collective entity of postcolonial critics themselves—the immediate problem here is one of demarcation and identification, for more often than not the amorphous method that goes by the name of postcolonial criticism is used by those working in existing fields, such as history, literature, anthropology, biblical studies, and so on. But let us assume for a moment that there are individuals who may be called postcolonial critics: Why would I want to argue that they are vanishing mediators? For they seem very much present and active, as this collection among many others attests. My point is twofold: firstly, postcolonial criticism is a distinctly academic activity, carried out by and large by people who work in tertiary institutions. Secondly, they seek, more than in many other approaches, to speak for and on behalf of those who lived under colonialism and who continue to live with its legacies. It is in this respect that they seek to become enablers and media of lost voices, whether human or textual, acting as transitional figures whose task, when complete, disappears from the scene. Yet, this vanishing act is as troubled as any other in which a trained critic acts as mediator for those not so trained. This can take the form of research into specific dimensions of the experiences and texts of colonized, especially indigenous, peoples, or the editing of volumes that seek to give nonacademic voices a place to speak, or critics may take on the task of representing the political aspirations of the people with whom they undertake research, and so on. It seems to me that the mediators' role needs to be factored into any consideration of postcolonial theory, especially in terms of the institutional form of such theory.

We can go further than this, however, by following Arif Dirlik's point: "'When exactly ... does the "postcolonial" begin?' queries Ella Shohat in a discussion of the subject. Misreading this question deliberately, I will supply here an answer that is only partly facetious: 'When Third World intellectuals have arrived in First World academe'" (Dirlik: 52). That is, those who practice postcolonial criticism may be found more often than not in the tertiary institutions of the so-called First World. Thus, Spivak and Said work at Columbia University, Bhabha and Dipesh Chakrabarty at Chicago, Ranajit Guha at the Australian National University, Moore-Gilbert at Goldsmith's College, University of London, and so on. In Australia, postcolonial critics are based mostly at the universities, as may be seen by the list of contributors to this volume: the universities of Sydney, Wollongong, the Australian National University, and Monash and La Trobe Universities. I do not want to argue that this betrays the political agenda of postcolonial criticism; rather, it is constitutive of the approach itself.

There is one last point concerning critics who make use of and engage in postcolonial theory: many of those drawn by postcolonial theory have some sort of political commitment, and perhaps engagement, that is somewhere between mild left liberalism and communism. In other words, postcolonial theory, in its perpetual search for oppositional strategies and tactics visited upon the colonizing power, has a political attraction for many. I would suggest that the identification of such resistance to the dominant hegemony is a political act in which the subject of research becomes a dimension, if not a focus, of the critic's politics.

Another vanishing mediator of postcolonial theory is history itself. This may appear an odd thing to write, for is not postcolonial theory very much concerned with rereading the history, art, texts, and practices of colonialism and its aftermath? But it is not this history that concerns me here: it is the history of the theory itself, of postcolonial theory. The rapid emergence of postcolonial theory with the work of Said, Spivak, and Bhabha has effaced the long precursor to this theory. It seems to me that this has happened not so much through a wilful neglect, as through the process of interpreting these older theorists. I think here particularly of Bhabha's appropriation of Frantz Fanon, or of Spivak's use of Marx. Others have fallen by the wayside, such as W. E. B. DuBois and Sol Plaatje at the turn of the century, although the former has been taken up by African American critics such as Cornel West. Bart Moore-Gilbert usefully reminds us of this longer critical history by distinguishing between postcolonial theory—that which we have now after Said, Spivak, and Bhabha—and postcolonial criticism—the longer history of the critique of colonialism. In fact, as I will argue in a moment, we need to go back to Marx and Lenin for the origins of this kind of criticism. The catch with Moore-Gilbert's distinction, however, is that the very notion of a tradition of *post*colonial criticism relies upon the more recent development of a postcolonial theory. That is to say, the idea of a history of this intellectual and political project seems to be enabled by the subsequent theory, which generates its own history. In this case the history itself—which happened without a distinct identifier such as "postcolonial"—does seem to vanish before the other history of postcolonial theory. What is needed, then, is a strategy for recovering this alternative history that simultaneously deals with the historical constructions of postcolonial theory.

Yet it was Marx and then Lenin who first developed a critical approach to what they variously called colonialism and imperialism. If Marx traced the way capitalism, for its very survival, had to expand, to "grow" (still very much the benchmark of economic success), beyond the confines of Europe and conquer ever new colonial spaces, Lenin, especially in *Imperialism, the Highest Stage of Capitalism,* developed an analysis of imperialism, or imperial capitalism, as the most advanced stage of capitalism up until that point. For Lenin, both "world wars" were conflicts between the European imperial powers, vying for global dominance, the struggle coming to head in the competition for the conquest of ever more territories throughout the globe.

I have arrived, then, at another vanishing mediator in both postcolonialism (the moment after colonialism) and postcolonial theory—Marxism. For after Lenin, the systematic theorization and critique of capitalist expansion, including colonialism, took place in the Marxist tradition. Key figures of earlier postcolonial criticism, such as Frantz Fanon, W. E. B. DuBois, and C. L. R. James, were all Marxist critics of colonialism. Of course, the whole tradition of Marxist theory, at least in the substantial portions of it that seek to analyze capitalism itself, is also *de facto* the critique of colonialism. Contemporary postcolonial theory cannot be considered adequately without coming to terms with this longer critical history.

Why has the strong Marxist dimension of postcolonial theory been lost? Its loss has been through a transformation that simultaneously erases its influence, section by section, like a chalkboard full of writing and diagrams. The process began with Said's use of Antonio Gramsci's notion of hegemony. In itself, Gramsci's theory was a significant step in the development of the Marxist theory of ideology: rather than the ruling ideas of an age being the ideas of the ruling class, understood as the class that is the ruling material force (Marx and Engels: 67), for Gramsci the ideas of the rulers are always shaky, contested, subject to challenge from below, from those who are ruled (see 268, 328, 348, 365, 370, 376). In the face of such perpetual challenges, the ruling class must work to ensure its dominance through repeated efforts to assert its own ideology. Hence the blatant propaganda (witness today advertising as such, or government advertisements that masquerade as "information"), the efforts to control the media, funding for activities such as sport that are deemed beneficial for national identity, and so on. For instance, in Australia, the success of the cricket team may be related reasonably directly to the massive amount of money given to the Australian Institute of Cricket, which sponsors and trains promising players from a young age. Similarly, the Australian Institute of Sport, with its government millions, was set up after Australia failed to gain a gold medal at the Montreal Olympics in 1976. The results have been somewhat spectacular since (the Sydney Olympics, the Australian Swimming Team, etc.).

In the period of colonialism such hegemony involved wholesale ideological work, ranging from racial theory, through military action and the production of belief in the superiority of the imperial centre, to Said's well-known "orientalism" (Said, 1978). But Said linked this in problematic fashion to Foucault's work on power, specifically the dispersed, capillary forms of power that never reside in the named and expected seats of power. One can see the connection—dispersed power and a threatened hegemony—but Foucault was not a Marxist, despite being a student of Sartre and a political activist. The absence of other categories crucial to hegemony, such as class, class conflict, and the crucial role of political economics, meant that the notion of hegemony was orphaned, drifting away from the conceptual context in which it made sense. So the first step in watering down the Marxist heritage in postcolonial theory was taken.

Even though Gayatri Spivak claims Marxism as part of her own theoretical and political position, it was her translation of Derrida's *Of Grammatology*, and especially the long and difficult introduction that she wrote, which brought deconstruction into the mix of what was becoming postcolonial theory. The subsequent appearance of *In Other Worlds* (1988) reinforced the prominence of Derridean deconstruction, along with Gramsci and Foucault via Said, as one of the theoretical strands available for critics wanting to forge a new approach. Finally, Homi Bhabha's work, especially *The Location of Culture*, introduced Lacanian psychoanalysis into the reading of colonial texts, particularly in relation to Frantz Fanon and the colonial period in India. Lacanian psychoanalysis became part of a contradictory hybrid along with other methodological elements—Gramscian hegemony, Foucauldian fragmented power, and Derridean deconstruction. One of the tasks in postcolonial criticism is to explore the contradictions of such an amalgam.

So, postcolonial theory sets one looking for the wealth of subversive material that remains buried and forgotten, such as Aboriginal literary resistance (see the essay by van Toorn in this collection), unexpected or unwanted appropriations of the Bible (see the essay by Johnston), or counterhegemonic moments in canonical texts (the essay by Singh on James Joyce). While this is an immensely fruitful and necessary task, I still want to ask: What next, after the resistance has been located, after the text deconstructs, after the Real has been glimpsed? Is this the kind of work that begins to make sense of the anticolonial movements and wars of independence, or do these acts of alternative agency remain ultimately futile, absorbed into the dominant system? In another place (Boer, 2001) I argue that the possibilities of anticolonialism came, in part at least, from the contradictory nature of European imperialism, providing colonized peoples with the physical, economic, and conceptual tools—individual subjectivity and agency, collective identity in a nation-state, racial and ethnic identity—that made anticolonialism possible in the first place. But my question remains: Is postcolonial criticism caught in a fruitful but limiting methodological mix?

However, by the time postcolonial theory achieved something of an identity and maturity, the Marxist heritage of postcolonial theory had vanished, and even Gramsci appeared less of a Marxist and more of a postcolonial critic *avant la lettre*. One of the agendas for subsequent work in postcolonial theory, it seems to me, is a recovery of this tradition that has been "left out," as Andrew Milner argues in relation to the history of cultural studies.

There is, finally, a vanishing mediator that is more directly the concern of this collection of essays, namely, the Bible itself. Apart from a very few notable exceptions—the debate over the use of the Exodus myth (Walzer; Said, 1988; Shohat; Schwartz) and Bhabha's "Signs Taken for Wonders" essay (102–22)—postcolonial criticism outside biblical studies (and even in this respect it is quite small) is notable for the complete lack of consideration of the Bible. There are obvious reasons for this: the concern to remove religion as a primary cause in dealing with colonialism, the fact that critics working with postcolonialism are not trained in biblical studies, nor even that interested. Such critics perhaps still assume that the Bible and biblical studies are inherently religious matters, the business of theological students and those who work for the church or synagogue. Yet this does not account for the absence of the Bible in postcolonial criticism, given its pervasiveness in colonialism and postcolonialism themselves, and given that an increasing number of people, from diverse backgrounds, now study the Bible without its religious connections.

In this case the Bible has indeed been a proper vanishing mediator: despite the crucial role of the Bible in colonialism, in producing the conceptual apparatus of the colonial nation-states of Europe and then later North America, it has made an extraordinarily hasty and unseemly departure, a retreat now firmly sealed by the criticism that seeks to reassess colonialism itself. And yet the marks and traces of its former presence cannot be so easily effaced: the mediator, apparently vanished, has left plenty of evidence of its former stay.

This volume attempts, in part at least, to redress this lack in postcolonial criticism. The obverse of this lack is the perpetual, if not overwhelming, presence of the Bible in colonialism and postcolonialism themselves. This volume is then an effort to bridge such a gap between the reality of social, economic, and cultural situations and the critical theory that seeks to analyse such situations and cultural products.

In shaping the volume, it seemed to me that more would be achieved by inviting nonbiblical critics working in postcolonial theory. There are a number of reasons for this. To begin with, a few biblical critics have worked on the question of the Bible and postcolonialism, in particular R. S. Sugirtharajah, Stephen Moore, Fernando Segovia, and Erin Runions. Laura Donaldson has edited an earlier volume of *Semeia* (1996), and R. S. Sugirtharajah edits the series "The Bible and Postcolonialism" from Sheffield Academic Press, in which four volumes have been published to date, two collections edited by Sugirtharajah (1998b, 1999), one edited by Segovia (2000b), and a monograph by me (2001). Sugirtharajah has written or edited a number of books that touch on the same issue (1995; 1998a; 2001). As I write, the first meeting of the "New Testament Studies and Post-Colonial Studies" consultation of the Society of Biblical Literature has had its first meeting. Fernando Segovia has recently published *Decolonizing Biblical Studies* (2000a), and Erin Runions's study of Bhabha and the Hebrew Bible will appear soon. Yet, this growing body of work has remained by and large within the discipline of biblical studies, although Donaldson also works in English literature (1992; 2001). To be sure, some of this work is being read by postcolonial critics outside biblical studies, as Anna Johnston's essay in this collection attests. It seems to me that such a disciplinary crossover should be the norm rather than the exception, that those interested in postcolonial theory in biblical studies and other disciplines should engage in discussion about the Bible in colonialism and postcolonialism.

On the other side, as I have noted, hardly any of those working in postcolonial criticism have considered the Bible. Naturally, biblical critics will want to argue for the importance of such a question, so it seemed better to ask critics from other disciplines without such a disciplinary advocacy for the Bible to write on the question, not only so that they and others in their disciplines might think about the Bible, but so that biblical critics might see how those from other fields deal with the Bible and postcolonialism in what is primarily a biblical studies journal. In order to move the discussion on a step or two further, the respondent, Gerald West, is a biblical critic. Inevitably, a collection like this will be varied, with contributions from politics (James and Seth), English (Johnston, van Toorn, and Jones), and literature (Singh and Docker), and a sole essay from biblical studies (Boer). Given the strongly geographic nature of postcolonialism, the best way to group these essays is in geographic terms. That is, some of them focus on the Bible and related questions within the colonized spaces themselves, such as India, the Pacific islands, and Australia. The remainder cluster around the colonial centres—the literature, politics, and religion of the colonial masters, if I may put it that way—with an agenda that both recognizes and strongly criticizes the importance of the Bible in such spaces.

So, I will begin with the formerly (or neo-) colonized spaces: the Pacific islands, Australia, and India. Anna Johnston's essay discusses in detail the complexities of Bible translation as a linchpin of the activities of the London Missionary Society (LMS) in the Pacific. Linking the evangelical tenor of the LMS, the printing press, and the emergence of textuality in oral cultures, Johnston tracks the justification of Bible translation by LMS workers in the mission field and the curiously skewed appropriation (in the eyes of the LMS) of the Bible by Pacific islanders. One can see in this essay some of the crucial moves of postcolonial theory working to full effect—a deconstruction of the colonizers' texts and power, the location of agency in colonized responses, often against the intentions of the colonizer, and the wholesale hybridity of the colonial interaction itself.

The next three essays have a distinctly Australian focus, covering Aboriginal appropriations of the Bible in the contested colonial space of Tasmania (van Toorn), the biblical constructions of Australia in explorer journals (Boer), and the use of biblical motifs in the contemporary Australian writing of Elizabeth Jolley (Jones). For some years now Penny van Toorn has undertaken groundbreaking research in the oppositional uses of literacy and textuality by Aboriginal people, who took up the tools of colonialism and used them against their colonial oppressors. In her paper she focuses on the alternative, unexpected, and oppositional uses of the Bible by Aborigines in Van Diemen's Land (Tasmania).

My own paper follows the texts of the so-called "explorers" of Australia—Mitchell, Sturt, Stuart, Eyre, Gray, and Giles—and the way their constructions of Australia were determined in large measure by the Bible and Christianity. Alongside the presence of Aborigines on every second page of their endless journals, I show the extent to which the Bible shaped their universe. The depictions of Australia by the explorers played a fundamental role in conceptions of Australia that remain powerful today, in all their possibilities and limitations. This essay is also a distinct intervention into other work on the explorers, work that is symptomatic of much postcolonial criticism in ignoring the key role of the Bible in the conceptualization, textuality, and politics of colonialism itself.

With Dorothy Jones's essay, the last in this trilogy of Australian-oriented essays, we move into some different territory: the use of biblical motifs by Elizabeth Jolley, a distinguished Australian writer. The solitary biblical motif that has made its way into postcolonial criticism is that of Exodus/Exile. The controlling use of this motif within colonialism took place with the first

European settlement of North America by the Pilgrims, for whom the flight from religious persecution and the occupation of another's land was inspired and saturated by biblical patterns of Exodus from "Egypt" and arrival at the "promised land." The model has reproduced itself in other key situations, ranging from the Boers in South Africa through to Zionism. Particularly in the context of modern Israel, the model has come under critique by Edward Said (1988, in response to Walzer) and more recently and broadly by Regina Schwartz in a critique of monotheism *per se*. In Australia Anne Curthoys, Deborah Bird Rose, and John Docker have criticized its use as a model that justifies dispossession of the people already in the land. However, I have argued (2001) that there is little early use of the Exodus motif in Australia, for the country was seen as a place of exile and oppression, a land that God did not bless at creation. However, Jones's paper indicates that the Exodus does begin to appear in later literature, becoming an extended metaphor in the work of Elizabeth Jolley, especially her novel *Milk and Honey* (1984). Here the focus is on refugee migrants from a war-torn Europe, although the use of Exodus is not to justify possession of a new land but to critique the very story itself as one of exclusion, barriers, and futile efforts to preserve identity.

The final essay that concerns the former colonial spaces is that by Sanjay Seth, in which the questions of textuality and education are central. Concerned to spell out some of the contradictions and tensions in the effort to educate Indian people (as if they did not have a long tradition of education and textual interpretation), Seth follows the changing policies relating to education and proselytizing in government and East India Company decisions. He also traces the various responses by Indians: for instance, parents felt education provided in English colonial schools would be enough to gain a government position, although they were wary of conversion to Christianity and withdrew their children before this might happen. But what underlies this essay is not merely the methodological moves of postcolonial criticism but the way the Bible appears both as a tool of education-for-conversion and as the groundwork for the question of textuality itself. In other words, the Bible is closely implicated in the English and European notion of education for, through, and by means of written texts. Of course, this comes into conflict with Indian traditions of textuality deriving from the Vedas. Might it be possible to argue that some of the tensions Seth traces come from the clash of two different textual and educational traditions, each one with sacred scriptures near the centre?

The last three essays, concerned as they are with the colonial centres themselves, appear toward the end. Not because the logic leads to this point, that postcolonialism still bows to the centre, but because the centre itself needs the most sustained critique.

James Joyce, a colonial voice close to the centre of the British Empire, is the focus of Amardeep Singh's detailed reading of part of *Ulysses*. Singh explores the way the Bible riddles this text, although in Joycean fashion the biblical material undergoes a series of transformations toward what Bakhtin calls "the material bodily lower stratum" (Bakhtin: 368). Here we find Bloom and Stephen juxtaposing their appropriations of the key biblical motif of the "promised land," the "Pisgah sight of Palestine." But Joyce's work is curious, for although it forms part of the Western literary canon, it is a distinctly anticolonial text, from Ireland, mapping Dublin, a colonized space. So here we find an appropriation of the Bible that profoundly alters it in the process, a distinct reading against the dominant modes.

John Docker takes a different tack, focusing on the work of Freud and, much less known but deserving of wider reading, Freke and Gandy's *The Jesus Mysteries*. "Freud" has of course been a crucial, if troubling, feature of Western, colonial thought, although again the threat from Freud is that his work can succeed in dismantling the ideology it appears to support. Thus, Docker reads Freud against himself, discovering in *Moses and Monotheism* a polytheistic Egyptophile who was fascinated with Moses, the Egyptian-become-Israelite and mythical founding figure, after Akhnaton, of monotheism. Docker's call is for an opposition to the domination, intolerance, and despotism of monotheism—that of the mythical figures of Moses and Jesus—and a reopening of the many-layered and cosmopolitan culture of polytheism over against a colonizing monotheism.

Finally, Paul James brings the critique back "home," as it were, to the European nation-state itself. Pursuing a research interest in the question of the state and the development of the nation-state, James argues for the centrality of the Bible in the European conception of the nation-state. The extraordinary myths that sought to connect distinct moments of biblical narrative with national identity—such as the Scottish Stone of Scone with Jacob's stone pillow in Gen 28:11—function as political myths, replete with enforced efforts at biblical antiquity. But showing the crucial symbolic role of such biblical pieces in the construction of the ideology of the nation-state is the achievement of James's essay. It would seem that the nation-state, the foundational unit for colonial expansion, would not have taken the form it now does without the Bible.

Our hope is that the discussion and debate begun here, by those interested in postcolonial criticism in different fields, may continue.

WORKS CITED

Bakhtin, Mikhail
    1984   *Rabelais and His World.* Trans. Helene Iswoldsky. Bloomington: Indiana University Press.

Bhabha, Homi
    1994   *The Location of Culture.* London: Routledge.

Boer, Roland
    2001   *Last Stop Before Antarctica: The Bible and Postcolonialism in Australia.* Sheffield: Sheffield Academic Press.

Curthoys, Ann
    1999   "Expulsion, Exodus and Exile in White Australian Historical Mythology." Pp. 1–18 in *Imaginary Homelands.* Ed. Richard Nile and Michael Williams. St. Lucia: University of Queensland Press.

Derrida, Jacques
    1980   *Of Grammatology.* Trans. Gayatri Chakravorty Spivak. Baltimore: Johns Hopkins University Press.

Dirlik, Arif
    1997   *The Postcolonial Aura: Third World Criticism in the Age of Global Capitalism.* Boulder, Colo.: Westview.

Donaldson, Laura
    1992   *Decolonizing Feminisms: Race, Gender, and Empire-Building.* Chapel Hill: University of North Carolina Press.

    2001   *Postcolonialism, Feminism and Religious Discourse.* London: Routledge.

Donaldson, Laura, ed.
    1996   *Postcolonialism and Scriptural Readings. Semeia* 75.

Gramsci, Antonio
    1971   *Selections from the Prison Notebooks.* Ed. Quentin Hoare and G. Nowell Smith. London: Lawrence & Wishart.

Jolley, Elizabeth
    1984   *Milk and Honey.* Freemantle: Freemantle Arts Centre Press.

Lenin, V. I.
    1950   *Imperialism, the Highest Stage of Capitalism.* Moscow: Foreign Languages Publishing House.

Marx, Karl, and Frederick Engels
    1976   *The German Ideology.* Moscow: Progress.

Moore-Gilbert, Bart
    1997   *Postcolonial Theory: Contexts, Practices, Politics.* London: Verso.

Rose, Deborah Bird
    1996   "Rupture and the Ethics of Care in Colonized Space." Pp. 190–215 in *Prehistory to Politics: John Mulvaney, the Humanities and the Public Intellectual.* Ed. Tim Bonyhady and Tom Griffiths. Melbourne: Melbourne University Press.

Runions, Erin
    2002   *Changing Subjects: Gender, Nation and Future in Micah.* Playing the Texts. Sheffield: Sheffield Academic Press.

Said, Edward
    1978   *Orientalism.* London: Routledge & Kegan Paul.

    1988   "Michael Walzer's *Exodus and Revolution:* A Canaanite Reading." Pp. 161–78 in *Blaming the Victims: Spurious Scholarship and the Palestinian Question.* Ed. Edward W. Said and Christopher Hitchens. London: Verso.

Schwartz, Regina
    1997   *The Curse of Cain: The Violent Legacy of Monotheism.* Chicago: University of Chicago Press.

Segovia, Fernando
    2000a   *Decolonizing Biblical Studies: A View from the Margins.* Maryknoll, N.Y.: Orbis.

Segovia, Fernando, ed.
    2000b   *Interpreting Beyond Borders.* Sheffield: Sheffield Academic Press.

Shohat, Ella
    1992   "Antinomies of Exile: Said at the Frontiers of National Narrations." Pp. 121–43 in *Edward Said: A Critical Reader.* Ed. Michael Sprinker. Oxford: Blackwell.

Spivak, Gayatri Chakravorty
    1988   *In Other Worlds.* New York: Routledge.

    1999   *A Critique of Postcolonial Reason: Toward a History of the Vanishing Present.* Cambridge, Mass.: Harvard University Press.

Sugirtharajah, R. S.
    1998a   *Asian Biblical Hermeneutics and Postcolonialism: Contesting the Interpretations.* The Bible and Liberation. Maryknoll, N.Y.: Orbis.

    2001   *The Bible and the Third World: Precolonial, Colonial and Postcolonial Encounters.* Cambridge: Cambridge University Press.

Sugirtharajah, R. S., ed.
    1995   *Voices from the Margin: Interpreting the Bible in the Third World.* New ed. Maryknoll, N.Y.: Orbis.

    1998b   *The Postcolonial Bible.* Sheffield: Sheffield Academic Press.

    1999   *Vernacular Hermeneutics.* Sheffield: Sheffield Academic Press.

Walzer, Michael
    1985   *Exodus and Revolution.* New York: Basic Books.

Weber, Max
    1992   *The Protestant Ethic and the Spirit of Capitalism.* Trans. Talcott Parsons. Intro. Anthony Giddens. London: Routledge.

THE BOOK EATERS: TEXTUALITY, MODERNITY, AND THE LONDON MISSIONARY SOCIETY

Anna Johnston
University of Tasmania

ABSTRACT

This essay works from the nineteenth-century textual archive of the London Missionary Society (LMS) toward contemporary issues within postcolonial theory. Its historical narrative is situated in the early LMS missions to the Pacific in the early nineteenth century, the first (and, arguably, the most widely publicised) missions of this Evangelical Protestant society. In both missionary narratives and, it would seem, in Islander cultures, the book came to represent an artefact of modernity and Western cultural capital in itself; particularly, for the missionaries, that holy book, the Bible.

Missionaries represented the introduction of the Bible into colonial cultures both as a symbol of modernity (brought into being by the machine of modern times, the printing press) *and* as a (colonial re-) instatement of the Bible's hallowed status as eternal, unchanging, and universal. The introduction of the Bible, then, works in missionary discourses within a kind of doubled discursive time. At the same time, the insertion of the Bible into colonial cultures also opens up a doubled *place* for the text—a place in imperial British culture and a place in indigenous culture. Translating the Bible—the first job for many missionaries in a new location—was an enormous task, and one that introduced a range of complex issues. As Steven Kaplan argues, "translation of the Scriptures into local languages both created new questions of interpretation and placed the texts firmly in the hands of the local population" (1995b:6). The act of translation thus made possible a variety of different interpretations, fundamentally uncontrollable by the missionaries.

This essay, then, uses the historical texts of the LMS missionaries to address a number of issues in contemporary postcolonial theory. It uses the "doubled time" of the Bible in colonial cultures to investigate the complex processes by which imperial agents sought to introduce modernity to indigenous cultures and the equally complex ways in which indigenous cultures, visible only partially through the imperial archive, sought to appropriate this knowledge for themselves. It also examines the central role that textuality played in the implementation of colonialism. As Simon Gikandi has argued, "texts were important and indispensible weapons in the imposition of rule and governance.... Texts provided the medium through which the crisis of both colonial and domestic identities were mediated" (xix).

In the nineteenth century, the Christian converts of Mangaia, one of the large islands of the southern Cook Islands, became known as *kai-parua* (book eaters) by their fellow Islanders and British missionaries, because of their time spent learning the word of the Christian God. Sir Peter Buck (also known as Te Rangi Hiroa, an indigenous anthropologist who profoundly challenged missionary versions of contact history on Mangaia) noted that the phrase meant "literally ... to eat the words of instruction: denotes to receive religious instruction. A word introduced by the early missionaries from the Tahitian language" (Savage qtd. in Buck: 55). These *kai-parua* emerge from the historical record as one of a group of Polynesians who adopted the Christian message brought to the region in the late eighteenth century by British Protestant missionaries, and can perhaps be seen as the forebears of the strong Evangelical cultures still existing in the Pacific today. Here, however, I want to examine the ideas surrounding a term like "book eaters" in terms of the issues that it raises in relation to the crosscultural encounter between Polynesians and British missionaries in the early nineteenth century.

This very brief narrative of the introduction of Christianity on one island in the Pacific resonates with other narratives and raises many questions. How did the *kai-parua* get access to this Bible that they are represented as so diligently ingesting? In what language were they reading the Bible? What levels of language facility did the missionaries have, in order to be introducing new words into the Mangaian vocabulary? Was it appropriate for Tahitian words to be introduced into a different culture—what meaning did this multiply crosscultural term have for the local people? What did the *kai-parua* really think about the Bible—what exactly was it that they were tasting in this text? In this essay, I will examine the introduction of the Bible into Polynesian communities by the London Missionary Society and trace this introduction of a print culture as a kind of metaphor for the introduction of a colonial regime that ideologically supported missionary intervention in Island cultures. In this essay, as in colonial narratives and in recent postcolonial theory, the Bible will operate as a multifactorial signifier. The Bible operates as an image of Christianity, of course, and specifically of the Evangelical Protestantism supporting foreign missions in the nineteenth century. It operates also as an image of the British civilising mission, as a blueprint for what the British considered the moral way of life. It operates also as a particularly colonial artefact: not just its heritage as a text deeply concerned with the colonialism of Israel, Egypt, Assyria, Persia, and Rome (Sugirtharajah, 1998a:19), but, more importantly here, as an artefact of the nineteenth-century British Empire. As Sugirtharajah has argued, "in the cultural milieu of the nineteenth-century missionary-imperial enterprise, the Bible was constituted as a colonial book, aligned with specific theological and missiological practices" (1998a:51).

Whilst British missionaries supported such acceptance of the Christian message through the Bible, they were also concerned that they were losing control of the message, the text, and the ways in which these might be used in a different cultural context. The metaphor of biblical learning being absorbed into the physical bodies of the Mangaians, for instance, makes clear the profound sense of transformation of the Christian message by indigenous believers. At the point of translation, too, the missionaries faced the possible loss of absolute control of the meaning of the biblical text. Whilst the missionaries were instrumental in the act of translation, they were reliant on "native informants" to teach them the local languages and to advise them on appropriate Polynesian equivalents for Christian concepts. Once the Bible existed in indigenous languages, the missionaries were no longer the sole, or even the most convincing, authority on this text. Whilst they strove to maintain this authority, as a symbol of their religious authority as evangelists, missionary narratives frequently give the sense that their authority is slipping away from them in the colonial context, that the Word is being translated in many more ways than they had anticipated or could control.

The answer to the question about what the *kai-parua* really thought about the Bible cannot be given in this essay. The texts under examination here are predominantly those produced by the missionaries and their nineteenth-century supporters. These texts provide a very filtered view of the *indigenous* history of missionary encounters, and, whilst I examine the missionary texts for their representations of Polynesian reactions, any straightforward insight into indigenous responses to Christianity are almost impossible to retrieve from the Evangelical texts. Rod Edmond queries: "Is it possible to get closer to the experience of contact from the native point of view? Can we, whilst still dependent on missionary texts, begin to construct a history of native subjects somehow distinct from colonial descriptions of them?" (123–24). The discomforting answer is, of course, that it is extremely difficult and highly problematic to read for indigenous agency or resistance or history through such highly mediated texts as those of colonial evangelisation. Thus, whilst I gesture at the ways in which Polynesians and others may have appropriated the Bible, such speculation *is* "gestural," in the sense of a formal acknowledgment of an important, other narrative, and in the sense of eliciting a response from those more qualified to attest to such issues.

This essay, then, uses the historical texts of the London Missionary Society to address a number of issues in contemporary postcolonial theory. It uses the "doubled time" of the Bible in colonial cultures (as both a symbol of modernity and a symbol of the return to Edenic purity) to investigate the complex processes by which imperial agents sought to introduce modernity to indigenous cultures and the equally complex ways in which indigenous cultures, visible only partially through the imperial archive, sought to appropriate this knowledge for themselves. It also examines the central role that textuality played in the implementation of colonialism.

The Bible in Polynesian Mission Cultures

Missions in the South Pacific have always held a special place within the history and memory of the London Missionary Society (henceforth referred to as LMS). The Society's first overseas mission was to what was then called Otaheite (later Tahiti), and considerable personnel, funds, and interest were invested in this area during the first half of the nineteenth century, the period under consideration in this essay. My discussions here focus on the LMS missions in Polynesia, originally established in the Society's first concerted move into the region at the end of the eighteenth century; in 1797 the LMS moved into Tahiti, Tongatapu, and the Marquesas, and from 1817–1822 they extended their influence to the Leeward Islands. After most of the missionaries left Tahiti by the end of the eighteenth century, a second, more successful Tahitian mission was initiated from 1811 onward. The Polynesian group is commonly assumed to include the islands of central and eastern Pacific, including Hawai'i, Samoa, Tahiti, and Tonga; and excluding Micronesia and Melanesia. As Nicholas Thomas notes of the geographic entity "Melanesia," "Polynesia" is "an artifact of colonial ethnology" (53), but the term is used here to establish a sense of congruence across these islands' experiences of LMS missionaries.

This case study operates as something of a limit case for the introduction of British Protestant Christianity, and its biblical texts, to colonial cultures. The Polynesian missions formed the first foreign enterprise of the Society and as such operated as something of a trial of Evangelical practices. The LMS's constituency of working- and middle-class Congregationalist Britons similarly make this society's actions indicative of the ground swell of British Nonconformism at this time. As Susan Thorne states, "the LMS was the principal institutional beneficiary of Congregational support for foreign missionary operations, and, in the words of one of its Leicestershire supporters, 'may be taken as a type of all the rest'"(13). The Pacific operated, during this period, as a very particular kind of colonial location—not formally under the jurisdiction of imperial powers such as Britain, the region was generally represented as a kind of *de facto* colonial space. Indeed, for much of the century, the missionaries there appear to have been acting as surrogate imperialists, though under their own impetus rather than because of any directive to do so from Britain. Whilst missionaries always had a somewhat ambivalent relationship with the imposition of imperialism, it is fair to say that missionaries in Polynesia formed their own versions of colonial states and, arguably, their intervention to some extent made possible the later wholesale colonisation of the region. Notably, the "bibles-and-muskets" phase has become a recognised historical marker in periodising Pacific history, even if, as Rod Edmond notes, it has become part of a less than productive "fatal impact" thesis of Pacific history (9–10).

Polynesia became the first testing ground for what became known as the dual processes of "Christianisation and civilisation" believed necessary for modern missions.[1] A crucial factor in this process was the introduction of textuality to the Polynesian missions. The eminent LMS missionary William Ellis, a fully trained printer, arrived at Eimeo with a printing press in 1816, and the press was eventually established on the island of Mo'orea in that year. Vanessa Smith notes that between June 1816 and May 1817 Ellis claimed to have printed nine thousand books, "after which the press was taken to Huahine, in the Leeward Islands. Presses were established in Tahiti in 1818, in Honolulu in 1822, in Tonga in 1831, in Rarotonga in 1834, in Fiji and Samoa in 1839, and in Micronesia by the 1860s" (70). The arrival of the press was seen by the Society as a crucial event in the development of the South Pacific missions and marked the second, more successful, phase of LMS missions in the region, dominated by men such as Ellis and the iconic martyred missionary John Williams. Many Evangelical narratives of the "South Seas" missions, like Silvester Horne's *The Story of the L.M.S.*, celebrate the event when "King Pomare set up the first types, and printed the first sheets, amid the most indescribable excitement and enthusiasm on the part of his subjects" (42). Naturally, these first sheets were translated copies of Scripture. In both missionary narratives and, it would seem, in Polynesian cultures, the printed word and the book came to represent iconic artefacts of modernity and Western cultural capital: particularly, for the missionaries, that holy book, the Bible.

The missionaries spent many of their early years in Polynesia attempting to learn and transcribe Polynesian languages because they believed that "there can hardly be education ... where the language of the people has never been written down" (Grant: 21). As Smith argues, "literacy enables the kinds of cultural boundary-crossing on which conversion depends" (71). Thus they intended to transcribe the oral

---

1 As Fernando Segovia has noted, Western missionary movements can be divided in two major periods: the first, from 1492, was instigated by the first European landfall in the "New World" and was predominantly Catholic; the second, from 1792, was primarily Protestant and involved the evangelisation of Africa and Asia, as well as other British colonial territories (58–59).

literature of the region into written form.[2] Their aim was to teach the local people Christianity in their own language(s), an aim that was moderately successful but not without its problems. For a start, the early LMS missionaries to Polynesia were not particularly well-educated—whilst their linguistic achievements were considerable given their lack of expertise, they had little experience to rely upon and basically had to invent an appropriate system as they went along. The LMS, particularly in its early years, prided itself on recruiting "godly artisans"—working-class men who possessed "industrial arts" and a sense of piety—rather than theologically trained gentlemen. As Niel Gunson explains, this was particularly the case in Polynesia:

> Many of the directors [of the LMS] held the view ... that because the Polynesians were comparatively uncivilized, the South Seas mission was more properly a field for artisans and the less intelligent or less scholarly volunteers. It is evident that the more scholarly, gifted and "respectable" missionaries were sent to India and the Orient. (96–97)

Early LMS missionaries often appear to have been profoundly surprised at both the complexity of Polynesian languages and the difficulties the Europeans experienced in learning and categorising them. Gunson notes that the Society's attempts to provide prior information to the Polynesian-bound missionaries were well-intentioned but flawed and that Rev. Samuel Greatheed's *Polynesian Grammar,* which formed the primary linguistic preparation for the LMS missionaries before they left for the mission field, was "naïve" (111–12). The missionaries' inexperience in linguistic work left them vulnerable to criticism from European travellers in the Pacific as well as from interested parties "back Home." William Ellis defended their work in his widely read *Polynesian Researches* of 1829, arguing that:

> The Missionaries have been charged with affectation in their orthography, &c. but so far from this, they have studied nothing with more attention than simplicity and perspicuity. The declaration and the pronunciation of the natives formed their only rule in fixing the spelling of proper names, as well as other parts of the language. (1:76)

---

[2] In the area of language and translation, it is important to emphasise the distinctive nature of linguistic work in Polynesia as opposed to other colonial locations such as India, the LMS's next mission field—Indian languages already existed in written forms, whilst Polynesian languages were primarily oral. The *type* of missionary linguistic work required in Polynesia was, then, quite different from that expected of missionaries in India. Consequently, linguistic work was represented quite differently in missionary texts about different regions and manifested itself in specific ways in the missionaries' conceptualisation of their endeavours.

Ellis's emphasis on these issues exemplifies the ways in which representation, language, and textuality were at the forefront of the missionaries' evaluation of their own work in the Pacific. As Rod Edmond notes, "a missionary's status, among both his own kind and the native population, depended heavily on his fluency in the local language" (117).

Early missionary narratives of the Pacific tend always to include a section detailing the orthographic and translation work in progress.[3] One suspects that the missionaries had been encouraged to believe that native language acquisition would be virtually effortless. By contrast, their accounts from Polynesia continually remarked on the complexity of the languages and the trials of learning them. Rev. Daniel Tyerman and George Bennet, members of a deputation travelling around the Pacific LMS stations in 1821–1829 (thus after a considerable amount of LMS experience in the area), repeatedly noted the sophistication of local languages. They wrote: "the Tahitian tongue lacks neither nerve nor copiousness; nor are opportunities wanting to display all its excellencies on glorious themes and great occasions—as in courts of justice, national and religious assemblies, but especially on Missionary anniversaries" (1:336). Elsewhere they admitted their difficulties in acquiring the language:

> We are daily learning for ourselves, from the lips of the natives, words and phrases of the language. By these means we have already a considerable vocabulary written down; which we often rehearse before our teachers of this class, who, sometimes seated in a circle around us, for hours together, exercise all their ingenuity and patience too, in giving us instructions, especially in the pronunciation, which is most difficult to catch, and delicate to use, there being a nicety and refinement to this, which our British friends would hardly believe in a language of uncivilised men. (1:85)

The presence of Polynesian teachers, translators, and informants was always evident in missionary accounts of language learning, though the narrators often attempted to downplay such evidence of Polynesian agency. Some gave Polynesian interlocuters considerable credit for their assistance. John Williams wrote of one Polynesian man: "Frequently he has sat eight or ten hours a day aiding me in this important work; and to him are we in a great measure indebted for the correctness with which we have been enabled to give the oracles of truth to the people" (161). However, the following extracts from Ellis's *Polynesian Researches* demonstrate his cultural biases when he discusses Polynesians and Europeans learning each other's

---

[3] See, for example, Ellis's *Polynesian Researches* (1:70–78); Tyerman and Bennet's *Journal* (1:338–39); and Williams's *Missionary Enterprises* (524–31).

languages. He condemned the Tahitians for picking up some English phrases from Europeans in the area, which

> they apply almost indiscriminately, supposing they are thereby better understood, than they would be if they used only native words; yet these words are so changed in a native's mouth that no Englishman would recognize them as his own, but would write them down as native words.... It was not in words only, but also in their application, that the most ludicrous mistakes were made by the people. (1:72)

Within a page of this comment, however, Ellis acknowledged the incompetence of *European* attempts to make themselves "better understood" by using native Polynesian words:

> Although amongst themselves [Polynesians were] accustomed to hear critically, and to ridicule with great effect, any of their own countrymen who should use a wrong word, mispronounce or place the accent erroneously on the one they used, yet they seldom laughed at the mistakes of the newly arrived residents. They endeavoured to correct them in the most friendly manner, and were evidently desirous that the foreigners should be able to understand their language, and convey their own ideas to them with distinctness and perspicuity. (1:73)

Ellis's reluctance to equate the two attempts at crosscultural communication, designating indigenous efforts as "ludicrous" and equivalent European efforts as instituting scholarly, intellectually generous interactions, suggests that his valuing of linguistic purity and learning was profoundly ethnocentric. Despite the generosity that Tahitians are portrayed as exhibiting toward European attempts to procure the linguistic and cultural capital of their culture, Ellis's conclusion remained that indigenous people corrupt the English language by making it sound "native," whilst European interlocutors could hope to achieve a "distinctness and perspicuity." Such internally inconsistent perspectives recur throughout missionary narratives and are indicative of the ways in which missionaries were often implicated in colonialist attitudes. In fact, as this report attests, a considerable amount of crosscultural exchange was being carried out by both Europeans and Polynesians.

Despite all these difficulties in language and translation, fair copies of biblical literature were produced in Polynesian languages, and the LMS missionary educators there relied on translated texts of Christian doctrine to bring about practical and basic reading and writing lessons, in addition to conversion. These texts were produced in considerable quantities and became a new crosscultural artefact in this contact zone (Pratt). E. Prout's *Missionary Ships Connected with the London Missionary Society* represented such Bibles as a kind of commodity and mobilised a metaphor of "freighting" missionary ships with religious texts. He wrote that "the *Camden* was freighted with five thousand Testaments in the language of the people—a gift more precious in their estimation than much fine gold" (55); and, later, that the *John Williams* was "freighted with 5,000 Tahitian Bibles, 4,000 *Pilgrim's Progress*, and other useful books, an iron chapel, printing materials, and iron tanks to receive the oil which the natives so willingly contribute to the Society" (70). Prout's metaphorisation of the Bible as a trade commodity was ironically realistic—missionaries invested these books with such significance that native communities picked up on their importance as cultural signifiers and artefacts, potentially without also adopting the biblical message that the missionaries intended. There is considerable evidence to suggest that these texts were incorporated into the gift economy of Pacific cultures. Prout described the LMS missionary Aaron Buzacott's arrival at Rarotonga with Bibles:

> So eager were [the local community] to possess the treasure, that Mr Buzacott could scarcely keep them from breaking open the boxes. And it was much the same at Mangaia and other islands, where all were ready, *not merely to possess, but to purchase at its cost price the Sacred Word*. (74, emphasis added)

Significantly, Prout's message about the appeal of books was intricately tied in with a message about the economics of missionary Christianity—the fact that local communities were prepared to actually pay for the Christian message seemed to imbue the project with particular success.[4]

Language and its acquisition were complex and fraught issues for LMS missionaries in Polynesia. Apart from the difficulties they experienced in learning languages in order to translate Scripture, missionary accounts of language learning reverberate with the anxieties of cultural outsiders. Missionaries in Polynesia were often amazed by indigenous peoples' facility with language learning, particularly in the area of oral learning. Often, this amazement seemed to be fuelled by the suspicion that Polynesians were in fact better and quicker in picking up the new (European) languages than the missionaries were in learning Pacific languages. Tyerman and Bennet's *Journal*, for example, noted that

> it is surprising ... with what diligence they commit to memory numerous chapters and whole gospels which have been rendered into their mother

---

[4] Of course, for the LMS missionaries such apparent willingness to engage in these transactions did indeed represent a thorough success. It seemed to indicate that the local people had been converted both to Christianity and to the capitalist market system that the missionaries endorsed.

tongue. Some who cannot read themselves can repeat almost every text which they ever heard, and even large portions of the New Testament, which they have learned by hearkening to others, while these read aloud to little audiences which they sometimes collect in the open air, under a tree, or in their family circles. (1:341)

This kind of bemused appreciation for Polynesian linguistic skills is quite common in missionary narratives. In most texts, as here, the appreciation is tempered with a kind of scepticism and suspicion: that is, specifically, a scepticism that Polynesians are only learning the words, rather than the meaning, of the Christian message (that they are mimicking without understanding—"mere parrots" in John Williams's terms [234]) and a suspicion that there are systems of Polynesian communication and educational networks that are beyond the control of the missionaries. The formalisation of a European-style school system attempted to counteract these indigenous systems of language and information diffusion, though missionaries seem always aware that European knowledges were being dispersed in different ways and for different purposes from those the missionaries intended. Tyerman and Bennet reported the desire of Polynesians for education and an awareness of its potential empowerment for them. They wrote of an encounter with one of the Matavai (Tahiti) chiefs on a day of baptism, where Upaparu "addressed Mr. Bourne in a very improper spirit, rudely demanding, 'What are you teaching us? And why do you not instruct us in English, and other things besides religion?'"(1:165). From such reported interactions it becomes evident that missionary education was recognised as valuable by local communities for their own purposes and that they resented the narrowly Evangelical curriculum endorsed by missionary educators.

Frequently the missionaries worried that their native informants were laughing at them, or misleading them, or not quite telling them the truth, or that maybe they were deliberately using language to evade missionary intervention. Rev. Murray, of the LMS Samoan mission, discussed the Samoan response to an early Evangelical address:

> Generally the address to us was couched in as soft and complimentary language as possible, but it was none the less decided on that account; though, till we became acquainted with Samoan politeness, we were apt to be misled by the first part of the speech, and fancy that we were about to gain our point. Sometimes we had almost a blunt refusal, but generally it was softened. (52)

Such crosscultural differences in discursive patterns and communication styles gradually became evident to the British, but missionaries such as Murray were continually troubled by the fact that Polynesian people seem to be saying one thing and meaning another. Frequently missionaries reported that Polynesians appeared to profess acceptance of Christian messages but then act counter to them. At the same time, missionaries expressed concerns with the ways in which local communities were adopting the Christian teachings. As Steven Kaplan argues, "translation of the Scriptures into local languages both created new questions of interpretation and placed the texts firmly in the hands of the local population" (1995b:6).

The Word: The Bible's Significance in LMS Cultures

In order to remain a viable part of the Society and to demonstrate a commitment to its overall project of "Christianisation and civilisation," the missionaries in Polynesia had to accept a complicit role within the economy of texts and discourses stipulated by the Society. Published missionary texts were drawn from the copious writings of the missionaries in the field—their letters, journals, reports, and memoirs formed the raw material that was then transformed into publishable material. They were produced in prodigious quantities by the missionary societies, keen to promote the Evangelical work of their colonial representatives, in order to justify their ongoing involvement in colonial projects and to ensure continued funding from governments and pious British individuals. As Jane Haggis describes it,

> The nineteenth century British missionary movement was a prolific producer of texts about itself and the lands and people it sought to transform. Not only did every Society have its periodicals, each aimed at a different audience: adults, women, "juveniles" and children; but a constant stream of pamphlets, leaflets and the like were distributed, often free or for only nominal charge, as well as the more substantial literature of books about the work in the various mission fields and lives of well-known missionaries. (90)

Missionaries were required at the very least to provide an annual account of their work at their mission. Mostly these annual reports were written up from the missionary's own journal, sometimes as a direct transcription but probably more frequently as "edited highlights." In the case of the LMS, these reports would be recycled in the Society's own quarterly *Chronicle* and later in the annual *Reports to the Directors*. In any discussion of missionary textuality it is important to maintain a kind of sceptical double-vision about the nature of the texts being examined. It becomes increasingly obvious when comparing the original manuscripts of letters from missionaries, for example, with their recycled versions in missionary chronicles or reports to directors, that such texts rarely remained unexpurgated or unedited. Indeed, the chain of potential editors of missionary texts is such that the relationship between the missionary *ur*-text and its subsequent manifestations is always uncertain. This interference with original texts is not exactly hidden, although the formal missionary publications certainly did not draw much attention to their editing of primary texts in the printed versions. Individuals, however, often noted the difference between the vision of the Pacific that missionaries had been prepared for and the actuality of their experience in the field. John Williams wrote:

> I have felt disappointed when reading the writings of Missionaries, at not finding a more full account of the difficulties they have had to contend with, and the measures by which these were met. It appears to me that a work from the pen of a Missionary should not contain just what might be written by one who has never left his native country, but a plain statement of the perplexities with which he has been compelled to grapple, and the means adopted to overcome them. (137–38)

Missionaries in Polynesia, therefore, were quite conversant with the notion that texts could be manipulated to affect public opinion and to produce social change. Of course, the Evangelical concentration on the figure of the individual reading the Bible had prepared them for such a view. Evangelical Protestantism placed particular theological importance on the relationship an individual should develop with his or her god and religion, based on individual reading of the Bible. As David Alderson has described the development of British Protestantism *against* Roman Catholicism,

> Protestantism clearly styled itself as a revolt from below against the deceitful, corrupt, and unjust system administered from Rome, and it did so in the form of vernacular languages which themselves materially signified opposition to a conspiratorially secret ecclesiastical system inimical to the individual and expressing itself typically in Latin. (7)

Deep within the foundations of British Protestantism, then, was the importance of being able to read biblical texts in one's own language. The corollary of this, of course, was the belief that the individual believer should be able to express and explore their religiosity without the intervention of a priest. As Alderson argues, this sense of religious individualism became a crucial part of a specifically racial historiography of England, where the distinctive nature of English social and religious development was located in the character of Saxons who "had brought with them an individualism in religion and forms of social organisation complemented by a virtually unique social commitment to democratic government" (10). The radical individualism of the Protestants, then, was dependent upon the "immediate relationship between the individual and God" (11). In the colonies, the missionaries sought to reproduce this intimate relationship between the "heathen" and the new Christian god, primarily through the texts of the Bible. Texts were undeniably items that could produce social change.

Whilst Catholic missionising might concentrate on teaching more verbally based, catechetical modes of religious conversion, Protestant work required the swift production of translated Scripture in local languages in order to effect conversion. By the end of the eighteenth century, Stephen Neill estimates, the Bible had been translated in whole or in part into more than seventy languages; by the end of the nineteenth century, complete translations existed in over one hundred languages and partial in roughly three hundred languages (253). As he notes, different mission policies (and theologies) meant that this translation was predominantly a Protestant achievement rather than a Catholic one. Missionary involvement in education, similarly, was targeted to getting the colonised individual to read. As Brian Holmes argues, "the first and most important aim of education ... was to make conversion possible. It could be done only if the Scriptures could be understood and preferably read. Bible study was the central aim of all Protestant mission education" (25). When William Ellis was provoked into responding to the accusation by the Russian critic of missionary endeavours, Captain von Kotzebue, that Christianity was being imposed on the Polynesians, rather than sought actively by them, he responded: "[Has he] never heard that the knowledge of *reading* is possessed by the majority of the population, and that the New Testament is translated and widely circulated amongst the people?" (qtd. in Smith: 79). The image of the Polynesian individual reading the Bible seemed to disprove von Kotzebue's point and confirm Ellis's view of the Polynesian as desirous of the Christian message and conversion.

There are a number of important theoretical points that need to be highlighted here. The first is the intense intellectual and emotional Evangelical investment in the "holy book," the Bible. Evangelical Protestantism placed great importance on the potential of biblical interpretation to effect religious conversion and to provide a blueprint for living an exemplary Christian life. For Evangelical missionaries out in the colonial field, the Bible came to be seen as capable of transferring not only the ideal model of religious life but also of "civilised" life—crucially, of British civilisation. The perceived power of this text was such that it promised to reproduce both Christianity and "civilisation"; as one nineteenth-century commentator noted, specifically in relation to imperialist incursions in Africa, "[w]e have the power in our hands, moral, physical, and mechanical; the first, based on the Bible; the second, upon the wonderful adaptation of the Anglo-Saxon race to all climates, situations, and circumstances ... the third, bequeathed to us by the immortal Watt" (qtd. in Headrick: 17). Here the Bible, race, and technology are brought into an invincible trinity as "tools of empire" (Headrick). Jamie Scott notes that "by the middle of the nineteenth century, under the double aegis of 'the bible and the flag,' governments, merchants, explorers, and other adventurers were exploiting the aura of ethical responsibility lent by religion to every effort to carry British civilisation to a benighted world" (xvii). The irony, of course, was that a crosscultural text such as the Bible could be seen to embody British-ness. As R. S. Sugirtharajah has argued, seeing the Bible as Britain's "greatest cultural product" was virtually nonsensical, as this was

> a book in which "not a single line was written, or single thought was conceived by, an Englishman." A collection of books which originated in West Asia, rooted in Mediterranean cultural values, clothed in the everyday imagery of Semitic and Hellenistic peoples, [had] now been assimilated by the English, reinscribed into their linguistic, poetic forms, and turned into a cultural artefact of the English people. (1998b:14)

Regardless, as Sugirtharajah argues elsewhere, the Bible came to be seen as an "ineluctable instrument of the Empire," one which was a key technology of colonial power (1998a:4).

Secondly, however, in the act of linguistic and cultural translation of the Bible in new colonial mission fields, Evangelical missionaries learned the hard way that the Christian message was not necessarily universal nor easily explainable to those of different cultural backgrounds; indeed, as later postcolonial theorists have argued, "the process of translation is the opening up of another contentious political and cultural site at the heart of colonial representation" (Bhabha: 33). In addition, the act of translation also opened up a variety of different interpretations, fundamentally uncontrollable by the missionaries. As Bhabha describes the missionary experience in translating into Indian languages:

> The written authority of the Bible was challenged and together with it a postenlightenment notion of the "evidence of Christianity" and its historical priority, which was central to evangelical colonialism. The Word could no longer be trusted to carry the truth when written or spoken in the colonial world of the European missionary.[5] (33–34)

The next section will address these issues of translation in some detail.

Thirdly, then, to some degree this *textual* crisis embodied the cultural and spiritual dislocation experienced by many of the LMS missionaries. The

---

[5] As Bhabha suggests, these linguistic problems in part led to the employment of native evangelists. Native catechists needed to be found, who brought with them their own cultural and political ambivalences and contradictions, often under great pressure from their families and communities. In Polynesia, native catechists became important members of the missionary community, particularly in making the first forays into new island communities. Indeed, men like Ta'unga, Fauea, and their fellow native missionaries were used as a kind of cannon fodder, frequently assigned to places where the missionaries expected physical threats to their safety. These indigenous catechists will not be examined in detail in this paper, though a study of them would provide an interesting counterpoint to the issues discussed here. See Smith for a brief discussion of native preachers (81–88).

first group of LMS missionaries to Polynesia were singularly unsuccessful in their evangelising attempts. In retrospect, the 1796 mission was ill-conceived and under-planned. Whilst the Society possessed some information about what their envoys might expect to encounter in the islands, individual missionaries seem to have been utterly confounded by the cultural differences they encountered and the extreme isolation they experienced. Assertive female sexuality frightened one missionary from staying more than one night at his appointed mission station, while several missionaries of the first LMS party deserted their stations to live with Polynesian women and their communities. Others decamped to Sydney when civil unrest and political resistance appeared to threaten their safety. Within the first five years of the Pacific missions almost all had thoroughly failed and, by the end of the eighteenth century, only seven missionaries were left in the entire South Pacific field (Neill: 252). Whilst these missionaries might not have been the most educated members of Evangelical congregations, their piety had to be strong and consistent in order to withstand the stresses of the LMS's selection and training processes. That they so consistently had their faith tested and found wanting by their colonial experience is incredible. I would argue that, particularly for these first LMS missionaries to Polynesia, the linguistic and textual crisis—where the supporting texts of their doctrine were unusable or unexplainable, and where communication was so limited and culturally laden—was an integral part of the missionaries' confrontation with their selves and the assumptions and expectations of their (white, religious, middle-class) culture, when forced to reconsider the basic criteria of civility, Christianity, and humanity in crosscultural encounters. As Bhabha suggests, "the hybrid tongues of the colonial space made even the repetition of the *name* of God uncanny" (101). The close attention that missionary texts pay to language collecting, learning, cataloguing, and interpreting reveals their deep investment in the linguistic and translation project as a measure of their success or failure.

Translation and Its Discontents

As noted earlier, translation into other languages opened up a space for colonial difference to emerge. Translation of the Bible was not an easy prospect in any mission field. Steven Kaplan describes translation in Africa as not merely the literal act of changing the language of the Bible but as a rather "more general attempt to express Christian ideas and concepts in an African idiom" (1995a:13). He attests to the complications of such a project, giving the example of the translation of the Bible into the Luba-Katanga language (in southeast Congo). The missionary here reportedly spent years looking for the right translation for "holy spirit"—one assumes a fairly substantial obstacle to the translation project. Local languages had equivalents that related to the African spirit world, but of course such terms were imbued with the wrong connotations. The missionary learned of the role of an official at the local court whose function was to meet those who had business with the chief, to find out what they wanted, to conduct them into the ruler's presence, and to act as their advocate and intercessor, and chose this mediating role as equivalent to Christian theology's Holy Spirit. He adopted the term and turned it to Christian usage in his translation (13–14). As Kaplan suggests, finding proper indigenous terms for producing a vernacular Bible was only a small part of translation work for missionaries—equally important and difficult was the identification of useful comparisons or analogies for explaining essential elements of Christian beliefs (14).

Such intricate problems have meant that biblical translation has been a foundational part of translation studies. However, as Tejaswini Niranjana has argued, the discipline of translation studies has largely ignored the colonialist ideology embedded in many of its foundational texts: "the refusal of translation studies to question these concepts is a refusal to examine the political consequences of translation rigorously" (63). Niranjana argues, with specific reference to India, that missionaries, anthropologists, and colonial administrators systematically collaborated in the consolidation of colonial domination, through their involvement in translation of both Indian and Christian texts. His analysis of the (colonial) politics of translation is, I think, an important one, for it emphasises the ways in which colonialism as an ideology, and as a part of what Marxist theorists would term a hegemonic culture, was bound up in missionary translations. As Niranjana argues, "the discourses of education, theology, historiography, philosophy, and literary translation inform the hegemonic apparatuses that belong to the ideological structure of colonial rule" (33).

R. S. Sugirtharajah has demonstrated the ways in which specific New Testament texts were mobilised to sustain and collude with colonialism and the colonial mission, again in the specific case of India, but with applications across the nineteenth-century mission field (1998b:95). He discusses the ways in which the texts of Matthew and Paul were particularly used in commentaries for Indian students, despite the fact that these texts had been "dormant and ... largely disregarded by the reformers [until] reinvoked in the eighteenth and nineteenth centuries during the evangelical revival which significantly coincided with the rise of Western imperialism" (95). As Sugirtharajah surmises of the imposition of a missionary pattern on the book of Acts during the colonial period, commentators were influenced by the significant changes in world politics wrought by imperialism and, in an act of eisegesis, "were reading these events back into Apostolic times" (103).

At the same time, though, translation should not be conceived of as a simple top-down application of colonialist power/ideology. As Bhabha suggests, translations in colonial contexts allow the possibility of a plethora of interpretations and decentre the European missionary as the sole interpretative authority. Sugirtharajah describes the Indian "Orientalist" phase of modern biblical interpretation, which has enabled Indian Christians to analyse ancient Indian texts as integral co-texts for biblical literature, to provide a sense of Indian-ness to those who were seen as somehow denationalised by the conversion to Christianity, and to establish a sense of authenticity despite being part of the Christian minority (1998a:4–8). Similarly, as many have noted, the missionary schools that taught the Bible, translated into indigenous languages, were often the very institutions from which many anticolonialist activists emerged. Among the imperialist ideologies other subversive ideas lurked, based on key Evangelical beliefs such as universal brotherhood, equality before God, and the potential for self-improvement. As Vicente Rafael argues, conversion can work dialectically in "one's submission to and incorporation of the language and logic of Christianity as the condition for possibility for defining and subsequently overcoming one's prior state of subordination, whether to a pagan past, a colonial overlord, or the local elite" (7).

The key issue here, though, is one of the authority to interpret the words of God. Translation opens up the potential for destabilising European authority; the response to such destabilisation is to reinforce dominant modes of interpretation or definition. Attempts to construe the biblical message in different ways were resisted strongly by many missionaries. Sugirtharajah has chronicled the contestation between Raja Rammohun Roy, a Bengali Brahmin, and Joshua Marshman, a British Baptist missionary at the Serampore mission (1998a:29–53). Rammohun Roy's production of a compilation of Jesus' moral sayings, published as *The Precepts of Jesus: The Guide to Peace and Happiness, Extracted from the Books of the New Testament, Ascribed to the Four Evangelists* in 1820, sparked an ongoing and fierce debate between the two men that continued throughout the 1820s and 1830s. Rammohun Roy's "crime" was to wrest Jesus "from his role at the focal point of missionary preaching, and reframe him as a wise and moral guide, as a 'Messenger of God' and a 'Spiritual Teacher'" (35). Marshman's response was one of moral indignation at the "liberties" taken with the biblical text and one that strongly resisted the consequent shifts in the biblical message in this new "translation." The missionary's belief in the monolithic, singular character of the Bible—as an authoritative text that brooked no interference (unless undertaken by missionaries)—was profoundly threatened by the Indian reinterpretation of "his" message. His authority, both physical and textual, was under threat. As Homi Bhabha has suggested, in such colonial conditions "the holiest of books—the Bible—bearing both the standard of the cross and the standard of empire finds itself strangely dismembered" (92). The ongoing, vociferous debates in the press and in private attest to the fundamentally unsettling nature of this attempt to reappropriate the biblical message, and particularly its potential to destabilise the Baptist mission to India. Sugirtharajah argues:

> at a time when missionaries were trying to utilize the Bible as a strategic resource to demarcate familiar colonial binaries, Christian and heathen, saved and damned, Rammohun Roy neutralized such dichotomizing perceptions by positing the *Vedas* and the Christian Scripture as part of a larger textuality, manifesting one revelation in two separate textual traditions. (1998a:38)

The increasingly "shrill and vitriolic" tone of Marshman's correspondence mirrors the increasingly uncomfortable and unnerved tone of the LMS missionaries in Polynesia, as well as other missionaries in other colonial locations (50). It is clear here that, for British missionaries, translation was meant to work in one direction only—from the imperial authority to the "needy" colonised populace—and the reversal of this progression had the capacity to undermine the imperial and spiritual projects supported by the missionaries. This reversal was, of course, a reversal of power relations, a refusal of the belief that "the colonizer has an inalienable right to explain and speak on behalf of the natives" (88).

The Double Temporality of the Colonial Bible

As the history of responses such as Rammohun Roy's *Precepts* demonstrates, the translation of the Bible—in both directions—opened up particular discursive spaces in colonial cultures. The arguments between Rammohun Roy and Marshman were essentially about the new divided place of the Scriptures, about the suddenly *double* nature of these texts. At the moment of translation, a new location for the Bible becomes possible. The Bible then can exist in two places at once, in two cultures at once, in two different temporalities at once. In this section I want to explore this issue of temporality in particular.

The first temporal dimension of the colonial mission was one of antiquity, of timelessness, and of tradition. The Bible is unarguably an ancient text. Revered by Evangelical Protestants for its antiquity, the Bible promised to be a blueprint for a life lived closer to God than the religions prior to the late eighteenth century (or the religions based in other cultures) had seemed to promise this body of believers. For the Evangelicals based in the British working and lower middle classes, who were beginning to feel the full effects of growing industrialisation and the breakdown of the feudal system, such a return to purer, biblical relations was welcome. When the missionary society most closely affiliated with this constituency, the LMS, chose Polynesia as their first foreign mission, this too fed into a sense of the archaic, the traditional, and the originary. One of the directors, Rev.

Haweis, "concluded that, of all the 'dark places of the earth,' the South Sea Islands presented the fewest difficulties, and the fairest prospects of success" (Williams: 2). These "dark places" of the nonimperial world were themselves perceived as historically prior to the flowering of European civilisation, as somehow anachronous places that had so far escaped the teleology of European notions of progress. Whilst the people of the South Pacific had encountered many more European explorers in the eighteenth century than ever before, the narratives of these explorers attested to the "traditional" lifestyles of the communities and established the stereotypical Romantic view of the islands, their people, and their social arrangements.[6] For the LMS, Polynesia offered a paradise similar to that imagined by many Europeans, but importantly the missionary vision of this paradise imagined that the closeness of the Polynesians to nature could be perceived as closeness to God. Early Evangelical fervour saw the Polynesians as in a "state of nature," which correlated to an originary "state of innocence." European visions of the Pacific, and other island communities being explored at this time, were also influenced by the idea that it might be possible to find the original Eden, as described in the Bible. The LMS missionaries believed they would, in some senses, travel back in time to the "noble savages" imagined by Rousseau and many others, and gradually bring them, through study of the Bible, forward to modern times.

The temporality of race, of course, formed the least palatable vector of the notion of antiquity. On the racial hierarchy that naturally placed the white European at its apex, colonised peoples were relegated to the lower rungs of a racial ladder, specifically *because* of their perceived "belatedness." This is what Bhabha has termed "that temporal caesura, the time-lag of cultural difference" (237): the European notion of historicity that placed the nonwhite world as historically prior to modern civilisation and that justified either intervention to "raise" it up to the temporality of modern Britain or neglect to ensure the "passing" of "dying races."

At the same time as the travel backward in time, then, the missionaries saw their mission as one of modernisation, of bringing modernity to the "benighted savages." This was the second temporal dimension of the colonial mission. During the early 1800s, British colonialism was very early in its influential "second empire" (generally understood as 1784–1867). The gradual expansion of British territories in places such as Australia, India, New Zealand, and the Pacific was in the process of becoming the modern world order that would dominate global politics by the end of the century.

---

6 Haweis's enthusiasm for the Pacific as the first LMS mission site was apparently due to his keen reading of Captain James Cook's *Journals*.

The Evangelical missionaries in Polynesia were at the vanguard of the new world and can be convincingly demonstrated to have played a critical part of bringing about this modernity. The Bible may have been an ancient text, but the Evangelical view of it was new. It was based on groundbreaking new ideas such as the importance of the individual, an agent with desires, rights, and responsibilities separate from those of the broader community. Class was no longer seen as the sole determinant of one's worth or one's access to a superior religiosity. Evangelical religion was the new, modern response to the new, modern times; this innovation was one of its strongest attractions for the growing urban working class and their middle-class employers in Britain. Evangelical activists applied innovative approaches to the age-old religious precepts and in doing so formed the new character of modern Christians—entrepreneurial, productive, assertive men of God.[7]

The Evangelicals used the technologies and ideas of the times to further their mission. They used the modern printing press and access to publication to disseminate their Evangelical intentions and achievements; as Cathcart et al. describe it, "the LMS exploited the resources of the printing press to the full. Anxious to win public support, it broadcast the minutest details of its operations through the pages of published tracts, reports, and the Evangelical Magazine" (25). The LMS took magic lanterns to the mission field, at a time when such technology was relatively new in Europe and even more so in the Pacific (Smith notes that John Williams deliberately took this technology in order to compete with Catholic missions in the region [59]). It transported printing presses, those icons of modernity and the democratisation of knowledge since Gutenberg's time, out to the colonies and continued the proliferation of what might be termed a knowledge economy there. It sought to represent the new British ideals of democracy, individualism, and the potential for "upraising" to those in other lands. In this context the Bible came to represent an artefact of modernity, one that was capable of "raising up" the "childlike" natives (childlike because they were in an "earlier" stage of development) to modern, independent, Christian nationhood. As Sugirtharajah argues of India, "[b]y prescribing Christian morality, [biblical] commentaries became the textual means for justifying the British occupation as the harbinger of civilization. In other words, Christianity was presented as a necessary appendage to the process of modernization, promoting a progressive outlook and contributing to alternative models of social behaviour" (1998a:59). Missionaries around the

---

[7] The gendered noun here is intentional: the corollary of the active Evangelical *man* of God was the domestic "helpmeet" wife. See Grimshaw, Haggis, Carey, Kirkwood.

colonial world used the Bible and Protestant teachings to "raise up" local communities, particularly in relation to issues such as the treatment of women and family structures. Despite the fact that the Evangelical views on such issues were relatively new in themselves, they introduced such social issues as key markers of modern civilisation.

John Williams explicitly advocated his Polynesian missionary work in such temporal terms:

> I am convinced that the first step towards the promotion of a nation's temporal and social elevation, is to plant amongst them the tree of life, when civilization and commerce will entwine their tendrils around its trunk, and derive support from its strength. Until the people are brought under the influence of religion, they have no desire for the arts and usages of civilized life; but that invariably creates it. (581–82)

Here the project of "raising up" colonised cultures is deliberately made an issue of temporality. Interestingly, Williams's design works from the organic metaphors beloved by missionary writers (their narratives are full of seeds being sown, fallow fields being planted, and jungles being cleared for later harvests) toward the industrialised world of commerce and civilisation (another key area of intervention for Williams in particular). The Christian "tree of life" is seen to bring forth modern, enlightened values, such as British civilisation, commerce, and goods: all markers of the modern British nation that will, in Williams's terms, transform the Polynesians into a modern, civilised people.

Again the temporal issues become particularly vicious in relation to race. When LMS missionaries encountered resistance, their early ideas of the racial purity or noble savagery of the Polynesians, for example, were challenged. When LMS missionaries in the Pacific were criticised because of the slowness of cultural transformation, the travellers Tyerman and Bennet defended them: "these islanders are, indeed, in a state of nature, but not of innocence; and the truth is that they are miserable, not happy, under it, for theirs is a state of nature fallen FROM innocence, without the possibility of recovery, except by the faith of Christ, and redemption through his blood" (1:438); "Alas! Such a race of 'Indians' never existed any where on the face of this fallen world, in a state of nature—or rather, in that state of heathenism in which the best feelings of nature are incessantly and universally outraged" (2:8). The temporal displacement has shifted here from an Edenic, prelapsarian vision of the Pacific to the fall; arguably, such a shift could validate a vision of the Pacific as the location of original sin. As Patrick Brantlinger argues,

> As Victorian social and political confidence waned, respect for "savagery" seems also to have waned.... The relatively naive racism of the

early decades of the century often found room for the noble savage...; increasingly it gave way to depictions of [indigenous people] in terms of a pseudo-scientific racism ... based on reductive versions of social Darwinism which did not mourn and sometimes explicitly advocated the elimination of "inferior races." (37)

The Bible, with its own complicated temporality, thus enabled this double time of colonial missions. The text of antiquity, now transformed, as previously discussed, into a British text of modernity and civilisation, itself embodied the paradox of double temporality. It enabled the evangelisation of indigenous cultures to inhabit a transitional or temporally ambiguous mode. The Bible could simultaneously return the "noble savages" to their Edenic state *and* "raise" them up to modern British standards. In this way the Bible functions as the primary text of the temporal caesura, of the time-lag of cultural difference. It introduces the break, the caesura, that enables cultural transformation under colonial evangelism. It brings about a new time in indigenous cultures, a time measured by notions of productivity, progress, and teleological development. As Greg Dening argues of the Marquesan Islanders, the introduction of this new time was a critical part of the evangelisation of the Pacific:

> They were savage because of their sense of time. Civilising them in its essence was giving them a different sense of time. This new sense of time was not just a concern with regularity, although that was important. Making seven days in a week and one of them a sabbath, making mealtimes in a day, making work-time and leisure-time, making sacred time and profane time laid out time in a line, as it were. It removed the irregularity of time in *mau* and *koina* with their peaks of intensity of preparation and participation and their troughs of inactivity. It removed the cyclical time of rituals in which a legendary past was re-enacted to legitimate and prolong the present. Most important in the new sense of time was a notion of progress and of a break-out from the present. A notion of progress called for a self and a social discipline informed by an image of the future. (264)

Conclusion: Biblical Discourses in Colonial and Postcolonial Texts

If the Bible operated as a primary, if complex, signifier within colonial missionary discourses, it has certainly continued this inheritance in contemporary postcolonial theory. For Homi Bhabha, arguably the most influential contemporary postcolonial theorist, the Bible is a central image for his analyses of textuality, colonial power, and the location of colonial cultures. For Bhabha, one of the "primal scenes" of the colonial encounter is the discovery of the English book in colonised lands—unsurprisingly, the emblematic book is the Bible. Bhabha's influential "Signs Taken for Wonders" circulates around the image of the Bible in India, much as his "By Bread Alone" circulates around the image of the chapati. In similar ways, the Bible and the chapati operate as condensed signifiers of British and Indian culture, respectively, and the debates surrounding these signs, the competition for their control, symbolise the intensely unsettled nature of the colonial environment.

Bhabha's essay re-narrates the story of an encounter near Delhi in May 1817 when the Indian catechist Anund Messeh found a group of about five hundred people reading and debating the Bible from a translated copy.[8] Messeh tries to convince the people that this text teaches the religion of the European Sahibs, but they resist his interpretation, feeling that it is God's gift to them, personally. Messeh tells them that "God gave it long ago to the Sahibs, and THEY sent it to us" (Bhabha: 103); he encourages them to be baptised, and, though they acquiesce to this as a possibility, they defer such an event and indicate their problems with the sacrament, because Europeans offend the food-based cultural practices central to Hindu morality. For Bhabha this story becomes one that demonstrates the potential for hybridity, where, for the missionaries, the "miraculous authority of colonial Christianity ... lies precisely in its being both English and universal, empirical and uncanny" (117), but for the potential Indian converts the Bible represents an opportunity to question and subvert colonial authority, to resist the imposition of imperial power, and to open up "a specific space of cultural colonial discourse" (120). Crucially, then, for Bhabha, the discursive conditions of colonialism become sites not only for undermining colonial authority but also for "actively enabl[ling] native resistance" (Young: 149).

For Sugirtharajah, this story becomes one that illustrates the foreignness of the Bible in Asia and the ways in which Asian Christian readings of this text have never been "easy, natural, [or] spontaneous" but always "a confected, mapped, or manufactured reading worked out amidst different cultures and multiple texts and undertaken inevitably from a situation of marginality" (1998a:124). For Robert Young, Bhabha's reading of Indian resistance is not entirely convincing:

> The question becomes whether it is the "colonial text [that] emerges uncertainly," whether the natives have in fact accepted the text but resist the much more obvious aspects of institutionalized imperial power.... To what extent has such recognition [of cultural difference] become

---

[8] The original version was published in the Church Missionary Society's *Register* in 1818. Sugirtharajah also retells this story (1998a:123).

"subversion"? And to what extent has hybridization occurred at all—as opposed to an ambivalence of the Christian text when placed in a new context? (210)

Young's fundamental question here is one that has haunted this essay: How was the Bible (and the Christian message, by extension) received by indigenous people, despite (or because of) its overt imperialist overtones? Vanessa Smith uses the same narrative (and Bhabha's analysis) in conjunction with evidence about cargo cults in the Pacific in the nineteenth century. She discusses the 1830s Siovili cult of Samoa, in which members produced a belief system syncretised from Christian and Polynesian religious practices, which used concepts such as the appealing foreignness of the missionaries and their religion, European artefacts such as the Bible, faith healing, and the imminent return of Christ to amass considerable local interest (88–97). Many of the "mimic practices" of the Siovili cult circulated around the Bible—from radical readings of the Bible that recuperated (and manifested) practices such as direct revelation, spirit possession, and speaking in tongues (discouraged by the missionaries) to the use of English books as props during services (93–94). In Smith's analysis, the Indian incident and the Samoan stand in direct relation as similar appropriations of the book: "the revelation received here by the natives of Delhi is cargo cult, image worship, satisfying the demand for a sign" (95).

In postcolonial theory, as in the colonial texts of the missionary experience, then, the Bible opens up the space for debate, for disagreement, for claims to authority, and for colonial difference to emerge. The correlation between colonial texts and postcolonial theory is not surprising, of course, given that the Indian case study is actually drawn from the colonial records of the Church Missionary Society. Curiously, few of these analyses seem to question the interpretative authority of the Messeh narrative—given other recognition of the ideological nature of missionary texts, it does seem a little strange that each of these analyses takes the base narrative as given and argues about the meaning embedded in that content. Regardless, though, all of these analyses illuminate the complex questions circulating around imperial texts in colonial cultures, as do the original colonial records. That these questions are intensified and focussed by the image of Bible is understandable. As the *ur*-text of nineteenth-century British culture, the Bible worked as the focal point for all debates about colonial discourse and textuality. As Simon Gikandi has noted, "texts were important and indispensible weapons in the imposition of rule and governance.... Texts provided the medium through which the crisis of both colonial and domestic identities were mediated" (xix). If this is true of texts in general, it is particularly so in terms of the Bible. The Bible was used as an important weapon by both missionary evangelists and indigenous people; it was both the mediator and, indeed, the producer of colonial and imperial crises of authority and morality. It stood in for the violence of colonialism at the same time as it stood against such violence, just as it both ameliorated and exacerbated the dispossession of colonised peoples. As the adage of the Xhosa of Grahamstown in South Africa expresses it, "When the whites came here they had the Bible and we had the land. Now they have the land and we have the Bible" (qtd. in Bowie: 16).

Works Consulted

Alderson, David
    1998   *Mansex Fine: Religion, Manliness, and Imperialism in Nineteenth-Century British Culture*. Manchester and New York: Manchester University Press.

Bhabha, Homi K.
    1994   *The Location of Culture*. London and New York: Routledge.

Bowie, Fiona
    1993   "Introduction: Reclaiming Women's Presence." Pp. 1–19 in *Women and Missions: Past and Present: Anthropological and Historical Perspectives*. Ed. Fiona Bowie, Deborah Kirkwood, and Shirley Ardener. Providence, R.I.: Berg.

Brantlinger, Patrick
    1988   *Rule of Darkness: British Literature and Imperialism, 1830–1914*. Ithaca and London: Cornell University Press.

Buck, Sir Peter (Te Rangi Hiroa)
    1993   *Mangaia and the Mission*. Ed. and intro. Rod Dixon and Teaea Parima. Suva, Fiji: Institute of Pacific Studies, University of the South Pacific, in association with B. P. Bishop Museum.

Carey, Hilary
    1995   "Companions in the Wilderness?: Missionary Wives in Colonial Australia, 1788–1900." *Journal of Religious History* 19:227–48.

Cathcart, Michael, Tom Griffiths, Lee Watts, Vivian Anceschi, Greg Houghton, and David Goodman
    1990   *Mission to the South Seas: The Voyages of the* Duff, *1796–1799*. Melbourne University History Monograph Series 11. Parkville, Victoria: The History Department, the University of Melbourne.

Dening, Greg
    1980   *Islands and Beaches: Discourse on a Silent Land: Marquesas, 1774–1880*. Chicago: Dorsey.

Edmond, Rod
    1997   *Representing the South Pacific: Colonial Discourse from Cook to Gauguin*. Cambridge: Cambridge University Press.

Ellis, William
  1829 *Polynesian Researches, During a Residence of Nearly Six Years in the South Sea Islands; Including Descriptions of the Natural History and Scenery of the Islands—with Remarks on the History, Mythology, Traditions, Government, Arts, Manners, and Customs of the Inhabitants.* London: Fisher & Jackson.

Gikandi, Simon
  1996 *Maps of Englishness: Writing Identity in the Culture of Colonialism.* New York: Columbia University Press.

Grant, Lewis Hermon
  1906 *School-Mates: Pictures of School-Time and Play-Time in the Mission Field.* London: London Missionary Society.

Grimshaw, Patricia
  1989 *Paths of Duty: American Missionary Wives in Nineteenth-Century Hawaii.* Honolulu: University of Honolulu Press.

Gunson, Niel
  1978 *Messengers of Grace: Evangelical Missionaries in the South Seas, 1797–1860.* Melbourne: Oxford University Press.

Haggis, Jane
  1991 "Professional Ladies and Working Wives: Female Missionaries in the London Missionary Society and Its South Travancore District, South India in the 19th Century." Ph.D. diss. University of Manchester, Faculty of Economics and Social Studies.

Headrick, Daniel R.
  1981 *The Tools of Empire: Technology and European Imperialism in the Nineteenth Century.* Oxford: Oxford University Press.

Holmes, Brian, ed.
  1967 *Educational Policy and the Mission Schools: Case Studies from the British Empire.* London: Routledge.

Horne, C. Silvester
  1894 *The Story of the L.M.S. 1795–1895.* London: London Missionary Society.

Kaplan, Steven
  1995a "The Africanization of Missionary Christianity: History and Typology." Pp. 9–28 in *Indigenous Responses to Western Christianity.* Ed. Steven Kaplan. New York and London: New York University Press.

  1995b Introduction. Pp. 1–8 in *Indigenous Responses to Western Christianity.* Ed. Steven Kaplan. New York and London: New York University Press.

Kaplan, Steven, ed.
  1995c *Indigenous Responses to Western Christianity.* New York and London: New York University Press.

Kirkwood, Deborah
    1993   "Protestant Missionary Women: Wives and Spinsters." Pp. 23–42 in *Women and Missions: Past and Present: Anthropological and Historical Perspectives.* Ed. Fiona Bowie, Deborah Kirkwood, and Shirley Ardener. Providence, R.I.: Berg.

Murray, A. W.
    1876   *Forty Years' Mission Work in Polynesia and New Guinea, from 1835–1875.* London: Nisbet.

Neill, Stephen
    1984   *A History of Christian Missions.* The Penguin History of the Church. Harmondsworth: Penguin.

Niranjana, Tejaswini
    1992   *Siting Translation: History, Post-Structuralism, and the Colonial Context.* Berkeley, Los Angeles, and Oxford: University of California Press.

Pratt, Mary Louise
    1992   *Imperial Eyes: Travel Writing and Transculturation.* London and New York: Routledge.

Prout, E.
    1865   *Missionary Ships Connected with the London Missionary Society.* London: London Missionary Society.

Rafael, Vicente L.
    1988   *Contracting Colonialism: Translation and Christian Conversion in Tagalog Society under Early Spanish Rule.* Ithaca and London: Cornell University Press.

Scott, Jamie [S.], ed.
    1996   *'And the Birds Began to Sing': Religion and Literature in Post-Colonial Cultures.* Cross/Cultures: Readings in Post/Colonial Literatures in English Series 22. Amsterdam and Atlanta: Rodopi.

Segovia, Fernando F.
    1998   "Biblical Criticism and Postcolonial Studies: Toward a Postcolonial Optic." Pp. 49–65 in *The Postcolonial Bible.* Ed. R. S. Sugirtharajah. Sheffield: Sheffield Academic Press.

Smith, Vanessa
    1998   *Literary Culture and the Pacific: Nineteenth-Century Textual Encounters.* Cambridge Studies in Nineteenth-Century Literature and Culture. Cambridge: Cambridge University Press.

Sugirtharajah, R. S.
    1998a   *Asian Biblical Hermeneutics and Postcolonialism: Contesting the Interpretations.* The Bible and Liberation. Maryknoll, N.Y.: Orbis.

Sugirtharajah, R. S., ed.
    1998b   *The Postcolonial Bible.* Sheffield: Sheffield Academic Press.

Thomas, Nicholas
   1991   *Entangled Objects: Exchange, Material Culture, and Colonialism in the Pacific.* Cambridge, Mass.: Harvard University Press.

Thorne, Susan
   1999   *Congregational Missions and the Making of an Imperial Culture in Nineteenth-Century England.* Stanford: Stanford University Press.

Tyerman, Daniel, and George Bennet
   1831   *Journal of Voyages and Travels by the Rev. Daniel Tyerman and George Bennet, Esq. Deputed from the London Missionary Society, to Visit their Various Stations in the South Sea Islands, China, India, &c., Between the Years 1821 and 1829.* Compiled by James Montgomery. 2 vols. London: Westley & Davis.

Williams, John
   1837   *A Narrative of Missionary Enterprises in the South Sea Islands: With Remarks upon the Natural History of the Islands, Origin, Languages, Traditions, and Usages of the Inhabitants.* London: Snow.

Young, Robert
   1990   *White Mythologies: Writing History and the West.* London and New York: Routledge.

BEFORE THE SECOND REFORMATION: NINETEENTH-CENTURY ABORIGINAL MEDIATIONS OF THE BIBLE IN VAN DIEMEN'S LAND

Penny van Toorn
University of Sydney

ABSTRACT

Adapting theories of dialogism developed by Russian theorists Mikhail Bakhtin and V. N. Vološinov, this paper points to an analogy between pre-Reformation and early colonial structures of power and knowledge. In both cases, language barriers made the Bible inaccessible to local language-speakers except as mediated and monologized through hierarchical institutions. The main body of the paper examines the means by which Aboriginal Australian engagements with the Bible were mediated during the 1830s on the Flinders Island Aboriginal Settlement off the northeast coast of Van Diemen's Land (now the Australian island state of Tasmania). Archival records suggest that the Bible (in the English language) played an important role in structuring power relations both between Aboriginal and non-Aboriginal people, and within the Flinders Island Aboriginal community. The Bible was used to promote cultural assimilation and was effectively monologized in a variety of ways. To elucidate this monologizing process, I analyse a series of sermons and other writings produced by two Aboriginal youths who mediated the Bible to their fellow refugees on Flinders Island. These manuscripts are amongst the earliest written compositions by Indigenous Australians. Ostensibly written by and for the Aboriginal residents of the Island, the sermons are ventriloquised documents produced by order of the Flinders Island Commandant, who deployed them as evidence supporting his specious claims to have educated, civilised, and christianised the Aboriginal people of Tasmania. Nonetheless, there are signs of an incipient dialogization of the Scriptures by non-alphabetically-literate Aboriginal preachers who disseminated biblical knowledge in their own traditional languages. These preachers sowed the first seeds of a "second Reformation" that sees Aboriginal theologians now decolonising the Bible, reading it in their own traditional languages, and bringing it into a zone of genuinely dialogic contact with traditional Aboriginal spiritual beliefs, cultural values, and political objectives.

Re-doing the Reformation

When the Council of Trent, in 1546, reaffirmed the Vulgate as the only authoritative version of the Bible, it was endeavouring to protect the long-standing monopoly of the Roman Church over certain spheres of knowledge and power. Exclusive use of the fourth-century Latin Bible meant that even as literacy levels rose and printed copies of the Bible proliferated, the laity still needed their parish priests to translate and carry God's Word to their ears. Protestant churches were founded on different readings of the Bible and in turn protected the Scriptures from semantic disintegration by establishing their own authority structures and hermeneutic conventions to regulate biblical interpretation. Nonetheless, the Reformation involved a fundamental split between the Roman Church, which continued to mediate between the Latin Bible and the non-Latin-speaking laity, and the Protestant churches, which encouraged people to read the Bible themselves in their own languages.

In colonial contexts, however, this aspect of the Reformation was undone. Latin and vernacular European Bibles were equally unintelligible to those whose homelands were annexed into Europe's modern empires. In Africa, the Americas, Asia, Oceania, and Australia, Catholic and Protestant missionaries alike had no *initial* option but to mediate between the Bible and the peoples they sought to christianise. In each new colonial mission field, the Word of God was at first—and often for many decades—carried to the ears of colonised peoples by European mediators, regardless of whether these mediators were Catholic or Protestant, or indeed whether they remembered that their own homelands in Europe had once been part of the Roman Empire, or that their own Vulgate or vernacular Bibles had been translated from Greek, Hebrew, and Aramaic manuscripts. Although mass production and distribution of biblical texts certainly facilitated the global dissemination of Christian doctrines, colonised populations were obviously prevented from reading the Bible for themselves until it was translated into their own languages and scripts, or until they acquired literacy in the language of the Bibles that were available to them. Like the pre-Reformation laity, colonised populations engaged with the Bible only as selectively mediated, translated, and transmitted to them by others.

The politics of biblical mediation in colonial contexts can be analysed in terms of the theoretical framework jointly developed by Mikhail Bakhtin (1981) and V. N. Vološinov (1973). Working at the time of Stalin's "Russianization" of the Soviet Union, Bakhtin and Vološinov perceived that all texts—and entire national languages—are subject to two competing but historically interrelated sets of forces. On the one hand they are shaped by centripetal, monologizing influences that work to centralise hermeneutic authority, suppress ambiguity and ambivalence, and curtail the practice of reading differently. On the other hand, they are subject to centrifugal, dialogizing influences that realize ambivalence and diversify interpretation. Both sets of forces were clearly operating both during the Reformation and in colonial contexts. The more widely the Bible was disseminated across cultural borders, the greater was the dialogizing pressure toward semantic fragmentation through translation and cultural recontextualisation, and the stronger in many cases was the reactionary monologizing impulse to hold that fragmentation in check.

According to Bakhtin and Vološinov, texts stay "alive" in human history only as long as they remain subject to semantic reappraisal through dialogue and debate. If a single authority monopolises the power to determine, mediate, and enforce scriptural meaning, the Bible becomes single-tongued, monoglossic, and monologic. When a text is permitted only to "say" the same thing to everyone under all circumstances, it becomes semantically ossified, stale, irrelevant, and oppressive. To remain "alive" and urgently meaningful, texts must remain dialogized—multitongued, multivoiced, and semantically contested. While the Bible is often referred to as *the* (singular) living Word of God, European and colonial history both suggest that the Word degenerates into dogma unless it is continuously "re-incarnated," as Walter J. Ong puts it (1977)—continuously revoiced, reheard, rewritten, reread, and reenlivened in human thought and debate. Semantically speaking, the Word "lives" only by remaining in a state of perpetual becoming. Its meaning continually unfolds through being dialogized through translation and recontextualisation in different linguistic, cultural, and historical settings.[1] Yet dialogization, when taken to the extreme, leads to semantic fragmentation and potential cacophony. In colonial contexts, uncontrolled dialogization also meant that colonial government and church officials lost their monopoly over the immense power and moral authority of the Bible.

Obviously, the struggle between centripetal and centrifugal forces unfolds differently in each region and each historical era. In some postcolonial contexts, language and literacy barriers have been overcome, and non-Western readers are now developing their own interpretations of the Bible. The Scriptures are being decolonised, and a second Reformation, global in scope, is now in the process of unfolding. This paper, however, looks at a time prior to this "second Reformation," when the indigenous peoples of Van Diemen's Land first engaged with the Bible both as material object and as verbal text. In archival records relating to the 1820s and 1830s, Indigenous Tasmanian dialogizations of the Bible can occasionally be

---

[1] For an analysis of this principle in Canadian Mennonite fiction, see van Toorn (1995).

glimpsed, but the monologizing impulse largely prevailed. What follows is an account of how the potential dialogicity of the Bible was actively suppressed by members of a colonial administrative hierarchy who prohibited translation, mediated the Scriptures selectively as a tool for cultural assimilation, and refracted their will to power through the voices of a tiny, formally educated Aboriginal elite.

The Text As Object—Red but Unread

Aboriginal societies have lived in Tasmania for over twenty thousand years, since before sea levels rose and cut off the island from mainland Australia (Ryan: 9). Dutch, French, and English explorers visited the island from 1682 onwards, and British and American sealers worked the Bass Strait islands from the late eighteenth century. The British first colonised Van Diemen's Land in 1803. The indigenous peoples of Van Diemen's Land experienced this influx of convicts and settlers as an invasion:

> They consider every injury they can inflict upon white men as an act of duty and patriotic, and however they may dread the punishment which our laws inflict upon them, they consider the sufferers under these punishments as martyrs of their country … having ideas of their natural rights which would astonish most of our European statesmen. (Gilbert Robertson [1828], qtd. in Ryan: 102)

By the 1820s Aboriginal resistance to the expansion of pastoral settlement was so effective that Governor Arthur imposed a state of martial law in 1828. This move amounted to a declaration of war. Arthur established six roving parties to hunt Aboriginal people out of the so-called settled districts. The military had powers to arrest Aboriginal people without warrant or shoot them on sight if they returned to the "settled districts." In early 1830, a bounty was placed on captured Aboriginal males and children, making "black-catching" a lucrative commercial enterprise. Later in the same year, two thousand men from the military, the police, and pastoral communities joined together to form the "Black line," a heavily armed human chain that moved across southeastern and central Tasmania in an attempt to make the land safe for colonists (Ryan: 102–13).

Meanwhile, outside the settled districts of the Tasmanian mainland and on Bruny Island in the southeast, a policy of conciliation was instigated. In early 1829, George Augustus Robinson, son of an East-end London brickmaker, was appointed to minister to the remaining members of the South-East tribe on Bruny Island. Over the next several years, Robinson also led a series of expeditions into the rugged Van Diemen's Land bush. With the help of a small party of Aboriginal guides and mediators, his "friendly mission" persuaded most of the Aboriginal bands remaining in the west, the north, and the northeast to come with him to a place of refuge where they would be looked after and protected from the incursions of the white man.

On 22 August 1831, George Augustus Robinson recorded an extraordinary moment in the history of his "friendly mission" to the people of northeastern Van Diemen's Land. Trekking through the bush, his party came upon a wooden dwelling, "the largest of the kind that I have yet met with in the whole of my travels" (Robinson, 1966:410). This structure and its surroundings "presented a remarkable scene." More surprising, however, was Robinson's discovery in this wild, remote setting of an artefact he saw as part of his own culture:

> All the ground in front of this habitation was thickly strewn with the feathers of the emu, and bones of this stately bird as also other animals such as the kangaroo covered the ground, which the natives had broken to pieces to obtain the marrow to anoint their head and body.... On searching about, found the claw of an emu and some red ochre, but what appeared to me the most extraordinary was finding some pieces of the leaves of the Common Prayer Book, covered with red ochre. On examining these I found them to contain parts of psalms 30, 31, 32, 33 and 96, and on reading the first five verses of the 31st psalm, I found it so peculiarly adapted to me that I could not help exclaiming, "Marvellous are thy ways, O Lord, and thy paths are past finding out"; and on reading the 33rd psalm at the 13th and 14th verses, "The Lord looked down from heaven and beheld all the children of men" &c, I thought them peculiarly applicable to this forlorn and hapless race of human beings.... Ere I left this celebrated spot I collected some feathers of the emu and the claws, which together with the fragments of leaves of the Common Prayer Book I brought away with me as mementoes of the circumstance. (Robinson, 1966:410)

Robinson's find repeats a motif that appears again and again in the literature of empire, a scene that Homi Bhabha has called "the sudden, fortuitous discovery of the English book" in the world's "dark, unruly places" (102, 107). Bhabha suggests that this moment of discovery exposes the potential ambivalence of the book, its dual aspect of being original, familiar, and authoritative but also aberrant, foreign, and vulnerable. In Bakhtinian terms, one might say that this moment of discovery discloses the tension between dialogizing and monologizing forces.

Unlike the Indian villagers who, in Bhabha's example, were alphabetically literate and had access to Bibles in their own language, the Van Diemen's Land Aborigines had no way of deciphering the Psalms as a verbal text. Nonetheless, they appropriated and transformed the text as a material object. Robinson discovered a book that was no longer a book, but a scattering of "leaves," coloured red—but unread. To Robinson, the *Book of*

Common Prayer epitomised English civilisation, Christianity, and colonial authority. Customarily the Prayer Book provided a script for Christian ritual. As I have suggested elsewhere, rituals and ceremonies are (in principle if not always in practice) the antithesis of carnivals (van Toorn, 1994). According to Bakhtin, carnivals temporarily do away with the distance ordinarily separating different voices and disparate varieties of discourse. All voices and discourses can potentially contextualize one another and can thus mutually dialogize or determine each other's meaning and authority (van Toorn, 1994:74–76). In English Protestant culture, the *Book of Common Prayer* would ordinarily have cocooned the psalmic text (and certain other parts of the Scriptures) within liturgical settings that monologized them by keeping potentially disruptive contextual influences at bay. In the Van Diemen's Land bush, however, the book had been displaced, dismembered, and torn away from its usual anchor points in English culture. The psalmic text was exposed to the transformative influences of one of the world's "dark, unruly places."

Robinson believed that the pages had been taken during a recent Aboriginal attack on a white settlement: "No doubt exists in my mind," he wrote, "but these are the people who have committed the recent outrages in the vicinity of Launceston and on the east bank of the Tamar, these leaves having been taken in their predatory attack upon the white inhabitants, together with other plunder" (Robinson, 1966:410). Red ochre played an important part in Aboriginal ritual life, so it is probable that the pages from the Prayer Book—part of the script for Christian worship—were used for different ritual purposes by the people of northeast Van Diemen's Land. Although these people would not have been able to decipher the words of the text, they covered the pages with red ochre, perhaps ritually appropriating the power of what they correctly saw as one of the white man's sacred instruments.

Upon finding the stolen Psalms, Robinson immediately repatriated the leaves back into the category of written text, subjecting them again to the rules of both iconic and phonographic recognition upon which their usage, authority, and meaning conventionally depended in his culture. On the one hand, he found the ochre-covered pages "most extraordinary" and quite alien; on the other hand, the words of the Psalms remained intimately familiar to him. Indeed, he read them as "peculiarly adapted to me" (Robinson, 1966:410). The first five verses of Psalm 31 ask God for protection from moral and physical danger ("come quickly to my rescue ... save me ... free me from the trap that is set for me"); the thirteenth and fourteenth verses of Psalm 33 describe God's gaze encompassing all humankind, including those whom Robinson called "this forlorn and hapless race of human beings" (1966:410). Robinson interpreted the found text as a promise of protection and a vindication of his dangerous conciliatory quest. His discovery of the Psalms of David in the Van Diemen's Land wilderness assured Robinson of God's omniscience and omnipresence. Although—or because—the text-as-object had been expropriated, Robinson effectively undid its otherness and restored its monologicity by reactivating the phonographic function of the script, and reassigning familiar meanings to the words of the Psalms.

The following day, Robinson reasserted his power to act as an authoritative transmitter of the Psalms to the Aboriginal people who served him as guides and mediators. In his journal he wrote:

> I could observe that I informed the natives attached to the service that the paper I had found in the wild natives' hut was pieces of the word of God, and some of them who spoke English requested me to read it to them and which I accordingly did, when they paid strict attention. On this subject I had often spoken to them. (1966: 411)

Robinson validated his own ministry to the Aborigines of Van Diemen's Land by pointing to the mission Aborigines as living proof that "natives" were capable of engaging "properly" with "pieces of the word of God," provided of course that such words were conducted into their hearing in appropriate ways.

Robinson's repatriation of the Psalms is evidence of his desire to make the Bible speak with a single voice in a single language. Throughout the colonial period, Aboriginal people in Van Diemen's Land, and in all other Australian colonies except South Australia, were not given access to the Bible in their own languages. Like priests of the Roman Church prior to the Reformation in Europe, colonial officials in Van Diemen's Land, sometimes aided by Aboriginal agents, carried the Bible—or a particular reading of it—to the ears of the Aboriginal people. Every effort was made to monologise the Bible or render it as a single-voiced text and to preserve the colonists' monopoly over the power of biblical knowledge. Every effort was made to prevent Aboriginal peoples from exploring what the Bible might say in the light of their own knowledge, culture, and social values. These efforts, however, did not prevent nonliterate Aboriginal people from appropriating and transforming the Bible as a ritual object, nor from challenging biblically based colonial viewpoints.

Before Aboriginal people were schooled into knowledge of alphabetic writing, their perspectives challenged orthodox readings of the Bible. Four weeks after discovering the ochre-covered pages in the bush, Robinson was resting at George Town in northeastern Van Diemen's Land. While there, he received a letter from John Batman, passing on a story told by a Captain Kneale, who had taken a six-year-old boy christened George Van Diemen to England a decade earlier in 1821. Robinson retold Captain Kneale's story in his journal:

> One night the boy was in conversation with him [Captain Kneale] and asked him who made the moon. He replied, God; God made everything. Then, looking steadily up at the Heavens for a few moments as if in deep reflection, he [the boy] said, do you see that star near the moon? He answered, yes. He replied, he supposed God made that star also? He replied, yes. Ah, said he, the moon's after that star and he will catch him too, and that he supposed the star was some poor black fellow and the moon would soon catch him. (Robinson, 1966:438)

When Captain Kneale told George Van Diemen that God made the moon and "God made everything," he was interpreting the beautiful night sky in terms of the first chapter of Genesis. In the wild beauty of Van Diemen's Land, Kneale perhaps glimpsed some remnant of an Edenic, unfallen world, a world confirming that God's creation was indeed "good," as is stated in Gen 1:18. The boy, by contrast, read the night sky in the context of his own people's experience. To him, moon and star were respectively predator and prey; they presented a picture of the way he and his people were being hunted down and killed or captured by the white man. George Van Diemen read the sky as an allegorical tableau of the bloody history of colonial race relations in Van Diemen's Land. He could not read the Bible for himself at the time and may not have known about the story of the fall. Yet by reading the night sky differently, he disturbed Captain Kneale's reading of Genesis, implicitly shifting the emphasis away from the goodness of God's creation and raising the possibility that colonialism as practised in Van Diemen's Land was a symptom of humanity's fallen state.

Genesis on Flinders Island

To house those Aboriginal people who accepted Robinson's offer of asylum, the colonial government in February 1833 set up the Wybalenna settlement on Flinders Island off the northeast coast of Van Diemen's Land, after several false starts on various unsuitable sites (Rae-Ellis: 107). The first translation of any portion of the Bible into an Indigenous Tasmanian language is ascribed to Thomas Wilkinson, who was appointed catechist at Wybalenna in June 1833. By mid-September of the same year, Wilkinson reported to Governor Arthur that he had translated "the principal parts of the first four chapters of Genesis" into the language of the Ben Lomond people (Wilkinson, qtd. in Plomley, 1987a:69). The Aboriginal people at Wybalenna belonged to several different language communities. Why did Wilkinson choose the Ben Lomond language over the others? The most likely explanation for his choice was the presence of a Ben Lomond boy, Walter George Arthur. Born in 1819 or 1820, Walter had been taken from his family at a young age and taught to read and write at the Orphan School in Hobart. In 1833, he appears to have been the only Aboriginal resident at

Wybalenna who was literate in alphabetic script and familiar with both English and the Ben Lomond language.[2]

Without acknowledging any assistance he may have received, nor considering the language differences that divided the Wybalenna Aborigines, Catechist Wilkinson proudly informed Governor Arthur that the people "seemed to understand his translation ... and showed an interest in what they heard" (Plomley, 1987a:69). Governor Arthur, however, judged the Ben Lomond translation "imprudent" (ibid.). While insisting that "scriptural religion should be the grand object of attention in the education of the aborigines" (Arthur, qtd. in Robinson, 1966:941n29), Governor Arthur thought it counterproductive to translate the Bible into the language of an "uncivilised" society. Plomley has observed that the governor "could not understand that the only way to enter the hearts and minds of the Aborigines was through their own language" (Plomley, 1987a:68–69). Governor Arthur believed that "the Bible is the most effectual mode of introducing civilization" (qtd. in Robinson, 1966:941n29), but he refused to countenance biblical translations into Aboriginal languages. For the governor, christianisation involved converting colonised peoples into "proper" interpreters of the Bible, not converting the Bible into a foreign text whose familiar meanings could be lost through "improper" assimilation into alien cultural contexts. To allow Catechist Wilkinson to facilitate the latter on Flinders Island was to throw away the colonising society's monopoly over the power of biblical knowledge.

Catechist Wilkinson was popular with the Aboriginal people but was considered an irascible bigot by his fellow officers. After becoming embroiled in conflict with Wybalenna Superintendent Lieutenant William Darling, and others, he was suspended from office in October 1833 and left the island permanently in April 1834 (Plomley, 1987a:69–70). No one else on Flinders Island attempted a *written* translation of any portion of the Bible into any of the indigenous Van Diemen's Land languages. George Augustus Robinson, who took over as superintendent of Wybalenna in October 1835, had once preached a sermon in the Bruny Island language in 1829 (Robinson, 1966:61). He did not repeat this experiment on Flinders Island, however, and strongly disapproved of attempts by the new catechist, Robert Clark, to preach in a pidgin English peppered with indigenous words (Robinson, 1987:319; 13 Dec 1835). Until 1838, when some Aboriginal men spoke in their own languages on their (mediated) understandings of the Scriptures, the Aboriginal people on Flinders Island engaged with the Bible

---

2 Walter George Arthur's Aboriginal name is not recorded in the written archive. I refer to him by his first name, "Walter," rather than his last name, "Arthur," in order to distinguish him from Governor Arthur, after whom he was presumably renamed.

only as interpreted by white officials, and by two young Aboriginal teaching assistants, Walter George Arthur and Thomas Brune, both of whom had been educated at the Hobart Orphan School.

The Bible became an instrument whereby the Aborigines on Flinders Island were inculcated into the English language and into a grotesquely degraded version of an English way of life. Walter George Arthur and Thomas Brune, together with Robinson and his officers, mediated the Bible in ways that implemented Governor Arthur's assimilationist agenda. The governor was especially concerned, for instance, that the Aborigines should observe the Sabbath. In September 1833, having admonished Catechist Wilkinson for his "imprudent" act of translation, Governor Arthur described the catechist's proper duties thus:

> Keep a school—have divine service twice on Sunday and ... have the effect of leading the Aborigines to see at least at an early period one striking particular of the Christian Dispensation—I mean the strict observance of the Sabbath—during which say they may readily be instructed that hunting and many other worldly pursuits give place to worship of an Almighty Creator. (Qtd. in Plomley, 1987a:68)

Governor Arthur's intentions were carried into effect by Superintendent George Augustus Robinson and those who served under him, especially the catechist Robert Clark, who had replaced Thomas Wilkinson in 1834. Having engaged with the Word of God primarily as mediated by their religious instructors and school teachers, the young Aboriginal men in turn passed on the Bible's messages to the rest of the Aboriginal people on the island. In October 1835, for example, Governor Arthur's preoccupation with the Sabbath was rearticulated in a short, biblically based lesson written by his namesake, Walter George Arthur:[3]

Lesson the first

> In six days the Lord made the Heavens and the Earth, the sea and all that there in is. And on the seventh day God ended his work, and he rested on that day. For this Reason we keep the Sabbath holy, because the Lord rested on that day. Six Days are for working, in which our Labouring is to be done; but the seventh day is a day of Rest. (ML, A7073, vol. 52, part 6, f. 51, 27 Oct 1835)

---

[3] This rewriting of Genesis is not signed, but Walter George Arthur was the only functionally literate Aboriginal resident at Wybalenna in 1835. Thomas Brune, the other young literate Aboriginal man, appears not to have arrived on Flinders Island until June 1836. See Ryan: 325, 327.

This lesson paraphrases Gen 2:2–3, which Walter had in all likelihood translated with Catechist Wilkinson two years previously. In the process of reinforcing the doctrine that God created the world, the passage functions as an instrument of cultural assimilation by teaching that the Sabbath should be observed as a day of rest. Walter was capable both of reading the Bible in English for himself and of copying out the verses verbatim from the Book. This "Lesson," however, is a paraphrase, not a verbatim copy of the Bible. Since its language differs from that of Walter's own biblical paraphrases and written compositions, it is probable that the paraphrase was not composed by Walter, but copied by him. Copying was the prevailing mode of developing the Aboriginal students' handwriting skills on Flinders Island. The model text was usually written out by the catechist. Walter's "Lesson" is evidently a copy of a paraphrase generated by the catechist, Robert Clark. Clark's mediation of Genesis prescribes the manner in which the Aboriginal residents should conduct themselves at the Wybalenna settlement—precisely as Governor Arthur would have wished. The governor's reading of the Bible was transmitted from the top down, throughout the colonial hierarchy. Governor Arthur's views shaped the way the catechist mediated the Bible to Walter, who in turn passed on the prescribed biblical messages to his countrymen.

Two years later, in the Wybalenna newspaper, the *Flinders Island Chronicle,* Walter again admonished the people to observe the Sabbath. This time he composed the text himself, yet invoked the authority not of the Bible but of his teacher, Catechist Clark. Governor Arthur had by this time been replaced by Governor John Franklin, but the biblically authorised assimilationist agenda continued. Taking it upon himself to extend the catechist's biblically grounded pronouncement about the Sabbath, Walter admonished the people to wash with soap and stop painting-up with ochre (an ironic reproach given that Catechist Clark's own standards of personal hygiene were notoriously lax[4]):

> And now my Dear friends I want to tell you and I saw some women carrying woods upon Sunday so I walk to ask Mr Clark if it is right to carry wood on Sunday no I don't think it is right to carry woods on God's day so that I am sure it is not right for any one to do such things in his day You should not play or work on that day you should not do anything on God day.... And also another thing you should not throw about the soap They have too much Mr Clark because when I am about the place I always see plenty of soap lying about I only want to put it down that you may all

---

[4] Robinson refers to Clark's "old, greasy dirty fustian jacket which he had worn until, as Mrs Nickolls observed, [it] would make excellent soup if boiled" (1987:319; 14 Dec 1835).

know that the soap is a fine thing to wash yourselves with and yet they
don't care for it no they would sooner put on that there clay stuff what they
have been always used and they like it better then they would have soap to
wash they faces.... (ML A7073, vol. 52, part 4, f. 39, 24 Oct 1837)[5]

Despite the biblical injunctions mediated through Robert Clark and Walter George Arthur, the nonassimilated Wybalenna residents had their own contextually determined views of the Sabbath. Everything relating to the Sabbath they termed "Sunday." Good cloth was referred to as "Sunday"; Bibles and Prayer Books were "Sunday books" (Robinson, 1987:318; 12 Dec 1835). Sunday or not, they were sent out to hunt for their food when the settlement's rations ran out, or when hostilities periodically erupted between the three main tribal groups (Ryan: 135). For the Aborigines, Sunday also meant the tedium of long, unintelligible church services. Seeing their boredom and drowsiness, Robinson considered adapting the liturgy, believing it was "absurd to persist in reading a set form of worship" (1987:314; 6 Dec 1835). Whether he could set aside the *Book of Common Prayer* was another question, however. He wanted to instigate "true worship" (ibid.) by making liturgical language more intelligible, yet he could not condone Robert Clark's attempts to mediate Genesis in pidgin as "God-a-mighty made us all, black and white fellows" (Robinson, 1987:319; 13 Dec 1835).

LITERACY, POWER, AND TRADITIONAL ABORIGINAL AUTHORITY STRUCTURES

The Flinders Island Aboriginal community was by no means homogeneous. A small group of adult Aborigines who had lived on the Bruny Island mission and guided Robinson on his treks through the bush lived in a separate area from the Western, Big River, and Ben Lomond peoples, between whom conflicts periodically arose. Fourteen women who had lived with sealers defied both Robinson and the Aboriginal men. Fourteen children lived apart from the adults in dormitories attached to the houses of the catechist and the storekeeper. These children were the main focus of Robinson's efforts to assimilate and christianise. Ranging in age from six to fifteen in 1835, they lived a regimented life, rising at half past six to wash and say prayers before assembling at seven o'clock to read the Bible with the catechist and his family. They breakfasted at half past seven, attended school until noon, and, after an hour's lunch break, returned to school until half past three. Between six and eight, they helped the adults at the evening

---

[5] Thomas Brune also used biblical quotations to urge the people to keep the Sabbath in his sermon of 21 Feb 1838. See ML A7073, vol. 52, part 6, f. 133. All quotations retain the spelling and grammar used in the original manuscripts.

school, then returned to the catechist's house for family worship before retiring to bed at nine o'clock (Ryan: 184).

Of these children, Walter George Arthur was the eldest, and Thomas Brune was between one and three years younger. These two teenage boys wrote virtually all the Aboriginal manuscripts now lodged in the Robinson papers at the Mitchell Library. Their writings consist of thirty-one issues of the *Flinders Island Chronicle* produced between September 1837 and January 1838,[6] thirty-one sermons written between September 1837 and July 1838, and an assortment of miscellaneous lessons and fragments. In these documents, many of which they read aloud to the assembled congregation, they carried selected parts of the Bible (in English) to the ears of the Aboriginal community at Wybalenna. George Augustus Robinson orchestrated these mediations. Whether trekking through the bush making contact with "wild natives" or imparting religious instruction to the inmates of the Wybalenna settlement, Robinson's recurrent *modus operandi* was to create and/or exploit divisions within Aboriginal society and to use a small group of known and trusted individuals to mediate between himself and the larger, less familiar, less predictable group. Walter George Arthur and Thomas Brune played an important mediatory role between Robinson and the wider Flinders Island Aboriginal community. Walter's and Brune's sermons and reports in the *Flinders Island Chronicle* also carried biblical doctrines to the ears of the larger Aboriginal community at Wybalenna.

While these two young men were conduits for the power of the colonial administration, they did not derive their authority from precisely the same source, and each had his own personal political agenda. Walter George Arthur was the son of Ben Lomond elder Drule.er.par, whom Robinson renamed "King George."[7] On Flinders Island, all of the tribal groups were in alien country. In contrast to Coranderrk Reserve established in Victoria in 1863, for example, where Woiworung leader William Barak was senior traditional owner of the country on which the reserve was situated, no one was on their home territory on Flinders Island. None of the groups residing on the island was invested with the power that flowed from ancient spiritual ties to the Wybalenna site. Killings and displacements from homelands had disrupted the kinship networks and broken the physical bonds to specific sections of country that traditionally structured inter- and intratribal social relations. Nonetheless, memory-ties, spiritual ties, and knowledge-ties would naturally have lived on, and there

---

[6] The first issue of the *Flinders Island Chronicle* is dated 10 September 1836; however, Plomley has corrected this dating to 1837 (1987b:1009).

[7] See Plomley (1987b:851), where Drule.er.par is named as Walter's father, but cf. 843, where Walter is not recorded among Drule.er.par's children.

is evidence to suggest that traditional ceremonial practices and power structures remained in place to some degree on Flinders Island.[8] Each of the main tribal groups retained an order of seniority that accorded authority to their elders. Robinson called the elders "kings" and was partially successful in securing their cooperation with his plans. Thus, in traditional Aboriginal cultural terms, Walter was the son of a man of high degree and had a certain social status, even though he had been taken from his family at a young age and had no recollection of his Aboriginal name.

Thomas Brune was in a rather different position. Born between 1820 and 1823 into the Nuenonne band on Bruny Island (Ryan:15–16), he was taken to the Orphan School in Hobart. Although he refers to being welcomed by "brethren and friends" upon arrival at Wybalenna, Brune appears to have had no close family on Flinders Island, and his social status is difficult to determine.[9] Within the kinship structures through which Aboriginal social identities and relationships are traditionally defined, he appears to have had no authoritative position from which to speak. However, political relationships at Wybalenna were relatively unstable and were complicated by Robinson's introduction of new forms of sacred and secular knowledge, new technologies of communication, and a pedagogical system where the young instructed the old, in direct contravention of customary practice in Aboriginal societies. In this context, a youth like Thomas Brune could create a niche for himself by using his language and literacy skills to mediate the power both of the Bible and of the secular colonial authorities. Although Brune was slightly younger than Walter and lacked the latter's kinship connections, both boys accrued power, social status, and authority through their closeness to the Flinders Island commandant, their knowledge of the English language, their ability to read and write, and their familiarity with the religious doctrines encoded in the white man's sacred book.

Walter and Brune both signed their writings with their names followed by the words "Aboriginal Youth Editor and Writer." Brune worked as a copy clerk for Robinson, and added "Clerk of the Commandant Office" to this title (*Flinders Island Chronicle*, 11 Oct 1837; ML A7073, vol. 52, part 4, f.

---

[8] On 8 November 1837, for example, Thomas Brune recorded in the *Flinders Island Chronicle* that "The Native men ... were singing bout their own country song." Ryan also states that "They hoarded ochre and performed ceremonial rites in secret" (185).

[9] In an untitled and undated text written by Thomas Brune, he states, "And when I came on Flinders Island I seen all my brethren and friends and were very glad to see them then when they saw me they were very glad" (ML A7073, vol. 52, part 6, f. 71). Trugernana, Wourraddy, and his sons David and Peter Brune were from Bruny Island, but their relation to Thomas Brune is not specified in any of the name-lists published in *Friendly Mission* or *Weep in Silence*, where only nuclear family ties are recorded.

31). Walter was referred to in the school reports as "Prince Walter" and later signed himself as "Chief of the Ben Lomond tribe" (Walter George Arthur to George Augustus Robinson, 1 Feb 1847; ML A7073, vol. 52, part 9, ff. 1–4). There are signs that the two young men were rivals at times. In the *Flinders Island Chronicle* of 2 October 1837, for example, Walter noted that "when I am in school I always see Mis Thomas Brune. Laughing and playing away in the middle of school" (ML A7073, vol. 52, part 4, f. 23). Being "put in the paper" like this was a mode of moral persuasion and a dreaded form of punishment that Brune and Walter were deputised to mete out. When, for example, they threatened to put the sealers' women "in the paper" for failing to clean their houses, Robinson recorded that the women "begged they would not be put in the paper, [and] said they might KARNY speak but not write. They seemed to have a great abhorrence of being put in the paper" (1987:489; 17 Oct 1837).

The earliest document bearing Thomas Brune's signature is a biblically based writing exercise dated 24 July 1836:

Protection
Protection Protec [*sic*]
                    23rd Psalm

The Lord is my shepherd: therefore can I lack nothing. He shall feed me in a green pasture: and lead me forth beside the water of comfort. He shall convert my soul: and bring me forth in the paths of righteousness for his Name's sake. (ML A7073, vol. 52, part 6, ff. 19, 21, 23)

In Thomas Brune's transcription of this section of Psalm 23, the archaic language of the King James Authorised Version has been simplified. In addition, in verse 3, "He *restoreth* my soul" has been changed to "He *convert* my soul," perhaps in an effort to adapt the biblical text to the mission context. These changes suggest that Brune was not transcribing directly from the Bible but rather, in accordance with common teaching methods of the time, was reproducing a copytext probably written by the catechist Robert Clark. Like Walter's, Brune's engagement with the Bible appears at this time to have been mediated rather than direct. Instead of having access to the entire text and copying out whichever parts he found most meaningful, Brune reproduced a passage chosen and edited by his teacher and may not have been aware of possible differences between the biblical text and Clark's copytext. In 1835–1836, the catechist's mediations determined which parts of the Bible were accessible, opening up some parts but closing off others. The Bible was thus effectively monologized. Until the people were able to read the entire text for themselves in an intelligible language, they had no way of knowing what they were missing, nor of deciding whether or how it might be meaningful or empowering.

For Thomas Brune, religious and political instruction were delivered simultaneously by Psalm 23. At the top of the page, above the transcribed psalmic verse, the word "protection" was written neatly in a copperplate hand, to be copied by Thomas Brune. Psalm 23 characterises God as a protector. While disease and high mortality rates made life for the Wybalenna Aborigines a fearful "walk through the valley of the shadow of death" (as in verse 4, before which Brune's transcription terminates), the official line was that the settlement was a safe, protected refuge where the Aboriginal people's needs were generously met by the grace of God and Commandant Robinson. The commandant certainly saw himself as fulfilling the role of a protector and was eventually to leave Wybalenna to take up the lucrative position of Chief Protector of Aborigines in the Port Phillip District (in what is now the Australian mainland state of Victoria). Discursively, Robinson inserted himself into the same position as God. In a sermon written in July 1838, Walter urged his Aboriginal audience to "obey the king and all that are put in authority under him to submit myself [corrected to "yourself"] to all my governors teachers spiritual partners and master and should order myself truly and reverently to all betters" (ML A7073, vol. 52, part 6, f. 129). The Bible was also used to explain why men such as Robinson and Clark had come from distant lands to christianise the Aborigines. Thomas Brune noted in three of his sermons that "Jesus Christ said a long time ago to his Disciples go ye and teach all nation baptising them in the Name of the Father and of the Son and of the Holy Ghost teaching them to observe all things whatsoever I have Commanded you and Lo I am with you always & even unto the end of the world" (ML A7073, vol. 52, part 6, ff. 73, 91, 93).

Formulaic Mediations

Walter's and Brune's sermons were a mixture of reportage, prayer, and moral exhortation. It is likely that they were imitating the preaching style of the catechist Robert Clark, whom Robinson described (with some irritation) as offering up "a mixed prayer and exhortation" (1987:319; 14 Dec 1835). Walter and Brune quoted from and wrote about the Bible in their sermons. Walter's sermon of 6 October 1837 situates the Wybalenna people at the centre of a moral and cultural tug of war between the Bible and the bush, the latter being the place where they hunted and continued their traditional ceremonies out of sight of the commandant:

> The people of Flinders Island ... are learning to read now as fast as they can but they all run away into the bush and get sick and they say they will never come home again no they say there is too much work for them to do....
> [I]f you lose what God hast told you in the Bible God wont like you Nay God would like you no more he will cast you out of his presence....

> Now my dear friends learn ... how to read this book and understanding it because there is no other [way] to get to God but by learning out of this book because there is no other book better than this Bible.
> Because the bible came from God and if it came from God it must be a Good book and those who learn of that book and understand it is a far better thing than into the bush and hunt for those things which is not of much Good. (ML A7073, vol. 52, part 4, f. 27)

Formulaic repetition is a common feature of Christian liturgy in general and of the sermon as a written genre designed for oral delivery. Walter's and Brune's sermons are unusually repetitive, however. Although each sermon contains some new material, certain messages are reiterated again and again, using set verbal formulae. Formulaic statements are shuffled around from sermon to sermon, like pieces of a mosaic that have been assembled in a variety of ways to form different configurations of the same basic picture. Some of the most frequently repeated formulae are invocations of the authority of the Bible. Over a ten-month period, for example, Walter and Brune told the Aboriginal community eight times, using an identical form of words, that "Jesus ... came into our world *to die for our sins according to the scripture*" (ML A7073, vol. 52, part 6, ff. 67, 75, 77, 93, 109, 113, 117, 131). On the one hand, it is important to acknowledge that what comes across as formulaic repetition in a set of archival documents that can be read at a single sitting may not have been perceived as such in the original context of reception, where each sermon was separated from the next by an interval of days or weeks. On the other hand, the exactness of these repetitions is striking precisely because an identical form of words echoes again and again across large intervals of time.

The repetitive, formulaic aspect of these sermons may be attributed to several causes. Walter J. Ong (1982) has noted that repetitive use of formulaic expressions is a distinctive characteristic of orally grounded discourse: where knowledge cannot be stored in written documents, it must be preserved through constant oral reenunciation in memorable, formulaic verbal units. Parts of the Bible were mediated to Walter and Brune, whose writings were designed for oral delivery to, and memorisation by, an audience who could not read alphabetic script.

A more likely explanation for Walter's and Brune's formulaic repetitions, however, lies in the catechetical instruction method whereby Aboriginal people learned Christian doctrines. Throughout the time Walter and Brune were writing their sermons, they were engaged both as teachers and learners in a repetitive catechetical teaching process that gauged "progress" on the basis of how accurately pupils could repeat prescribed forms of words in answer to set questions. Scriptural education at Wybalenna centred on repetitive, ritualised, ostensibly dialogic exchanges that in effect imposed a monologic reading of the Bible.

The Double Positioning of Speakers and Audience

By early 1838, Thomas Brune was reading the Bible for himself and reporting some of his findings in his sermons:

> And now my friends there is a passage in John's Gospel the third Chapter "for can a man be born again when he is old can he enter the second time into is mother's womb and be born"
> Jesus said except a man be born of water and of the spirit he cannot enter into the kingdom of God....
> And now my friends I was reading in my house and I saw a verse in the chapter
> And now my friends if we are good in Christ well he would give us his word
> And now my brethren who is it that gave us the word Jesus Christ gives us his word and none [other] Do you know that Jesus Christ pardon all your sins The people of Van Diemen's land they are learning about God and his son Jesus Christ
> Do you think my friends that God is very good yes my friends and don't you think that Jesus is very good Yes and my friends don't you know that there is three persons in the Godhead perhaps you might say who are they why I should say the Father Son and Holy Ghost there are all one the Father his equal to the Son and the Son is equal to the Holy Ghost and these three all agree in one
> And my friends there is in the scriptures it says "Thus saith the Lord of hosts consider your ways" do we consider our ways No my friends don't consider our ways No my friends we do not ... and do let us pray to God for he will pardon our sins and if we do not well we have that place which burns for ever and ever
> And now my friends let us love the Lord thy God with all thy heart with all thy soul and with all thy strength love thy Neighbour as thy self
> Thomas Brune Aboriginal Youth Editor and Writer.
> (Sermon, 7 Feb 1838, ML A7073, vol. 52, part 6, f. 81)

This sermon illustrates several features typical of both Brune's and Walter's writings. First, Brune's authority derives in part from the fact that he has read the Bible for himself. As well as delivering God's word to the Aboriginal congregation, Brune's direct biblical quotation functions to authorise him as a speaker. Quotations verify his claim that "It tells me in the Bible" (Undated sermon, ML A7073, vol. 52, part 6, f. 93). The question is: Did the Bible tell Brune anything different from the readings imposed by the colonial authorities? And if different readings did, on occasion, take shape in Brune's mind, would he have been punished for transmitting them to his countrymen?

A second notable feature of Brune's sermon (and Walter's sermons too) is that he speaks *for*, as well as *to*, the congregation. He asks rhetorical questions, a monologic form of pseudo-exchange in which the speaker answers the questions for his audience. The rhetorical questions in Brune's sermons pretend to activate a dialogue, but the dialogic form serves only to mask the monologic way in which the Scriptures are mediated and re-mediated in the Flinders Island context. In this respect, Brune's rhetorical questions are entirely congruent with the catechetical method of teaching that situates teacher and pupil in a pseudo-dialogic context that does not allow the latter a separate, autonomous voice.

A third conspicuous feature of both Brune's and Walter's writings is the oscillation between first, second, and third-person plural pronouns: the Aboriginal audience is referred to as "we," "you," and "they." Use of third-person pronouns was particularly prevalent in the *Chronicle,* although the practice also occurred in the sermons. Why did Brune and Walter need to tell the people of Flinders Island what they themselves had been doing? Given that the sermons and *Chronicle* issues were both read out loud by their authors to the people assembled at the evening school, why did Brune and Walter adopt the apparently absurd practice of referring to their audience as "they" rather than "you," even to the extent of referring to themselves in the third person?[10]

These pronoun shifts may be accounted for in two mutually non-exclusive ways, First, they show Brune's and Walter's sense of the multiplicity and mutability of their own social positioning. In his sermon of 7 February 1838 (quoted above), Brune begins in the first person ("And now my friends if *we* are good in Christ well he would give *us* his word"), but shifts between the second, first, and the third person in "Do *you* know that Jesus Christ pardon all *our* sins. The people of Van Diemen's land *they* are learning about God and his son Jesus Christ." In oscillations such as these, Brune and Walter shift between different speaking positions, crossing verbally back and forth between being at one with all indigenous Van Diemonians, being part of some groups but not others, and being on the side of Robinson and his officers. Brune and Walter are multivoiced individuals who shift between different subject positions.

A second explanation of Walter's and Brune's pronoun shifts is that they are conscious of writing for more than one audience. Brune and Walter were often required to make fair copies of the texts they composed. Some of the neatest copies have the words "Copy to Report" written in the margins in Commandant Robinson's handwriting. Although ostensibly written for an Aboriginal audience, Brune's and Walter's writings were produced under orders from Robinson and were appropriated by him for enclosure in

---

10 For example, in the *Flinders Island Chronicle,* 2 Oct 1837, ML A7073, vol. 52, part 4, f. 21.

his official reports. One of Brune's sermons ends with a glimpse at its own circumstances of production: "I cannot write no more on this paper Commandant hast directed me to do it and I will do it and obey him what he says to me" (Sermon, 13 Feb 1838, ML A7073, vol. 52, part 6, f. 83). In terms of their content, form, and language, Brune's and Walter's writings served as proof of the success of Robinson's program of civilisation and christianisation. Ostensibly they were reports *on* Aborigines *by* Aborigines, yet in effect they were double-voiced documents that had been ventriloquised by Robinson, and they were aimed at a distant, non-Aboriginal group of addressees—the governor of Van Diemen's Land and his superiors in London who, as Robinson well knew, would eventually read his reports and enclosures.

Learning by Imitation

Thomas Brune urged his countrymen to "learn the words of God" (Sermon, 22 Sept 1837, ML A7073, vol. 52, part 6, f. 67). The question is: What exactly did "learning" mean in the Flinders Island context? To implement Governor Arthur's wish that scriptural religion be the "grand object of attention" in Aboriginal education, Robinson introduced three types of schools on Flinders Island: a day school for the children and women, an evening school for adults of both sexes, and a Sabbath school. Catechetical dialogues—teaching the pupils by having them give rote answers to set questions—was the main form of instruction used in the schools. Teaching occurred through ritualised verbal exchanges or pseudo-dialogues wherein the correct answers were prescribed by the questioner. Robinson was a long-time advocate of Dr. Andrew Bell's teaching method, which he had briefly outlined in a letter describing his amelioration program to Governor Arthur (15 April) in 1829.[11] Bell had developed his system of teaching in Madras in southern India, his aim being to produce "good subjects, good men, good Christians." The more advanced pupils taught the less advanced, and the main method of learning was by "repetition which took hold of the mind" (Bell, qtd. in Robinson, 1966:102n21).

No mode of education produces entirely predictable outcomes, especially in crosscultural contexts. Repetition, copying, and mimicry may, on the one hand, serve as valid learning methods, as in traditional Aboriginal societies where people learned how to do things from generation to generation by imitating their elders. Copying may, on the other hand, consist of

---

11 "The school to open and conclude with prayer. Dr Bell's system to be adopted, as far as practicable. The children to be taught the English language" (Robinson, 1966:56).

empty, mechanical repetition, as several non-Aboriginal historians have noted when suggesting that the Aboriginal pupils did not internalise, utilise, or retain what they had learned at the Flinders Island school (see Plomley, 1987a; Ryan; Rae-Ellis). Some postcolonial theorists have highlighted the subversive potential of verbal copying that almost (but not quite) conceals its parodic intent (see Bhabha: 85–122). Others have noted the difficulty of distinguishing between acts of deliberate parody committed by colonised subjects and parodic qualities assigned retrospectively at the moment of reading by postcolonial critics (McClintock: 63–64). Finally, one might ask whether, strictly speaking, exact copying is possible at all, since every repetition is a recontextualisation and every copy a re-creation because it is also implicitly a translation into what might be called the "language of now."

While there is evidence indicating that the Wybalenna Aborigines maintained some of their own traditional beliefs and cultural practices on Flinders Island, it is difficult to know today—as it was difficult for Robinson in his time to know—precisely what they "learned" in the classroom. Robinson's records were highly selective and biased; his career depended on telling his superiors whatever they wanted to hear. Likewise, the Wybalenna Aborigines were compelled to play out rituals of subordination before the colonial authorities; to avoid trouble, they told Robinson and his officers whatever they wanted to hear.[12]

What seems clear, however, is that during 1837–1838, Robinson lost faith in the catechetical schooling method and had to exercise all his ingenuity to keep up the charade of success before his superiors. Testing the pupils in January 1837, he received some unpleasant surprises. Some Aboriginal pupils were deviating from the script. Having asked the pupils, "Who is God?" one woman replied "Eve" and "heaven"; Davey Bruny corrected her, saying, "God is a spirit, is not a woman; God is a white man" (Robinson, 1987:417; 20 Jan 1837). The previous day he had asked "Who made me?" and one of the pupils had answered "the Devil." Robinson then offered five shillings to anyone who would get up and pray (417; 19 Jan 1837). The following year, after testing the pupils orally, Robinson recorded that some of the people, "when asked whether they liked the examination ... replied 'that they did not like it, did not like the "damnation."'" Robinson explained that "This of course was a mispronunciation" (535; 23 Feb 1838).

In the latter half of 1837, shortcomings of schooling-by-imitation were becoming increasingly obvious. In July, Robinson demoted the literate

---

[12] For a thorough analysis of how both dominant and subordinate groups engage in performances of control and subordination, see Scott.

Aboriginal boys, other than Brune and Walter, from teachers to class monitors. He also formed the adults of both sexes into a separate class where they would be "instructed in religious information, reading being considered by me superfluous" (1987:467; 1 Aug 1837). In October 1837, Robinson reported that the surgeon, James Allen, had begun to "depreciate and underrate the intellectual acquirements of the aborigines. He condemns the mode of tuition and does not attend the evening school" (483; 5 Oct 1837). Allen soon left the island, but his replacement, Matthew Walsh, together with Robinson's son, George, also "found fault with the subject and manner of instruction" (496; 14 Nov 1837; Rae-Ellis: 126). In early December, Robinson discovered that the west-coast people misunderstood the concept of heaven, believing that "when they die they go to PONE.DIM, i.e. a country a long way off to England and that they then appear as white people" (1987:507; 4 Dec 1837). Around the same time, Walter George Arthur was discovered to have suffered a moral lapse: he was found in bed with Mary Ann, a young woman of mixed descent who taught at the school (506; 2 Dec 1837). Robinson married the couple in March of the following year, but after the ceremony, the Aborigines "mispronounced" the toast to the couple's "good health" as "go to hell" and drank "to the health of all" with words that sounded to Robinson suspiciously like "go to hell all of you." Thinking perhaps that such miscopying might reflect badly on him, Robinson explained the difference away by noting that "the natives find it difficult to pronounce the 's'" (543; 16 Mar 1838). Whether such mispronunciations were accidental, or deliberate and strategic, it is difficult to tell. What is clear, however, is that Robinson saw the political danger of the latter possibility. In order to maintain an appearance of proper order and control, he explained away the difference—the recalcitrant otherness of the voicing—as an inadvertent error.

In January 1838, the new governor, Sir John Franklin, made a short visit to Flinders Island with his wife and their retinue. Now Robinson's achievements would be put to the test. Robinson orchestrated the visit very carefully so as to hide anything that was not consistent with his glowing reports of success in christianising and educating "the natives." When the governor and his party inspected the school, "the natives were well assembled in new garments accompanied by their teachers." After roll call and an opening prayer by Thomas Brune, teaching commenced. Immediately, Robinson sensed danger and "speedily stopped this part and ordered singing" so that the visitors would not perceive how little educational progress had been made (1987:526; 26 Jan 1838).

Vivienne Rae-Ellis has argued that, like the classroom display, Robinson's written records and official reports were instruments of deception. In the records of the school examinations carried out in mid-February 1838, each question and correct answer was recorded for each pupil in the same neat, clerical hand within ruled grid-lines. The report is a chilling record of a dialogue scripted entirely from one side. After the Aboriginal pupils had learned the correct answers by rote, the examination ostensibly verified their understanding of scriptural doctrines by recording their replies in writing. In effect, the teachers ventriloquised the pupils' answers. Robinson used the examination records as "an additional voucher to my reports and other conclusive evidence of the superiority of the plan pursued at this settlement to every other that has been adopted towards the Australian savages" (1987:535; 22 Feb 1838). By enlisting the services of his family and officers to serve as teachers in the school, and recording the examination results for each class under the relevant teacher's name, Robinson implicated the teachers in his deception. Any who dared to contradict his glowing reports, or declined to endorse his records, would be calling their own competence into question.

In April 1838, however, in one of his last sermons at Wybalenna, Thomas Brune spoke openly of the inferiority of schooling on Flinders Island in comparison with the education he had received at the Orphan School in Hobart. In an uncharacteristically autobiographical vein, he wrote:

> I was took when I was young and I was brought to the [Orphan] school and I was taught to read the Bible and I understood it and I was taught to cipher and I was taught to learn the geography and the grammar and the catechism all them did I learn
>
> And then my friends I was come at Flinders Island and when I came on it and then two or three days afterwards I began to lose all the instruction what I have learn
>
> I am dunce that I cannot say anything at all
> (Thomas Brune, Sermon, 20 April 1838, ML A7073, vol. 52, part 6, f. 135)

The catechetical method imposed a colonial reading of the Bible as a sort of "dead quotation" (Bakhtin: 344) that ostensibly wiped away and replaced the voice, knowledge, and world view of the pupil.

Older Men's Re-articulations of the Bible

Brune and Walter were not the only Aboriginal males to convey biblical teachings to their countrymen. A handful of men, who could read only at an elementary level, also mediated Christian doctrines in their own languages to their people. Between February and April 1838, Robert Clark recorded English translations of these men's addresses at the weekly meetings for prayer and mutual instruction. Ranging in age from their mid-twenties to their mid-forties, these men may already have attained a degree of seniority in traditional Aboriginal cultural terms, but it is difficult to know whether their authority as mediators was a cause or an effect of their existing social standing. In any case, the mediated nature of their received biblical knowledge did not prevent them from assuming mediatory roles themselves. They may not have been fluent in English, nor been able to read the ornate, archaic English of the printed biblical text. Nor were they schooled to a level where they could compose written sermons and reports for the *Flinders Island Chronicle*. What they did, however, was address the Wybalenna Aborigines on biblical themes in the Aboriginal lingua franca of Wybalenna, as well as in the traditional languages of the Big River, the Northern, Western, and Bruny Island peoples. The men's usual practice was first to address their own people in their own first language, then address the community as a whole in the lingua franca. In line with both Aboriginal and European traditions, women and girls did not address the assembled community. Their role was to translate the men's speeches into English. The English translations of the Aboriginal men's addresses recorded in the archival records are in fact the words uttered by the female translators.

The youngest of the male orators were two Big River men, Dow.wring.gi ("Leonidas," also named "David"), and Drue.mer.ter.pun.ner ("Alexander"), and a north-coast man, Drine.ne ("Neptune").[13] Estimated to be in their mid-twenties, these three were inclined to castigate the people from positions of moral superiority. On 10 March 1838, Leonidas urged the people to "Love the Bible, it is a good book, it is God's book. Why do not you all learn to read God's book? It tells you plenty about God, about Jesus Christ. You are too lazy to learn (qtd. in Robinson, 1987:726n1; Journal Annotations, 10 Mar 1838). One week later, Neptune told the people, "My brothers and sisters, why do you forget God? ... You do not like God. I love God.... [Y]ou are too fond of doing what is bad Learn to read the Bible. It is a good book. It is God's book ... " (qtd. in Robinson, 1987:728n1; Journal Annotations, 17 Mar 1838).

Noemy (Mar.wer.reek) was from western Van Diemen's Land. Aged in his mid-thirties, he was appointed by Robinson to the role of constable in August 1836. One of his duties as a constable was to curb what Robinson saw as sexual promiscuity, a role that may have translated in his own cultural terms into the senior men's traditional responsibility to control younger men's access to women. In February 1838, Noemy was examined with two others by the chaplain Thomas Dove, who remarked on "the accuracy and extent of their scriptural knowledge." Dove found that Noemy was capable of easily reading words of one syllable and answered correctly a range of questions such as "Who made you? Who is God? What

---

[13] George Augustus Robinson renamed almost all the Wybalenna Aborigines, giving them names from the Bible, Greek and Roman mythology, and British history.

is the soul? Does it survive the body? What kind of place is heaven?" He also correctly answered questions "relative to the creation of man, his original state and character, the cause of his expulsion from paradise, the story of Cain and Abel, the deluge and the great objects for which Jesus Christ came into our world" (qtd. in Robinson, 1987:724n2; Journal Annotations, 22 Feb 1838).

Noemy was described by Chaplain Dove as "not merely an eloquent but an elegant speaker" (qtd. in Robinson, 1987:733n1; Journal Annotations, 14 Apr 1838). Robinson also remarked on his oratorical skills. Like Brune and Walter, he was familiar with biblical doctrines. Unlike them, he is unlikely to have read the Bible for himself, nor did he compose his addresses in writing, although he sometimes spoke with a small book in his hand, "a primer, on which his eyes occasionally dwelt as a relief whilst he collected his thoughts" (Robinson, 1987:491; 21 Oct 1837). Noemy used a combination of English, the Western language, and the Aboriginal lingua franca of the settlement. On 24 February, he urged the Western people "to live peaceably together, not steal from each other nor tell lies, nor scold each other." He then shifted to the lingua franca to urge the Wybalenna women in general to "not scold one another, clean your houses early in the mornings, do not be sulky, out your bad tempers away from you, love God, love Jesus Christ, do not remain too long in the bush when you go for firewood, doing what is bad (qtd. in Robinson, 1987:724n1; Journal Annotations, 24 Feb 1838). Like Neptune's addresses, Noemy's were translated into English by Pignaburg ("Bessy") and Ta.ne.e.ber.rick ("Clara").

The oldest orator, Wourraddy ("Doctor"/"Count Alpha"), was from Bruny Island and had accompanied Robinson on this treks through the bush in the early 1830s. His addresses to the Wybalenna Aborigines were translated into English by Pie.yen.kome.yen.ner ("Wild Mary"). In April 1838, he addressed the Aborigines' weekly meeting for prayer and mutual instruction, using the Bruny Island language to relate a narrative of what had happened to all the Van Diemen's Land tribal groups:

> The white men have killed us all; they shot a great many. We are now only a few people here and we ought to be fond of one another. We ought to love God. God made every thing, the salt water, the horse, the bullock, the opossum, the wallaby, the kangaroo and wombat. Love him and you go to him by and bye. (Qtd. in Robinson, 1987:733n1; Journal Annotations, 14 Apr 1838)

Wourraddy's narrative of a shared Aboriginal historical experience announces the birth of a new, pan-Tasmanian indigenous social consciousness, possibly based on Jesus' commandment to "love one another" (John 15:12). Today, Aboriginal people from all parts of Tasmania refer to themselves as "Pallawah," a word that means "people" in Wourraddy's Bruny Island language.[14]

On the same day as Wourraddy delivered the above address, Clark's report of the Aborigines' "weekly meeting for prayer and mutual instruction" recorded that a native youth read Matthew 2 and "translated some of the leading facts into the language of the settlement" (qtd. in Robinson, 1987:733n1; Journal Annotations, 14 April 1838). By April 1838, Governor Arthur's earlier prohibition against translating the Bible into Aboriginal languages appears to have been forgotten. Biblical doctrines were being channelled to the Wybalenna Aboriginal community through several Aboriginal voices speaking different Aboriginal languages, in addition to Walter's and Brune's English sermons. These new, non-English renditions of biblical doctrine represent the tentative beginnings of a second reformation, a decolonisation of the Bible in Van Diemen's Land. In the context of the Wybalenna Aborigines' historical experience of being decimated, displaced, and crushed violently up against groups from other parts of Van Diemen's Land, Wourraddy's injunction to "be fond of one another" possibly appropriates one of Jesus' central teachings as a foundation for an incipient Aboriginal nationalism.

Crucial here is the fact that, if Wourraddy was using John 15:12, he was not deauthorising the Bible, but instead appropriating its power and harnessing its truth value to a new postcolonial agenda. He was rearticulating the Bible both in the sense of revoicing it, and in so far as he was linking it onto Aboriginal needs. In Bakhtinian terms, Wourraddy was not engaging with the Bible as an "externally authoritative text" whose power derived from remaining single-tongued (monoglossic), semantically unambiguous (monologic), and monolithically separate from contaminating contextual influences.[15] Instead, if Wourraddy was using the Bible, it was as an "internally persuasive discourse," a discourse that wins allegiance on the basis of its dialogic engagement with what learners already know, value, or desire (Bakhtin: 345–46). If Wourraddy was transmitting Jesus' message to the Wybalenna Aborigines, it was as Bakhtin describes:

> interwoven with "one's own word." ... [T]he internally persuasive word is half-ours and half-someone else's. Its creativity and productiveness consist

---

[14] See Robinson's sermon of 31 May 1829, in the Bruny Island language, where he translates "Parlerwar" as "native" (1966:61).

[15] Authoritative discourse "remains sharply demarcated, compact and inert.... [I]t is fully complete, it has but a single meaning.... [I]t demands our unconditional allegiance, [and] ... permits no play with the context framing it, ... no spontaneously creative stylizing variants on it.... It is indissolubly fused with its authority—with political power, an institution, a person—and it stands or falls together with that authority.... It is by its very nature incapable of being double-voiced; it cannot enter into hybrid constructions" (Bakhtin: 343, 344).

precisely in the fact that such a word awakens new and independent words, that it organizes masses of our own words from within, and does not remain in an isolated and static condition.... [I]t enters into inter-animating relationships with new contexts.... [I]n each of the new contexts that dialogize it, this discourse is able to reveal ever newer ways *to mean*. (Bakhtin: 345–46)

Conclusion

On a tiny island in Bass Strait, off the northeast corner of Tasmania, the beginnings of biblical translation and recontextualisation tentatively initiated a process of appropriating the Bible for Aboriginal Australians. Today, although it would be overly optimistic to say that Australia has entered a postcolonial era, there are some Aboriginal communities where the Bible is no longer consumed entirely "in a Western cup" (Grant: 164).[16] Third Church Aboriginal Christianity replaces the notion of "conversion" with metaphors of productive entanglement and transformation of Indigenous and Western traditions. In parts of Australia, the gospel is no longer viewed as a Western cultural artefact, and as Aboriginal theologian Djiniyini Gondarra maintains,

> We no longer see Him as the white man's God or a God that the missionaries brought to us, but He is our God who has lived with us in history. But not only in history, He is living with us now in the person of the Holy Spirit. He has given us the vision for the Aboriginal Church to think and theologize the gospel in the language and culture of the people. (Gondarra 1986:13–14)

Unlike the catechetically schooled Aboriginal residents of Flinders Island in the 1830s, Djiniyini Gondarra is in a position to assert: "We cannot go on answering someone else's questions" (ibid.).

---

[16] Some of these new Aboriginal Christian contexts are explored in Harris, Swain and Rose, and the Rainbow Spirit Elders.

WORKS CITED

Bakhtin, M. M.
    1981   *The Dialogic Imagination.* Ed. Michael Holquist. Trans. Caryl Emerson and Michael Holquist. Austin: University of Texas Press.

Bhabha, Homi K.
    1994   *The Location of Culture.* London and New York: Routledge.

Gondarra, Djiniyini
    1986   *Let My People Go.* Darwin: Bethyl Presbytery.

    1996   "Aboriginal Spirituality and the Gospel: Introduction." Pp. 41–53 in *Aboriginal Spirituality: Past, Present and Future.* Ed. Anne Pattel-Gray. Sydney: Harper Collins.

Grant, Cecil W.
    1996   "The Gospel and Culture: An Aboriginal Perspective." Pp. 162–86 in *Martung Upah: Black Australians Seeking a Partnership.* Ed. Anne Pattel-Gray. Sydney: Harper Collins.

Harris, John
    1990   *One Blood: 200 Years of Aboriginal Encounter with Christianity.* Sutherland: Albatross.

McClintock, Anne
    1995   *Imperial Leather.* New York and London: Routledge.

Ong, Walter J.
    1977   "Maranatha: Death and Life in the Text of the Book." Pp. 230–71 in *Interfaces of the Word.* Ithaca and London: Cornell University Press.

    1982   *Orality and Literacy.* London: Methuen.

Plomley N. J. B.
    1987a   "A History of the Flinders Island Aboriginal Settlement." Pp. 1–292 in Plomley, 1987b.

Plomley, N. J. B., ed.
    1987b   *Weep in Silence.* Hobart: Blubber Head.

Rae-Ellis, Vivienne
    1988   *Black Robinson.* Melbourne: Melbourne University Press.

Rainbow Spirit Elders
    1997   *Rainbow Spirit Theology: Towards an Australian Aboriginal Theology.* Blackburn, Vic.: Harper Collins.

Robinson, George Augustus
    Robinson's papers are cited frequently. They are held in the Mitchell Library, Sydney. (E.g., ML [Mitchell Library] A7073, vol. 52, part 6, f. 51.)

1966   *Friendly Mission: The Tasmanian Journals of George Augustus Robinson 1829–1834*. Ed. N. J. B. Plomley. Kingsgrove: Tasmanian Historical Research Association.

1987   "The Flinders Island Journal of George Augustus Robinson." Pp. 293–788 in Plomley, 1987b. (Citations include the date of the journal entry.)

Ryan, Lyndall
    1996   *The Aboriginal Tasmanians*. 2d. ed. St. Leonards: Allen & Unwin.

Scott, James C.
    1990   *Domination and the Arts of Resistance*. New Haven and London: Yale University Press.

Swain, Tony, and Rose, Deborah Bird, eds.
    1988   *Aboriginal Australians and Christian Missions*. Bedford Park: Australian Association for the Study of Religions.

Van Toorn, Penny
    1994   "Mastering Ceremonies: The Politics of Ritual and Ceremony in Eleanor Dark, Rudy Wiebe, and Mudrooroo." *Australian and New Zealand Studies in Canada* 12 (Dec): 73–89.

    1995   *Rudy Wiebe and the Historicity of the Word*. Edmonton: University of Alberta Press.

Vološinov, V. N.
    1973   *Marxism and the Philosophy of Language*. Trans. Ladislav Matejka and I. R. Titunik. New York and London: Seminar Press.

Explorer Hermeneutics, or
Fat Damper and Sweetened Tea[1]

Roland Boer
Monash University

ABSTRACT

Following the texts of the so-called "explorers" of Australia—Mitchell, Sturt, Stuart, Eyre, Grey, and Giles—I show how their constructions of Australia were determined in large measure by the Bible and Christianity. Apart from finding Aborigines on every second page of their endless journals, I indicate the extent to which the Bible shaped their universe. The depictions of Australia by the explorers played a fundamental role in conceptions of Australia that remain powerful today, in all their possibilities and limitations. This essay is also a distinct intervention into other work on the explorers, work that is symptomatic of much postcolonial criticism in ignoring the key role of the Bible in the conceptualization, textuality, and politics of colonialism itself.

We celebrated the day [Easter] with a luncheon of fat damper and sweetened tea.

Leichhardt: 190

After having celebrated Whit-Sunday with a double allowance of fat cake and sweetened tea....

Leichhardt: 252

Having completed this last morsel, I occupied myself for a little with my journal, then read a few chapters in the New Testament, and having fulfilled these duties, I felt myself as contented and cheerful, as I had ever been in the most fortunate moments of my life.

Grey, 2:60

The "explorers" of Australia traversed a country full of distance and Aboriginal people, pretending that they were the first to "discover" the

---

[1] This is a modified form of chapter 2 in my *Last Stop before Antarctica: The Bible and Postcolonialism in Australia* (Sheffield: Sheffield Academic Press, 2001). Permission for republication granted by Sheffield Academic Press.

vast stretches of Australia: Mitchell in New South Wales, Sturt in both New South Wales and South Australia, Eyre in South Australia, Leichhardt in Queenland, Stuart across the centre, and Giles through the deserts of South and Western Australia. It is an endless trek of perpetual wandering, tracing, tailing, trailing, although now it can be done via the tracks themselves as well as the explorers' journals, which were formative in the construction of how the land and its people were and are viewed, in the construction of "Australia" itself. Those texts yield some distinct surprises, particularly in the way the Bible permeates them in so many ways, ranging from explicit biblical references to what might be termed a biblical imaginary, a construct of perception that rendered the foreign, antipodean Australian land, flora, fauna, and people in terms that were comprehensible, that is, in biblical terms. The Evangelical Grey is perhaps the most obvious, citing distinct moments of biblical study and reading, or at least he writes that he did so:

> It may be asked, if, during such a trying period, I did not seek from religion that consolation which it is sure to afford? My answer is,—Yes; and I farther feel assured that but for the support I derived from prayer and frequent perusal and meditation of the Scriptures, I should never have been able to have borne myself in such a manner as to have maintained discipline and confidence amongst the rest of the party: nor in all my sufferings did I ever lose the consolation derived from a firm reliance upon the goodness of providence. (1:381)

To be sure, this was not a solitary occurrence, avid Bible student that he was:

> The safety of the whole party now depended upon my forming a prompt and efficient plan of operations, and seeing it carried out with energy and perseverance. As soon as I was out of sight of Mr. Smith and Coles, I sat down upon the shore, to reflect upon our present position....
> I determined not to decide hastily between these plans, and in order more fully to compose my mind, I sat down and read a few chapters in the Bible. (1:393–94)

Out of the half dozen major texts—journals, crucial not only in the gathering of scientific information in a haphazard way, but also for the burgeoning travel and tourist literature—a number of items in what might be termed explorer hermeneutics emerge. None of them more than amateur students of the Bible, although Eyre was the son of a clergyman, they thereby produced some striking signals not only of the way the Bible influenced their modes of perception but also of how the Bible itself was read and understood. Despite their differences, there are some common motifs that appear in their scribblings, particularly the notion of the call, divine strength, relief from trouble (especially the finding of water), antiquarian evidence, particularly with reference to the indigenous people met at nearly every step of the way, and then the providential, all-surveying, all-knowing eye (what used to be known as the gaze). And in all of this the overwhelming reference, despite Mr. Grey's reading of the New Testament, is the Hebrew Bible.

Implicit Israelites

Ernest Giles, least orthodox out of them all and thereby at the other pole from Grey, gives voice to a sense of calling to the explorer vocation. Giles indulges in theological and philosophical reflection, including gentle questions on orthodox Christian ideas such as the nature of heaven (1:237–38; see also 2:118–19). All of this takes place when he is under fever, but it is not clear whether this is a strategy to avoid theological censorship, the fever of his later writing, of the trip itself, of reflection and thought, of.... Yet Giles writes that he felt divinely appointed, called, anointed even, to the task: a heavenly choir with angelic harps sings—echoes of the shepherds at Christmas and a prophetic calling: "Be bold of heart, be strong of will, for unto thee by God is given, to roam the desert paths of earth, and thence explore the fields of heaven. Be bold of heart, be strong of will, and naught on earth shall lay thee low" (2:155).

To support such a notion of calling, that most ideologically suspicious of theological categories, the sense of strength from "Providence," the "Creator," the "Almighty" (rarely, if ever, "God") pervaded the ideological construction of the world of the explorers. They felt clearly that God was guiding them and keeping them out of danger (at least, those who were not killed or who did not die of thirst, hunger, or exposure, as nearly every expedition experienced). The devout Grey is a model of pious strength:

> It is only those who go forth into perils and dangers, amidst which human foresight and strength can but little avail, and who find themselves, day after day, protected by an unseen influence, and ever and again snatched from the very jaws of destruction, by a power which is not of this world, who can at all times estimate the knowledge of one's own weakness and littleness, and the firm reliance and trust upon the goodness of the Creator which the human breast is capable of feeling. Like all other lessons which are of great and lasting benefit to man, this one must be learnt amidst much sorrowing and woe; but, having learnt it, it is but the sweeter from the pain and toil which are undergone in the acquisition. (1:381)

For Grey, a perfect reliance on "the goodness of God" and "the merits of our Redeemer" is a "sure refuge and certain source of consolation" (1:394). The Scriptures themselves provide him with a sense of resignation and contentment at his present fate, sure as he is that his Redeemer will either rescue him or have him die by starvation.[2]

Giles, in his characteristic way, uses the Bible while shifting the emphasis to human initiative. Thus when talking of the burden of leading the other people on his journey and the strain it induced after their 325-mile trek without water across the desert by camel, writes "I gathered some support from a proverb of Solomon: 'If thou faint in the day of adversity, thy strength is small'" (2:155).

Apart from a general sense of calling and of divine providence and strength, there is a distinct evocation of divine assistance in moments that were felt to be rescues from imminent death—inevitably associated with the finding of water (and the subsequent destruction of aboriginal water supplies as the horses and, for Giles, camels, were watered). There is a repeated focus on water, a struggle to locate that which seems to keep the many tribes whom they meet alive, their campfires at night indicating not only their presence but also the fact that they seemed to know where the water was (see Eyre's reflections [1845 1:351]). Indeed, all the explorers obsess about water. Grey runs short within minutes of landing on the West Coast, being totally unprepared (1:69–71).

Giles, travelling completely blind—despite the presence of Aborigines about him—through some of the most arid territory in the world, identifies thirst as "that dire affliction that besets the wanderer in the Australian wilds" (1:75) and then connects Providence and water closely with each other: "It is in circumstances only such as we had lately been placed in that the utter hopelessness of all human efforts is truly felt, and it is when relieved from such a situation that the hand of a directing and beneficent Being appears most plainly discernible, fulfilling those gracious promises which he has made, to hear them that call upon him in the day of trouble" (1:365; see also 2:120). The footnote to this then quotes Isa 41:17–18; 43:19.[3] In

---

[2] "By the influence these [Bible readings] imparted, I became perfectly contented and resigned to our apparently wretched condition, and, again rising up, pursued my way along the beach to the party. It may here be remarked by some that these statements of my attending to religious duties are irrelevant to the subject, but in such an opinion I cannot at all coincide. In detailing the sufferings we underwent, it is necessary to relate the means by which those sufferings were alleviated; and after having, in the midst of perils and misfortunes, received the greatest consolation from religion, I should be ungrateful to my Maker not to acknowledge this, and should ill perform my duty to my fellow men, did I not bear testimony to the fact, that under all the weightier sorrows and sufferings that our frail nature is liable to, a perfect reliance upon the goodness of God, and the merits of our Redeemer, will be found a sure refuge and certain source of consolation" (Grey 1:393–94).

[3] "When the poor and needy seek water, and there is none, and their tongue is parched with thirst, I the LORD will answer them, I the God of Israel will not forsake them. I will open rivers on the bare heights, and fountains in the midst of the valleys; I will make the wilderness

general, Giles, despite his lack of orthodoxy, is "[s]incerely grateful to the Almighty for having guided us through so many difficulties, and for the inexpressible relief afforded to us when so much was needed, but so little expected" (2:69). And this after his aboriginal "boys" (see below) had killed his overseer and he had been left all but stranded in the desert before coming upon the whaler, Mississippi.

Charles Sturt, Evangelical Anglican with a divine mission to explore Australia, also feels that it is Providence that has protected him and his party on so many occasions from calamity, neglecting to mention the stupidity that got him into the situations from which Providence was then obliged, good Christian gentleman that he was, to rescue him : "Something more powerful, than human foresight or human prudence [of which he seemed to be singularly lacking], appeared to avert the calamities and dangers with which I and my companions were so frequently threatened; and had it not been for the guidance and protection we received from the Providence of that good and all-wise Being to whose care we committed ourselves, we should, ere this, have ceased to rank among the number of His earthly creatures" (Sturt, 1833 2:6).

Ironically, Leichhardt, who disappeared into the desert never to be seen again, says "an Almighty Protector had not only allowed us to escape [privation] hitherto but had even supplied us with an abundance" (Leichhardt: 235). Indeed, Leichhardt opens up another window on the explorers, for whom Providence was not always so kind, nor did they always feel so much in the good register of the Almighty Protector. Thus, Giles found himself identifying with Pharaoh during the plagues of Egypt: when afflicted by ants, mosquitoes, and flies, he wonders why Moses had not thought of these plagues. Indeed, he would delight in a cool, watery plague of frogs.[4]

John McDouall Stuart, succumbing to scurvy on the long trek from Adelaide to the Gulf of Carpentaria (despite the many Aborigines they met on the way who were remarkably free of scurvy), invokes the Almighty to help him: "I feel myself getting weaker and weaker every day. I hope that the Almighty will have compassion on me, and soon send me some relief. He is the only one who can do it—my only friend" (454). Passages like these in fact provide some relief in the staccato, frenetic journals of Stuart. They are as frantic as his five major journeys in rapid succession, attempting to cross the continent from south to north, and as his subsequent devotion to alcohol.

---

a pool of water, and the dry land springs of water" (Isa 41:17–18 NRSV). "I am about to do a new thing; now it springs forth, do you not perceive it? I will make a way in the wilderness and rivers in the desert" (Isa 43:19 NRSV).

4 "Whatever could have obfuscated the brains of Moses, when he omitted to inflict Pharaoh with such exquisite tortures as ants, I cannot imagine" (Giles, 1:236; see also 310).

Nothing embellishes his journals, including revision (unlike Giles's flourishes), and all he is concerned with are water, the horses, food, illness, continually hostile natives, and the direction of the fucking wind. Even when he is in the depths of despair, evoking the biblical psalms of complaint or laments and riddled with disease, these concerns may still be found: "What a miserable life mine is now! I get no rest night nor day from this terrible gnawing pain; the nights are too long, and the days are too long, and I am so weak that I am hardly able to move about the camp. I am truly wretched. When will this cease? Wind, south-east" (Stuart: 453). It seems as though "my friend," the "Almighty," has deserted him; the wind had not.

Apart from points of experiential contact with the Bible, the explorers made a very different use of these texts. They became a resource for comparison with aboriginal culture and behaviour. Yet the comparison was quite specific, antiquarian, seeking to present aboriginal people as ancient as those civilizations felt to be represented in the Hebrew Bible.[5] The most extensive antiquarian use of the Hebrew Bible is found with Thomas Mitchell, Surveyor-General of New South Wales, who systematically grids the Aborigines he meets and knows with the Bible, alongside other ancient sources. For instance, after the narrative description of mourning by aboriginal women and their singing, he quotes Pope's *Iliad*, Homer, and Jer 9:17–18: "Call for the mourning women that they may come, and let them make haste, and take up a wailing for us, that our eyes may run down with tears, and our eyelids gush out with water" (Mitchell, 1839 1:118–19). All of this functions as proof that such practices once existed in other, ancient places, sucking back the Aborigines in question into a similar time frame.

Once there, a swarm of other practices see them more at home in the Hebrew Bible and among its peoples. This is the case with other burial customs, such as cutting for mourning, especially about the head. The reference here is to Jer 48:37 (via the cryptic citing of "Harmer" [Mitchell, 1839 2:346]), although the Jeremiah text actually refers to the shaving of head and beard and the cutting of hands, rather than the head. A little slippage, but the connection is made, this time with mourning Moabites in an oracle against them.

So also with the use of burial mounds. Mitchell notes their use along the Darling after the ravages of smallpox, a burial practice comparable to the Bedouin Arabs of Mt. Carmel. A string of biblical texts are then referred to but not quoted. "See also" he writes, "2 Kings xxiii. 16—1 Kings xiii. 2 and Isaiah xxii. 15–17" (1839 1:254). However, whereas the first and last texts refer to tombs on a height, 1 Kgs 13:2 speaks of sacrificial practices on the

---

5 Ryan (136) argues that this is an orientalist move, following Said's delineation of the term. In part this is the case, but I think the ancient biblical trope has other functions as well.

"high places," apparently understood by Mitchell as sepulchers rather than altars (unless human sacrifice is meant, but even this is not quite the same thing as burial).

The dead return, as it were, a little later, where, after narrating the finding of some graves in which there was evidence of occupation of the tomb, Mitchell writes in a note: "Isaiah lxv.4. *Who remain among the graves.* 'The old Hebrews are charged by the prophet Isaiah with *remaining among the graves and lodging in the monuments.*'—See *Lewis's Origines Hebraeae,* vol. iii. p. 381" (1839 2:105). Apparently the understanding is that a close relative remains with the body until it is decayed. Here the text of Lewis (no further references are provided for this half-identified piece) is used to interpret the biblical text, although the text itself comes as part of a condemnation of the practices of the rebellious Israelites, which include sacrificing in gardens, offering incense on bricks, eating swine's flesh and abominable broths (Isa 65:3–4). Sinful Israelites maybe, but still Israelites.

Apart from burial and the treatment of the dead, there is the use of smoke signals on mountaintops in order to send messages. Mitchell notes: "This mode of communicating intelligence of sudden danger, so invariably practised by the natives of Australia, seems quite in conformity with the customs of early ages as mentioned in Scripture [Jer 6:1]. 'O ye children of Benjamin, gather yourselves to flee out of the midst of Jerusalem, *and set up a sign of fire in Beth-haccerem:* for evil appeareth out of the north, and great destruction.'" (1839 1:129). Indeed, there is a hint of an unconscious enrollment of the Aborigines in the ranks of the amorphous and disparate numbers of Israel itself.

The web tying the natives in with ancient Israel strengthens with comparisons relating to bodily ornaments, reverence for elders, cooking, magical stones, hunting methods, housing, and the carrying of children. Thus, the wearing of a bracelet of corded hair as a sign of royalty links the Aborigines in with 2 Sam 1:10,[6] again via Harmer's ready reference to "Oriental practice" (Mitchell, 1839 1:265). The authority of old men and women, characteristic among Aborigines Mitchell meets, sees them obeying the command of Lev 19:32[7] (2:346). The specific cooking reference is to the use of hard clay mounds instead of stones, regarding which Mitchell quotes the Hebrew Bible again: "'And Jacob said unto his brethren, Gather stones: and they took stones, and made a heap, and they did eat there upon the heap.' Genesis xxxi. 46." (2:81). Of course, even though the particular Aborigines Mitchell meets

---

[6] Here, the reference to the "armlet that was on his arm" is that of King Saul, claimed to have been taken from a slain Saul in the words of the Amalekite produced in this text.

[7] "You shall rise before the aged, and defer to the old; and you shall fear your God: I am Yahweh."

use hard clay, this is in replacement of the more usual stones, a patriarchal approach to cooking, although in the context of a covenant meal between Jacob and Laban in the biblical text. Stones are also at issue in relation to "magical" practice and reverence. Writing that the natives carry crystals of quartz and other shining stones that are highly valued, especially the "coradjes" or "priest," Mitchell refers to Gen 28:18, which, in the midst of the story of Jacob's stop and dream at what was named Bethel, speaks of his taking the stone on which he had put his head, setting it up as a pillar and anointing it.

As for hunting methods, particularly the use of spears, axes, and nets, Mitchell invokes the enigmatic Isaiah once again, in a note: "Isaiah xxiv. 17.—*Fear, and the pit, and the snare, are upon thee*" (1839 2:153). Ever full of the trivia Mitchell is seeking, Harmer comes to the rescue in relation to a poetic text that renders judgement on the whole earth, no less: "These images are taken from the different methods of hunting and taking wild beasts, which were anciently in use. The snare or toils were a series of nets, enclosing, at first, a great space of ground, in which the wild beasts were known to be; and drawn in by degrees into a narrower compass, till they were at last closely shut up and entangled in them." Having cited Harmer, Mitchell himself closes, in the shadow of this authority, with "This is precisely the method adopted by the Australian natives at present for the same or similar purposes" (2:154).

Even the housing made and used by Aborigines has its connection with the Israelite Feast of Booths, at least the practice of making and living in the huts themselves. Indeed, it is their "mode of life, as exhibited in the temporary huts made of boughs, bark, or grass" that may be compared not only to the Arabs, but ultimately the command of Nehemiah to the Israelites (or, more specifically the Judeans), after the "return" from Babylon and the "re-establishment" of Judah, recited in Neh 8:15[8] (2:343).

Finally, in a whole series of aboriginal-Israelite links, including mourning and burial practices, smoke signals, bodily ornaments, reverence for elders, cooking, magical stones, hunting methods, housing—in short, a collection of key social features—there is the mode of carrying children: "We trace a further resemblance between this rude people and the orientals, in their common method of carrying children on their shoulders; and the sketch of Turandurey with Ballandella so mounted (Pl. 24. page 69) affords the best illustration of a passage of Scripture, which has very much puzzled commentators." The note quotes Isa 49:22[9] (2:347).

---

[8] "Go out to the hills and bring branches of olive, myrtle, palm, and other leafy trees to make booths [*succoth*], as it is written" (NRSV).

[9] "Thus says the Lord GOD: I will soon lift up my hand to the nations, and raise my signal to the peoples; and they shall bring your sons in their bosom, and your daughters shall be carried on their shoulders" (NRSV).

The only exception to the resolute focus on the Hebrew Bible appears in Mitchell's discussion of what he calls rituals of repulsion. After a spear was pointed at one of the party, and a green twig at Mitchell, "He [an Aboriginal] and the boy then threw dust at us, in a clever way, with their toes. These various expressions of hostility and defiance, were too intelligible to be mistaken" (1:245–46). A footnote then connects this with "the early history of mankind," specifically the Hebrews. So "King David and his host met with a similar reception at Bahurim.—'And as David and his men went by the way, Shimei went along on the hill's side over against him, and cursed as he went, and threw stones at him, *and cast dust.*' 2 Sam. xvi.13. So also we read in Acts xxii.23, 'They cried out, and cast off their clothes, *and threw dust into the air.*'" Wider comparisons to rituals of repulsion are made to the "Turks," "Oriental customs," and Num 12:14, but what interests me is the sole New Testament reference in the explorer texts, depicting the response of the Jews in Jerusalem to Paul's sermon in the temple. Indeed, this text traces its way through into Eyre's journal, published some two years after Mitchell's, although not referring to it. Eyre narrates a standoff, produced through Eyre's overseer kidnapping a woman for a couple of days to find out about "water": "yet they had established themselves in the close proximity of our encampment [at a depot], and repeatedly exhibited signs of defiance, such as throwing dust into the air, shouting, and threatening with their weapons." He footnotes the same text, Acts 22:23 (1845 1:83).[10]

This turn to Eyre indicates that Mitchell is not alone in this use of the Bible, especially in a way that makes the Aborigines implicit Israelites (or Jews in the case of the Acts passage). Eyre, for instance, casts himself in terms of Saul and natives as David, during the long pursuit of the former by the latter in 1 Samuel 21–30: while doing meteorological observations he finds that he has lost a horizon glass, a piece of canvas, spade, parcel of horse shoes, axe, tin dish, ropes, grubbing hoe, and other smaller things left outside the tent. He then reflects how close the natives had come under cover of night. They must have seen him lie on the ground, he reflects, to read the stars and then write by candle in his tent. "The only wonder with me was that they had not speared me, as they could scarcely have been intimidated by my individual presence" (1845 1:143; compare 1 Sam 26:8–9). They can come so close to him, like David to Saul in the camp, yet they deign not to kill him, although the effect was almost the same, for "[t]hey had, however, in their turn, produced as great an effect upon me, and had at least deprived me of one night's sleep" (1:144).

---

10 One other New Testament exception is found with Sturt, but there is no direct biblical reference here. He casts himself in messianic terms, finding in one diseased aboriginal camp that "The lame had managed to hobble along, and the blind were equally anxious to touch us" (1833 2:135).

Grey also comes to the party. He speaks, for instance, of manna, but his signified is somewhat skewed in a characteristic nineteenth-century scientific reading. For the manna found on the trees resembles, he feels, the medicinal stuff prevalent in Europe, although in Australia it is mottled red or brown, firm and sweet (2:273). And in another part, after describing a cave painting of an extraordinary figure with a yellow headdress, he writes in a note: "This figure brings to mind the description of the Prophet Ezekiel:—'Men pourtrayed upon the wall, the images of the Chaldeans pourtrayed in vermillion, girded with girdles upon their loins, exceeding in dyed attire upon their heads, all of them princes to look to, after the manner of the Babylonians of Chaldees, the land of their nativity.'—Chap. XXIII.14, 15" (1:215). And then he relates how the naming of children from some circumstance connected with their birth is a custom "prevalent equally amongst the most ancient nations of whom any records are preserved, and the modern Australians." Evidence comes in the form of Gen 30:11, "'And Leah said, A troop cometh, and she called his name Gad;' &c. &c. &c." (2:343).

Indeed, it is both Mitchell and Grey who make explicit the identification I have been tracing, one negatively, the other less so. For until now I have tailed what has been an unconscious element in a more deliberately antiquarian, archaicizing move by the explorers, who sought to link the Aborigines with the earliest human beings and thereby place them lower on the evolutionary scale, closer to animals. Yet the unconscious has a habit of surfacing. So, Mitchell speaks of an aboriginal face with "features decidedly Jewish, having a thin aquiline nose, and a very piercing eye, as intent on mischief, as if it had belonged to Satan himself" (1839 1:270). If this identification is demonic and Jewish, Grey sees them in a much better light. Although subincision is a practice he finds unique,[11] it is circumcision that makes the Aborigines, and others who practice, purer and more faithful children of Moses:

> The injunctions contained in Deuteronomy, ch. xxiii, ver. 12, and 13, are literally fulfilled by the natives in several parts of the continent. In addition to my own testimony on this point, I will refer to "Wilson's Voyage round the World," p. 165, where he states, "They are cleanly in their manners, and, in some respects, superior to the Europeans, fulfilling the injunction of Moses

---

[11] Assuming the greater ability of those who know Latin to handle the reference, as well as the politeness of avoiding direct reference in English, he describes it as "*Finditus usque ad urethram à parte infera penis,*" noting that "This extraordinary and inexplicable custom must have a great tendency to prevent the rapid increase of the population; and its adoption may perhaps be a wise ordination of Providence, for that purpose, in a country of so desert and arid a character as that which these people occupy" (1:213).

in the twelfth and thirteenth verses of the twenty-third chapter of Deuteronomy.... They also conform strictly to the injunctions in Leviticus, ch. xv. ver. 19. (2:344; see also Leichhardt: 413–47)

Yet, it is not just Aborigines who seem to become Israelites in these texts, for the explorers themselves have a tendency at odd times to go native, for survival if nothing else. The curious Eyre, infamous for his brutal repression of a mutiny in the West Indies after his time in Australia, begins to use native names for things and places, rather than the exclusively English names normally provided in the frenzy of Adamic naming, such as Yeer-kumban-kauwe (1845 1:284). He starts to dig for water like natives and describes its procuration from a tree root (1:350–51). But Eyre is notable for raising issues of dispossession and for his calls, paternalistic to be sure, for an inquiry and means to prevent the abuse and decline of Aborigines. In contrast to Sturt, who sees them as scarce, diseased, starving, animal-like, cannibals (1833 1:114; also 2:222), Eyre concludes that our presence in the land is an act of intrusion and aggression, that Aborigines can't comprehend the English presence, the taking of the land and ignorance of their laws. He feels their violent reactions perfectly justified (1845 1:163–72). Even theological justification for rapid aboriginal death and decline is criticized:

> It is most lamentable to think that the progress and prosperity of one race should conduce to the downfall and decay of another; it is still more so to observe the apathy and indifference with which this result is contemplated by mankind in general, and which leads to no investigation being made as to the cause of this desolating influence, or if it is, terminates, to use the language of the Count Stzelecki, "in the inquiry, like an inquest of the one race upon the corpse of the other, ending for the most part with the verdict of 'died by the visitation of God.'" (1:x)[12]

A Providential Eye?

One final item of explorer hermeneutics that comes through in these journals is the most elite of the senses that have been separated out from the amorphous territory of human perception, namely, sight. Here the discussion moves into wider theological zones than the biblical texts alone, yet the issue of sight, the eye, the eyeball with its nervous wiring that reaches back

---

12 Even Mitchell describes "my friends," the Dharuks, as the "first inhabitants" who are "deprived of the liberty which they formerly enjoyed." He also sees the inevitable march forward of what he feels is a superior civilization (1839 1:10).

to the brain, is crucial for the hermeneutics in which I am engaged. For how the explorers saw Australia (the subtitle of Simon Ryan's book that is so important for this section) is not only influential for the way they read the Bible but is also determined by a certain biblical or theological imaginary, a way of constructing the seen in terms of a framework in which theological and biblical categories were fundamental.

But let me begin with the gaze and its problems.[13] The mention of "gaze" (or now the more favoured "eye") will activate a whole area of cultural criticism, ranging from gender and its construction in film theory, through Freud's scopophilia and Foucault's work on the panopticon to an increasing interest in the role of the gaze in postcolonial criticism. In fact, the particular department of the gaze that interests me here is the colonial gaze, the "cartographic eye" as Simon Ryan has dubbed it.

Read some more and make it relevant: my interlocutors here are Michel Foucault, particularly his well-known "panopticism," a term he derives from Jeremy Bentham's panopticon, a prison in which the prisoners may be seen without seeing their centralized warder and in which the warder sees but cannot be seen. Following Bentham's suggestions for its use in education, industry, hospitals, and so on, Foucault traces a transition to panopticism, which, along with the suburban home, family car, weekend sport, deodorant, and heterosexuality, has become a necessary marker of everyday bourgeois life—a surveillance of life rather than the feudal policing of death (modelled by public executions). Apart from Foucault and Bentham, there is the strong influence of David Spurr's *Rhetoric of Empire*, especially his discussion of "surveillance" as a colonial discourse. Finally, in Ryan's *The Cartographic Eye* there is the sustained study of the various discourses by which the European explorers of Australia constructed Australia and its people as a place for narrative possession.

The motif that binds these different theoretical sources together is the look from the height, the view from the mountain, the elevated and enlarged eye that roves and controls, the phallic eye that winks its seminal influence over tracts of the earth's surface. Thus, Bentham's jailer looks over the prisoners from the central tower, Foucault's panopticism operates from the privileged central place, Spurr's journalists survey foreign lands from

---

[13] There is a general question—obviously pertinent to this chapter but also much wider—that perpetually bothers me in all the contemporary perusal of the visual. It is a sort of class identification of the senses, a hierarchy in which sight, hearing, and speech, once they have been separated off from one another, attain a higher status than touch or smell. Indeed, sight may now be in a class of its own, and if it is by sight that the panopticon was supposed to work, then seeing is the sense most closely tied in with the bourgeoisie at this historical juncture. That the early explorers of Australia relied primarily on sight only reinforces my point.

hotels, helicopters, or heights, Ryan's explorers seek out rise after rise to gain strategic (and scenic—but are they not one?) and descriptive advantage, and God himself, or rather, Providence, provides the ultimate perspective. In the words of Mitchell: "the visible possibility of overlooking the country from any eminence, is refreshing at all times, but to an explorer it is everything" (1848:157–58).

Yet, what drew me to these texts in the first place is a curious conjunction of Foucault, Bentham, and Australia, all around the infamous panopticon. Despite my profound ambivalence about Australia (do I not always wish to draw closer to the global "centre"?), I remain intrigued by any passing connections, moments when others speak about it. So it is with Jeremy Bentham and the panopticon, for in a work—itself a couple of long letters published together and then later appearing in the Collected Works—entitled *Panopticon versus New South Wales,* he argues at laborious length against transportation and in favour of his dearly beloved panopticon prison. Bentham—whom Marx called "the arch-Philistine ... that soberly pedantic and heavy-footed oracle of the 'common sense' of the nineteenth century bourgeoisie intelligence" (1976:758)—spent two decades or more of his time and money drawing up plans for a prison, factory, school, or asylum in which a central tower enabled surveillance of a series of individual cells. While the observer is able to see the inmates, they are not able to see the observer. Further, each cell is lit by a window on the other side of the surveillance window so that the warder can see each inmate, as in a theatre. The power of the panopticon—the all-seeing device—is not that the jailer actually observes all the time, but that he or she is able to do so. The inmates do not know when the jailer, or teacher, or doctor, or, more recently, surveillance camera, is looking, but the knowledge that they may be doing so is as good as if they were.[14] In short, surveillance becomes reflexive, the inmates becoming their own warders. The inmates are "caught up in a power situation of which they are themselves the bearers" (Foucault: 201).

Comparing the prison built on panopticon principles in Pennsylvania with transportation to New South Wales, Bentham, not unexpectedly, finds the prison wins on the counts of using the convicts as an example, reformation, incapacitation or the prevention of further offence, deterrence from escapes, compensation, and economy. His prison leads to industry, frugality, and sobriety rather than general depravity, drunkenness, and debauchery. One may be forgiven for thinking that Bentham is in fact

---

14 "[T]he greater chance there is, of a given person's being at a given time actually under inspection, the more strong will be the persuasion—the more *intense,* if I may say so, the *feeling,* he has of his being so" (Bentham, 1995:44).

advocating New South Wales, especially since transportation went ahead while Bentham failed to have his prison built in England.

However, in a dialectical twist that makes one think of Žižek, Michel Foucault suggests that it was in fact the panopticon, or its principle, that won out. In *Discipline and Punish* Foucault digs up, as it were, the transition from power over death to power over life; the slide from public executions to prison timetables (to recall once again the well-known opening to this book); the rotting away of public, overtly violent, and highly ritualistic forms of power and the new growth of covert violence, surveillance, and systematic control; the vast and gore-stained transition from the feudal lords and kings to the bourgeois modern state of capitalism, with its institutions of discipline—prison, school, hospital, asylum, and factory. Bentham himself presented the panopticon as a widely applicable, and cheap, idea.[15]

The panopticon becomes panopticism, the telltale mark of new arrangements of power: "What would you say, if by the gradual adoption and diversified application of this single principle, you should see a new scene of things spread itself over the face of civilized society?" (Bentham, 1995:95). For Foucault the panopticon is a signal of a seismic shift in systems of power: as part of the slow, conflict-ridden move from feudalism to capitalism, the operation of power slides from public and exemplary forms to subtle forms of observance and observation. Bentham himself was a strong campaigner for the abolition of capital and corporal punishment, as well as universal suffrage and the secret ballot. Yet these show the internal contradiction of the new arrangements of power: while the principle was one of egalitarianism (what will later be seen as the fundamental equality of everyone as a consumer), the very structures of bourgeois society ensured that such a society was anything but egalitarian, that it was structurally and hierarchically in favour of the middle class. In other words (and to move beyond Foucault to Jameson), whereas the rhetoric of the bourgeois revolution was one of the liberty and equality of all people, the middle class positioned itself so that when the cheques came to be cashed, when the peasants and the newly formed working class demanded their cut, the bourgeoisie used its new-found strength to avoid paying its debts to precisely those who had helped it win in the first place (the 1848 revolutionary movements in Europe

---

[15] The panopticon for Bentham is not merely a prison, as his elaborate title suggests: "Panopticon; or, The Inspection-house: Containing the Idea of a New Principle of Construction Applicable to any Sort of Establishment, in Which Persons of any Description Are To Be Kept Under Inspection; and in Particular to Penitentiary Houses, Prisons, Poor-houses, Lazarettos, Houses of Industry, Manufactories, Hospitals, Work-houses, Mad-houses, and Schools" (1995:29). Bentham, half in jest, even suggests it as a way to preserve the virginity of "young damsels," by transferring them to a strict inspection-school (1995:90).

constitute the moment of this shift). The egalitarian drive was unable to be realized. So Foucault:

> Historically, the process by which the bourgeoisie became in the course of the eighteenth century the politically dominant class was masked by the establishment of an explicit, coded and formally egalitarian juridical framework, made possible by the organization of a parliamentary, representative régime. But the development and generalization of disciplinary mechanisms constituted the other, dark side of these processes. The general juridical form that guaranteed a system of rights that were egalitarian in principle was supported by these tiny, everyday, physical mechanisms, by all those systems of micro-power that are essentially non-egalitarian and asymmetrical that we call the disciplines.... The contract may have been regarded as the ideal foundation of law and political power, panopticism constituted the technique, universally widespread, of coercion. (222)

Panopticism does not "stick out," as it were: in contrast to the power of kings and lords, it works its way into the very flesh of social interaction. It is, for Foucault, "capillary," entering into the smallest extremities of the social body.

However, what Foucault does not draw out is that the panopticon is a profoundly theological idea. In a remarkable introduction to *The Panopticon Writings* (Bentham, 1995), Miran Bošovič shows how the panopticon may best be seen as a transmutation of the idea of God into particular, bourgeois and utilitarian forms. In a reading that connects Bentham's theory of fictions with his panopticon writings, Bošovič argues that the production of the panopticon is the production of God. Even though Bentham exempts God from the category of nonentities, in which are included ghosts, the bane of Bentham's life, God of course is precisely such a nonentity.[16] The key to all of this lies in the relation between prison warden, or inspector, even public spectators, and the inmates, students, patients, or whatever. For the inspector's authority relies on not being seen by the inmates: they think the inspector is present, ever vigilant, that they are constantly being watched, but they can never see the inspector. If they did, then this would lessen the

---

16 A conclusion Bentham allows in an extraordinary footnote. After discussing, in the main text, that God is a supreme superhuman entity—"sanctioned by revelation; sanctioned by the religion of Jesus as delivered by the apostle Paul"—and that, since no one has seen God, God must be an inferential real entity, Bentham then notes: "Should there be any person who, incapable of drawing those influences by which the Creator and Preserver of all other entities, is referred to the class of real ones, should refuse to him a place in that class, the class to which such person would find himself, in a manner, compelled to refer to that invisible and mysterious being would be, not as in the case of the human soul to that of fictitious entities, but that of non-entities" (1995:120). The convoluted syntax here partly obscures the conclusion drawn by Bošovič.

effect of his absence and unravel the whole arrangement, for the direction of the inspector's eyes, as well as his presence and absence, would be noted. Although the inspector can see and hear (through elaborate voice pipes) all that goes on, it is absolutely essential that the inspector, his movements, comings and goings, remain hidden from the inmates, even during chapel, and Bentham goes to great lengths, by means of elaborate lanterns with holes, colored and smoked glass, the production of a silhouette and a trap-door beneath, to ensure that this is the case (1995:105–9). What counts is the "*apparent omnipresence* of the inspector" combined with "the extreme facility of his *real presence*" (45). This is, then, the fiction that lies at the heart of the panopticon—perpetual surveillance. But does not the inspector become, with omniscience, omnipotence, and omnipresence being added to the ability to see everywhere, more and more godlike? "What has to be staged in the panopticon for the gaze of the prisoners is reality itself, i.e. God. Whereas the innocent are deterred from offending by real punishment, by the real suffering of the punished, the prisoners in the panopticon are deterred from transgressing by the fiction of God" (Bośovič: 11). Yet, it is a hidden God, *deus absconditus*, one who by definition cannot exist. God exists as long as his subjects believe so, in the same way that the authority of the inspector exists as long as the inmates believe he is there and watching. The repeated invocations of Providence by the explorers of which I will speak in a few moments take on a distinctly new hue in this light.

For the veins and capillaries of the explorers also flowed with the new panopticism as they surveyed the land. Over against the general and quite unremarkable practice of climbing hills to look around I would like to set the new eyes that gradually looked upon lands, "old" and "new," as things to be measured, mapped, controlled, and possessed. And it is the visual that is dominant: Ryan speaks of "exploration methodology's heavy reliance on sight" (87). But not merely the visual—it is the view from a height: "The cartographic necessity of gaining elevation and seeing great distances offers a particular point of view and demands the arrogation of a visual power over the land, opening it for inspection" (88). This opens up the vast area of cartography and its transformation into a "precise" discipline that relied on a different set of ideological assumptions from those earlier ones that depicted the world and its various sectors according to religious or theological categories. What is interesting here is that such a change in the practice and theory of cartography coincides by and large with the rise of the bourgeoisie, the development of modern science, and the complex minute patterns of surveillance and the policing of life and the body that Foucault designates as panopticism.

I want to focus, however, on a certain set of practices that became the norm in the era of classical and imperial capitalism as the various European colonial powers set out to conquer those areas of the globe outside Europe itself. Thus, the Royal Geographical Society in England sponsored a string of expeditions in the "new" lands that attempted to traverse them from one end to the other, or to "penetrate" their interiors. All the while the various explorers were expected and compelled to keep verbal and graphic traces of their moves, experiences, and reflections in various diaries and journals. These were subsequently published, under the auspices of the society in question, with the expected advancement of the career of the explorer in question. The range of what was surveyed in these texts—land forms, flora and fauna, indigenous people, the impressions of the writer, potential places of settlement—ensured that at least the impression of comprehensiveness had been achieved. Ryan usefully traces the ideological constructs that operated in such observation: the aesthetic ideals of the picturesque (active alteration of the land according to codes of looking), panoramic (perceptual construction of the land according to similar codes), mimeticism (since this was the high period of realism), and perspectivism. Often, however, the agenda was one of pastoral profit and human settlement: Where were the best pasture lands, the best possibilities for grain and especially grazing, where might the squatters and farmers be able to move in the new worlds for the maximum gain of the industries back "home"?

But how might all of this be designated as panopticism? To begin with there is the view from the height, the *sine qua non* of the aesthetic category of the panoramic. The best possibilities for a surveying view were to be had on any rise—ridges, hills, if not the occasional mountain itself. Mountains presented either a barrier that hindered further surveying and possession of the land—as in the perpetual question in the first convict colony in Sydney about what lay beyond the "Blue Mountains"—or as a peculiar vantage point from which to view the land about. This may take a number of forms: the first view of a valley or plain upon passing over a ridge; the distant rise that is finally attained after much effort; the mountain that is desirable as a place of aesthetic advantage (the beauty of the view and the aesthetic code of the picturesque); and the mountain as best point for surveillance itself.

Time and again the explorers mount a mountain, ascend an ascent, clamber up a climb. For instance, in a little over a hundred pages, Eyre crests Mt. Deception (1845 1:64–65), Termination Hill (87), Mt. Searle (117), Mt. Distance (126), Mt. Hopeless (127–30), Baxter's Range (139), Mt. Hill (151–52), and Mt. Hall (193). When he is not on them, he sets his bearings by them (1:110). Although Eyre finds the desert views disconcerting, "the realization of my worst forebodings," rendering the expedition futile (1:118), Giles likes his eagle eye: viewing Birthday Creek (Ernabella) from a nearby mountain he crows, "We had a perfect bird's eye view of the spot.... Having completed our survey, we descended barefooted as before" (1:170). And so it goes on from explorer to explorer: Grey climbs a ridge "and a magnificent view burst upon us" (1:161); "... and there burst upon my sight a most enchanting view" (2:28); the country "lay like a map at our feet" (2:180). Sturt names the directions in which he looks, as though the land it itself were a map, NE, SE, SW, NW (1833 1:25–27). Leichhardt, upon Mt. Stewart, "obtained a very extensive view from its summit," being able to espy "as far as the eye could see" (113). And of course Mitchell embodies all of them, surveyor-general that he was, ascending every hill with a utilitarian purpose, such as Warrawolong, north of Wiseman's Ferry in what is now the Yengo wilderness (1839 1:9–10).

Further, the view from the height gives control. Explorer texts favour military terms such as "command" (see Ryan: 89–91). Apart from repeated references in the journals about commanding positions or views, the question of control also surfaces when there is a contest (real or otherwise) with Aborigines for the high ground, as when Eyre found that the natives had taken a position a little higher and more commanding than his (1845 1:237–38).

With this visual, and at times belligerent, control comes the idea of possession and ownership. The land is possessed, in proxy as it were, for the British-style estates and manors that are to follow. Certain vantages are more than the means of visual control and possession of the land viewed; they themselves become desirable for their commanding prospects. So, Grey writes of Western Australia, "I painted in fancy the rapid progress that this country would ere long make in commerce and civilization, and my weakness and fatigues were all forgotten" (1:163). He also reflects on the territory's commercial prospects (1:265–88) and the "Overlanders" who made the first treks to dispossess the Aborigines (2:183–204). The progress is so rapid that Eyre can note, after narrating his initial journey through the fertile land north of Adelaide in 1840, that by the time he revises his journals for publication some five years later "all this country, and for some distance to the north, is now occupied by stations" (1845 1:38). Of course, he had prophesied this himself: "I however felt conscious that within a few years of the moment at which I stood there, a British population, rich in civilization, and the means of transforming an unoccupied country to one teeming with inhabitants and produce, would have followed my steps" (1:359). Like all prophecy, it was all the more true having been written after the event— *vaticinium ex eventu*.

Alongside this conjunction of vision and power is the desire and requirement for meticulous detail, the minute recording of a whole range of items that were regarded as significant. Indeed, the explorers' journals often read as the early, faltering efforts of the later, apparently more sophisticated ethnographers and anthropologists who were to comb the world in search of the most authentically aboriginal tribe. This is particularly true of Grey's accounts (1:11–20, 37–64, 202–5, 238–64; 2:116–80, 207–388, 391–482) and those of Sturt (1833 1:ix–lxxx, 105–6, 151–81; 2:50–55, 249–56; 1984:118–264;

see also Leichhardt: 351–61; Mitchell 1839 1:xvii–xxi, 14–16; 2:340–415; Stuart: 484–507), interspersed as they are with smatterings of linguistic material (lists of words with English "equivalents"), descriptions and inventories of specimens of flora and fauna, natural history, climate, nature of soil, landforms, commercial opportunities, advice for other explorers, and of meticulous observations on Aborigines, their appearance (including the presence of lighter-skinned people), life, customs, burial practices, law, kinship, ritual, life span, production, preparation and consumption of food, song and culture, and details of cave paintings and styles—in short, a list comparable to the web of biblical references that I noted above, particularly with regard to the natives.

Not only do these practices signal the functioning of panopticism in the activity of English explorers of Australia, but they also suggest that panopticism is crucial for the exercise of colonialism. That this is not restricted to exploration or the early stages of colonial expansion is suggested by David Spurr's *The Rhetoric of Empire,* which begins with a treatment of surveillance as one of the prime motifs by which journalists perceive and process the lands they visit and report about. The act of surveillance is made invariably from a height, although for these contemporary "explorers," that height may be as much a hotel tower, helicopter, or aeroplane as the mountain of former surveyors of lands that were open for "possession." The way surveillance operates may well be problematized—the reporter may question the surveying function in the process of doing it—yet the action itself remains in place.

I have taken some time with this, since it seems to me that not only is the panoptic gaze a particular production of consolidating capitalism, but it is, as I argued above, a distinctly theological notion. Its ideology, in other words, is one that is constructed in theological terms. With the explorers this happens in two ways. First, the land, traditionally presented in cartography about Australia as a blank, is textualized. It is both a *tabula rasa* on which the explorers must inscribe themselves and a text that speaks of the Author of nature. The divine signification, common enough in nineteenth-century European writing, is also applied to Australia, of which God also is the author (see Ryan: 123).

Secondly, the depiction of surveillance, whether in writing or illustration, often includes the explorer: the explorer appears as knowledge gatherer and as surveyor, viewed by yet another eye, which is immediately that of the writer/illustrator and reader. The explorer is, in other words, there in the picture: the writer writes himself, or the drawer draws himself, into the text. But this superior eye, the one that sees the explorer seeing is not only the writer (explorer) or reader, but often God. "The point of view of the eye of God is not simply a well-worn trope, but continues in the explorers' texts the association of height and surveillance" (Ryan: 91–92). God is the ultimate watcher, the last in a hierarchy of vision. Not only does this justify the explorers' role, giving divine approval, but it provides reasons for survival itself:

> in the wide field of nature, we see the hand of an over-ruling Providence, evidence of care and protection from some unseen quarter, which strike the mind with overwhelming conviction, that whether in the palace or in the cottage, in the garden, or in the desert, there is an eye upon us. (Sturt, 1849 2:92)

The panoptic view of God is then a wider theological position—the eye of Providence—that applies in the explorer's own experience. The explorer looks upon the land, and especially the Aborigines, as though he were the Divine, or perhaps Bentham's inspector (so Ryan: 133). But the explorer is also one item in that greater vision that only God can command. Colonial exploration is but a particular example of this larger practice, which is then watched over by God. Of course, at the same time, God's eye is constructed in terms of the explorer's panoptic view: "The eye of God looking down on the solitary caravan, as with its slow, and snake-like motion, it presents the only living thing around, must have contemplated its appearance on such a scene with pitying admiration" (Giles 2:318).

This, finally, is an elision of explorer and God, usually through vision. So Giles writes of a "currugated range … spread by the great Creator's hand" which was rescued by him and his companion, Tietkens, "from its former and ancient oblivion" (1:282). Without being seen, it may as well not exist: their act of viewing is comparable to that of creation.

It is not for nothing, then, that the favoured term for God is "Providence," the one who sees before, or who sees ahead. So Sturt, in a speech reiterated by Eyre:

> Nevertheless, gentlemen, I shall envy that man who shall first plant the flag of our native country in the centre of our adopted one. There is not one deed in those days to be compared with it, and to whoever may undertake so praiseworthy and so devoted a task, I wish that success, which Heaven sometimes vouchsafes to those who are actuated by the first of motives—the public good; and the best of principles—a reliance on Providence. (Eyre, 1845 1:9)

One must not actually desire to be the first to plant the flag, since that smells of naked competition, but must be drawn above all by the equation of the public good and a reliance on Providence. Only then, as is proper under Providence, will one be duly rewarded with the other prize.

It goes without saying that Providence, or "Heaven," has the commercial good of both (South) Australia and England at heart: "Go forth, then, on your journey, with a full confidence in the goodness of Providence; and may Heaven direct your steps to throw open the fertility of the interior, not only for the benefit of the province, but of our native country" (*South Australian Register,* 20 June 1840, qtd. by Eyre, 1845 1:20). With the heavenly being clearly with his party, hidden in the saddlebags perhaps, Eyre can leave the outcome of the expedition to such a goodly force. "The result we were willing to leave in the hands of that Almighty Being whose blessing had been implored upon our undertaking, and to whom we looked for guidance and protection in all our wanderings" (28).

And so my discussion folds back to its earlier theme of the reliance on the Almighty Being, Providence, Heaven, or whatever, particularly in rescue from moments of dire distress, recklessness, and plain stupidity. Eyre again:

> Such are the mysteries and inscrutable ways of providence and so impossible is it for man's private comprehension to estimate the result even of his own simplest actions, still less to judge of the more general ordinations of Divine Wisdom. In my progress thro' life I have frequently found trivial circumstances conduce to important events, and influential occurrences take place when least expected; an experience no doubt shared in by others, but which I think ought to teach us to distrust ourselves and our own judgement and to place full reliance on the wisdom and goodness of God, who can, and in his own good time often does, make plain and clear what once seemed dark, inexplicable or unimportant. (Eyre, 1984:214)

If readers look hard enough through the lines of the text, it may be possible to discern the diminutive silhouette of Bentham himself, casting his controlling eye over his prison, school, infirmary, or whatever. For this text is soaked with the transformation of the central theological notion of Providence in terms of panopticism, with its focus on the trivial and everyday, the use of these by God to produce great events in a person's life, momentous occasions from the minutiae of life, and the shedding of light and reason on the dark and inscrutable. Yet is it not the case not only that the perception of God here is determined by such panoptic categories but also that the theological traditions of divine surveillance, foreknowledge, and predestination influenced the construction of panopticism, and thus of the ways the explorers saw the land?

In the end, the Providential eye that oversaw the explorers' strange wanderings also monitored the spread of Christianity—inextricably tied in with civilization and English commerce—throughout the globe. Ever Evangelical, Grey writes: "Christianity and civilization are marching over the world with a rapidity not fully known or estimated by any one nation; the English are scarcely aware what has been effected by their own missionaries and commerce, and they are utterly ignorant of what has been already done, and is now doing, by the Americans, Dutch, and Portugese" (2:224).

A Queer Land?

Let me close, however, on a different note, a little more surreptitious but all the more intriguing. A recurring feature of postcolonial study is the argument that the colonial land is gendered as female, lying recumbent, awaiting penetration by the male explorer's eye and caravan. That is to say, colonial desire is in many respects also sexual desire. Freud's designation of woman as the "dark continent" only adds to such an argument, although it is also compounded by the overlapping of colonial and precolonial patriarchy, and by the complicity of Western white feminism in the exclusion of colonial women (Mohanty: 196–97). Yet, one of the weakest arguments in recent work on the explorers is to argue that their desire for Australia is the sexual desire of colonial male for exotic female. Indeed, Ryan's attempt to make this argument turns, symptomatically, from the explorer texts on which he focuses to colonial fiction (196–205). Michael Cathcart has also attacked this idea, suggesting that Sturt's famous passage about a veiled central Australia draws not so much upon the notion of the veil of a harem girl as upon the veil of the holy of holies in the temple of Jerusalem, where the greatest mystery was hidden from view, until it was torn in two with the death of Christ in the Synoptic Gospels. Devout and Evangelical Anglican that he was, knowing his Bible, Sturt viewed the centre as the hidden, mysterious, divinely charged place, the holy of holies from which the female was excluded:

> Men of undoubted perseverance and energy in vain tried to work their way to that distant and shrouded spot. A veil hung over central Australia that could neither be pierced nor raised. Girt around by deserts, it almost appeared as if nature had intentionally closed it upon civilised man, that she might have one domain on earth's wide field over which the savage might roam in freedom. (1849 2:2)

Like Christ, his duty was then to break through the curtain to this mystery as well. For Cathcart, Sturt "was imagining 'the centre' as a place of Christian mystery which he alone could reveal" (7).

However, if the female is largely excluded from the explorers' desire—in part due to the aridity of much of the land, in contrast to the America discussed by Kolodny—then what form does that desire take? A queer desire, it seems to me. In this light, the bands of men travelling together for months on end become homosocial bands, bonding and squabbling as they travel, thirst, starve, and explore. The land is rarely soft and receptive, but rather harsh, unforgiving, testing them: in short, manly. The explorers pit their strength against a tough land; some lose, some win, but it is a contest of man against man. Yet, as any reading of such masculine contests will attest, a queer desire inflects such contests. Homosocial groups and homo-social contests are also the place of homosexual desire, and the paradigmatic case of this is Giles and his Aboriginal helpers.

Most of the time Giles treats Aborigines as no better than cannibals; troglydites, cave dwellers, he calls them. However, he does like black males: so, he begins his expeditions buying one, after patting his head and admiring his curly hair, only to lose him later on: "I suffered another loss," he laments, "as a bright little black boy called Fry, a great favourite of mine, with splendid eyes and teeth, whom I intended to bring with me as a companion for Tommy, was also dead" (2:157). Tommy, on the other hand, was drawn by Giles from his initiation rites, making them partners in conspiracy as Giles took advantage of the adolescent's rebelliousness. Giles keeps him with him for the trip from Port Augusta to Perth: he cuts off his initiation hair growth, allows him near women, and so on, so that he can have him for himself and that the elders will reject Tommy. When a group of sexually inquisitive native girls follows the party at the beginning of the return trip from Perth to Adelaide, Giles notes Tommy's reluctance to be with them, "though they tried very hard to make love to him," as Tommy, "being a very good-looking boy, was an object of great admiration to a good many of them" (2:270). In the end, however, Giles "was anxious to get rid of them; they were too much of a good thing" (2:272). Other boys and young friends appear: in 1882 on a trip to the Everard range he has a black boy with him, Billy, and a "very young friend" named Vernon Edwards (2:331).

Giles cannot refrain from commenting on his ability to attract the boys to him. So, when he meets a small group of aboriginal males, he writes: "This old party was remarkably shy; the elder boy seemed a little frightened, and didn't relish being touched by a white man, but the youngest was quite at his ease, and came up to me with the audacity and insouciance of early youth, and pulled me about. When I patted him, he grinned like any other monkey" (2:326). And then there is the remarkable poem to youth, recited as a waking dream: "O lovely youth, with thine arrowy form, and slender hands, thy pearly teeth, and saintly smile, thy pleading eyes and radiant hair; all, all must worship thee" (2:154).

WORKS CITED

Bentham, Jeremy
    1843   *Panopticon versus New South Wales: Or, the Panopticon Penitentiary System, and the Penal Colonization System, Compared. In a Letter Addressed to the Right Honourable Lord Pelham*. Pp. 173–248 in *The Works of Jeremy Bentham*, vol. 4. Ed. J. Bowring. Edinburgh: William Tate.

    1995   *The Panopticon Writings*. Ed. and intro. M. Bošovič. London: Verso.

Bošovič, Miran
    1995   "Introduction: 'An Utterly Dark Spot.'" Pp. 1–27 in Bentham, 1995.

Cathcart, Michael
    1997   "Eyes of the Beholders." *The Australian's Review of Books* 2 (March): 6–7.

Eyre, Edward John
    1845   *Journals of Expeditions of Discovery into Central Australia and Overland from Adelaide to King George's Sound in the Years 1840–1; Sent by the Colonists of South Australia, with the Sanction and Support of the Government: Including an Account of the Manners and Customs of the Aborigines and the State of Their Relations with Europeans.* 2 vols. London: T. & W. Boone.

    1984   *Autobiographical Narrative of Residence and Exploration in Australia 1832–1839.* Ed and intro. J. Waterhouse. London: Caliban.

Foucault, Michel
    1979   *Discipline and Punish: The Birth of the Prison.* Trans. A. Sheridan. New York: Vintage.

Giles, Ernest
    1889   *Australia Twice Traversed: The Romance of Exploration, Being a Narrative Compiled from the Journals of Five Exploring Expeditions into and through Central South Australia and Western Australia from 1872 to 1876.* 2 vols. London: Low, Marston, Searle & Rivington.

Grey, George
    1841   *Journals of Two Expeditions of Discovery in North-West and Western Australia, during the Years 1837, 38, and 39, under the Authority of Her Majesty's Government Describing Many Newly Discovered, Important, and Fertile Districts, with Observations on the Moral and Physical Condition of the Aboriginal Inhabitants.* 2 vols. London: T. & W. Boone.

Kolodny, Annette
    1975   *The Lay of the Land: Metaphor As Experience and History in American Life and Letters.* Chapel Hill: University of North Carolina Press.

Leichhardt, Ludwig
    1847   *Journal of an Overland Expedition in Australia, from Moreton Bay to Port Essington, a Distance of Upwards 3000 Miles, During the Years 1844–1845.* London: T. & W. Boone.

Marx, Karl
    1973   *Grundrisse: Foundations of the Critique of Political Economy (Rough Draft).* Trans. M. Nicolaus. Harmondsworth: Penguin, in association with New Left Books.

    1976   *Capital: A Critique of Political Economy.* Trans. B. Fowkes. Intro. E. Mandel. Harmondsworth: Penguin, in association with New Left Books.

Mitchell, Thomas Livingstone
- 1839 *Three Expeditons into the Interior of Australia; with Descriptions of the Recently Explored Australia Felix, and of the Present Colony of New South Wales.* 2d ed. 2 vols. London: T. & W. Boone.
- 1848 *Journal of an Expedition into the Interior of Tropical Australia: In Search of a Route from Sydney to the Gulf of Carpentaria.* London: Longmans.

Mohanty, Chandra Talpade
- 1993 "Under Western Eyes: Feminist Scholarship and Colonial Discourses." Pp. 196–220 in Williams and Chrisman.

Ryan, Simon
- 1996 *The Cartographic Eye: How Explorers Saw Australia.* Cambridge: Cambridge University Press.

Spurr, David
- 1993 *The Rhetoric of Empire: Colonial Discourse in Journalism, Travel Writing, and Imperial Administration.* Post-Contemporary Interventions. Durham, N. C.: Duke University Press.

Stuart, John McDouall
- 1865 *The Journals of John McDouall Stuart during the Years 1858, 1859, 1860, 1861, & 1862, When He Fixed the Centre of the Continent and Successfully Crossed It from Sea to Sea.* Ed. W. Hardman. 2d ed. London: Saunders, Otley & Co.

Sturt, Charles
- 1833 *Two Expeditions into the Interior of Southern Australia, during the Years 1828, 1829, 1830, and 1831: With Observations on the Soil, Climate and General Resources of the Colony of New South Wales.* 2 vols. London: Smith, Elder & Co.
- 1849 *Narrative of an Expedition into Central Australia, Performed under the Authority of Her Majesty's Government, during the Years 1844, 5 and 6 Together with a Notice of the Province of South Australia, in 1847.* 2 vols. London: T. & W. Boone.
- 1984 *Journal of the Central Australian Expedition.* Ed. and intro. J. Waterhouse. London: Caliban.

Williams, Patrick, and Laura Chrisman
- 1993 *Colonial Discourse and Post-Colonial Theory.* Hemel Hempstead, England: Harvester Wheatsheaf.

Surveying the Promised Land: Elizabeth Jolley's *Milk and Honey*

Dorothy Jones
University of Wollongong

ABSTRACT

The Bible proved a significant resource for European imperialism both in aiding colonisers to impose their own culture on those they conquered and in justifying their annexation and administration of other peoples' territory. Metaphors drawn from biblical accounts of the garden of Eden and the promised land offering a new home to Jews who had been held captive in Egypt were mobilised in relation to European colonisation. In the biblical context, these motifs emphasised God's cherishing or protection of chosen people to the exclusion of all others and so could be used to justify many forms of containment and exclusion in a colonial situation. The garden of Eden and the promised land also resonate as metaphors within a postcolonial context, and writers have drawn upon them when exploring issues of personal, national, and communal identity. Elizabeth Jolley engages in such exploration in her novel *Milk and Honey* as she presents Australia, not through the eyes of newly arrived colonists, but from the viewpoint of refugee migrants escaped from Europe during World War II. In a novel permeated with biblical allusion, she portrays the costs both of cultural and social exclusivity and of breaking down barriers erected to preserve identity.

One foot in Eden still, I stand
And look across the other land.
The world's great day is growing late,
Yet strange these fields that we have planted
So long with crops of love and hate.
Time's handiworks by time are haunted,
And nothing now can separate
The corn and tares compactly grown.
The armorial weed in stillness bound
About the stalk; these are our own.
Evil and good stand thick around
In the fields of charity and sin
Where we shall lead our harvest in.
(Edwin Muir: 227)

Biblical images of the garden of Eden, paradise lost, the promised land, and the kingdom of heaven still haunt the Western imagination, although in a secular age, many people dismiss the Bible as a past relic, unaware how far it continues to shape our perceptions of the world. Regina Schwartz, however, claims it "encodes Western culture's myths of collective identity," showing that sacred categories of thought still linger, transformed into secular ones (6). Biblical language, motifs, and narrative pervade centuries of European art and literature. One especially potent image, the garden of Eden and its loss, has generated innumerable plot lines where characters attempt the impossible task of recovering that state of primal innocence and bliss. Sometimes, on the other hand, the enclosed world of Eden, no matter how idyllic, appears so restrictive it prompts an urge to escape. Whether as point of origin or ultimate goal, Eden becomes associated with journey, quest, or pilgrimage and, as a result, its story sometimes fuses imaginatively with the later biblical narrative recording the Israelite wanderings through the wilderness in search of the promised land. While inspiring artists, these narratives also generated political metaphors defining nationhood and justifying imperial expansion. A wide variety of past social and political movements have claimed the Bible's endorsement, and it has proved particularly significant for imposing European culture on indigenous peoples, whilst colonists drew on biblical narrative to justify appropriating their territory.

This paper examines the importance of Edenic and exodus imagery in colonial expansion, with particular reference to Australia, while focusing on its use in one postcolonial text, the novel *Milk and Honey* (1984), whose author, Elizabeth Jolley, uses it to delineate the plight of a group of refugee European migrants living there after World War II. Jolley begins an autobiographical essay on her schooldays:

> Our headmaster often said he knew which boys and girls would hand in their Golden Treasury of the Bible (2 Vols) on leaving school and which boys and girls would keep them as a spiritual guide for the rest of their lives. (1992:27)

Even without the author's half humorous acknowledgment that she still retains the "two grey nondescript books" (1992:30), her fiction reveals how influential the Bible has been. Jolley shows herself well aware of limitations inherent in the Western humanist tradition, sardonically observing it in collision with popular culture; nevertheless, she regularly invokes its great musical and literary masterpieces (the Bible among them), representing these artistic achievements as a profound source of imaginative, spiritual, and moral inspiration. *Milk and Honey* contains significant reference to works by Rilke and to Mozart's music, particularly his Requiem Mass, but biblical allusion pervades the entire novel.

Jolley's title derives from the verse in Exodus which also serves as an epigraph—"and to bring them up out of that land unto a good land and a large, unto a land flowing with milk and honey" (3:8). Biblical narratives of Eden and its loss, the Israelites' Exodus to the promised land, the rivalry between Cain and Abel, together with allusions to the Song of Songs and images of labouring in the vineyard, all contribute to the novel's structure and range of meanings. Events in the life of the Old Testament patriarch Jacob are configured in the experience of his namesake, the novel's protagonist. Biblical reference contributes to *Milk and Honey*'s rich fund of imagery but, more importantly, it reinforces the novel's moral weight. The narrative explores interactions between Australian and European culture in the lives of characters who, forced to move countries, maintain an uneasy balance between past and present worlds, the old existence and the new. But although Jolley's characters are buffeted and manipulated by circumstances beyond their control, the author also emphasises how ultimately they must assume responsibility for their own choices. Failure to do so results in catastrophe, internal exile, and the destruction of a yearned-for paradise.

After the expulsion from Eden, God warns Adam he will return to the ground from which he has been taken—"for dust thou art and unto dust thou shalt return" (Gen 3:19). In her prologue to *Milk and Honey*, Jolley compares political upheaval in Europe to a great wind sweeping away "the soot and the dirt, the horse manure, the brickdust and the thistledown" forming it into innumerable cones of debris that descend to earth in another hemisphere where most disintegrate and mix with "the dust of the new place." But some cones press closer together, determined to remain unchanged, sustaining themselves by drawing "on the fragments of other such cones." Among the principal characters are a migrant family—Leopold Heimbach, his unmarried sisters Tante Rosa and Tante Heloise, his daughter Louise, and his son Waldemar—who escape from Vienna to Australia during World War II. Jacob, the novel's narrator, also from an Austrian family settled in Australia, is introduced into their household aged thirteen to receive the musical instruction his father, uncle, and aunt all believe he merits. The Heimbachs, devoted to music and to one another, while eking out a meagre living through music lessons and dressmaking, depend heavily on money they receive for his board and tuition. Consequently, Jacob is manipulated with tender devotion to become firmly enmeshed within the family and ultimately corrupted by it while being caught in the clash of cultures.

Jolley's narrative keeps moving between present and past, tracing Jacob's movement from innocence through corrupt self-absorption to experiencing the pain of loss and dispossession. He recalls a many-layered past—young manhood, adolescence, early years living with his father in their country vineyard, and a still earlier period before his mother's death.

He also records yet more distant memories relayed to him by the Heimbachs of their life in Europe before and during the war. Past recollections are filtered through the consciousness of the man Jacob develops into, so the vision of the uncomprehending child and adolescent is incorporated within that of the man who has acquired painful, lacerating knowledge. But, mired in self-delusion, he is a far from reliable narrator, and it is possible certain key events, in a novel where realism merges with elements of fairy tale and gothic romance, project his own fevered imaginings, especially when we eventually discover that he recounts his narrative from inside a mental hospital, though whether he is there as patient or worker is unclear.

The situation of the Heimbachs in *Milk and Honey*, yearning for the lost paradise of home and seeking to recreate it in a new land, is characteristic of peoples who leave their homelands for new countries whether as conquerors, colonists, or refugees. Like Eden on the one hand and the kingdom of God on the other, paradise lies simultaneously far behind and well ahead. This double vision of a past and future paradise infuses the whole history of European colonisation. The earthly paradise "epitomises our dream of order: natural organisation with no frictions, no tensions of any kind" (Hughes: 104), and, for centuries, people hoped it might either be rediscovered or, in some way, recreated. Maps and treatises throughout the Middle Ages and Renaissance located the garden of Eden "now east, now west, now on an island, now behind or upon a mountain—but always remote, always inaccessible" (Giammatti; 4). A possibility of actually finding it helped prompt some early European voyages of discovery. As hitherto unknown plants from the New World were brought back to Europe, some thinkers speculated that, after the fall, the contents of Eden must have been scattered throughout the world and believed that including them in newly established European botanical gardens would result not only in a living encyclopedia of plants but in the recreation of the original garden itself (Prest: 9).

Yet Eden, representing both paradise and paradise lost, is an ambivalent location since it is largely defined by the harshness and evil it excludes. The cultivated garden is contrasted with the surrounding wilderness where the ground brings forth "thorns and thistles," but when the Eden metaphor is applied to newly acquired colonial territory, distinctions between garden and wilderness prove somewhat tenuous. Thomas Mitchell, describing his exploration of inland Australia, has no doubts, triumphally asserting a God-given right to the land.

> this highly interesting region lay before me with all its features new and untouched as they fell from the hand of the Creator! Of this Eden it seemed that I was the only Adam; and it was indeed a sort of paradise to me. (Gibson, 1992:14)

From the vantage point of the Colonial Office, however, Sir James Stephen, in a speech of 1858, sees these new territories as wilderness that British settlers will transform into paradise. "You can therefore understand how it is that they make their way to the ends of the earth, finding the land before them as the desolate wilderness, and leaving it as the very garden of Eden behind them" (283). From the settlers' perspective, Eden more often resembled the country they had left behind. Susanna Moodie writes of Canada in her memoir *Roughing It in the Bush:* "The unpeopled wastes of Canada must present the same aspect to the new settler that the world did to our first parents after their expulsion from the Garden of Eden" (251–52).

In Jolley's novel, the Heimbach family, ensconced in Australia's land of milk and honey, consider themselves exiles, who, though not Jewish themselves, have been forced to leave Austria because of Leopold's Jewish wife whom they never fully accept as a family member. In Genesis, the loss of Eden represents a universal condition of exile with humanity excluded forever from its true home. But this loss also foreshadows another quite specific exile experienced by a particular nation. "The paradisal garden is an idealised, and lost, land of Israel" (Schwartz: 50). Dispossessed and homeless, after fleeing slavery in Egypt and suffering innumerable trials in the wilderness, the Israelites arrive in that abundant land flowing with milk and honey promised by God in recompense for their sufferings and to reward their faith in him. But the promised land is already inhabited by peoples who must in turn be conquered and dispossessed. Regina Schwartz explores this paradox.

> Possession implies domination. Defining identity in terms of territory produces two myths that are the two consequences of possessing (or dreaming of possessing) land: either a people take the land from another people (conquest) or the land is taken from them (exile). Narratives of conquest and exile are the logical elaborations of a doctrine of land possession. But conquest and exile are not simply opposites. Exile also serves as a kind of retrospective justification for conquest. (51)

The history of white settlement in Australia is also permeated with biblical images of Eden, exile, and the promised land. Mythic imagination had focused on the region long before Europeans set foot there. The Celtic Otherworld or Underworld, a "place and source of health, youth, wealth, wisdom, perpetual spring and summer, fruits and feasts, music and joy" was sited in the southern hemisphere (Bird Rose: 195). Ross Gibson demonstrates how ancient images of an earthly paradise inspired and haunted many journeys of exploration to and within Australia so that, despite the harsh realities they encountered, colonists often "developed a paradoxical ability to tolerate disappointment while continuing to expect some Australian felicity" (1984:37). In Britain some regarded Australia as a promised land flowing with milk and honey where the poor might emigrate to lead a prosperous existence abroad (Lansbury: 157–58). But for many of its European inhabitants, Australia represented exile rather than a land of promise and, given the numbers transported there as convicts against their will, a more appropriate analogy was with Adam and Eve driven from paradise. "The Expulsion myth situates Home as Eden, the monarch as God, and the convicts as sinful fallen people doomed to a life of toil and sweat amidst thorns and thistles" (Bird Rose: 205).

Noting white Australia's myth of victimhood, where battlers combat adversity in a hostile land, Ann Curthoys demonstrates how biblical motifs of expulsion from Eden and entry into the promised land fit neatly together in Australia to obscure white aggression and justify the conquest of Aboriginal territory. She concludes that much non-Aboriginal hostility to indigenous land claims relates to long-standing fears of homelessness, that such claims "may somehow affect their own land holdings, whether rural farm or urban home" (36). Eden and the promised land are powerfully linked with concepts of home, the place of belonging, but in nations established as imperial possessions home becomes highly problematic. Where is it located—in the country of origin or the land of settlement? In sheltering its inmates, home is defined through exclusion: "it is in the heyday of British imperialism that England gets defined as 'Home' in opposition to 'The Empire' which belongs to the English but which is not England" (George: 4). Not surprisingly, a metaphysical homelessness often persists well after former colonies become independent, as New Zealand poet Allen Curnow indicates in concluding his poem "House and Land" with the lines, "what great gloom / Stands in a land of settlers / With never a soul at home" (Curnow: 39).

At first sight, the refugee family in *Milk and Honey*, poor and marginalised in their host country, have little connection with the imperial conquest of Australia and the dispossession of its native population. But they too are convinced of their inherent superiority to their Australian neighbours and have few qualms about exploiting others in defence of their own exclusivity. The Heimbachs (the name means home stream) are fiercely attached to the ideal of home, the safe place "built on a pattern of select inclusions and exclusions ... a way of establishing difference" (George: 2). Their true home, their paradise, is their pre-war world of European high culture and social refinement, which they seek to recreate and maintain within their own household by excluding the new environment as far as possible. "It is not easy with one's needs and refinements to adapt to a new country. It was all so strange, language, customs, climate, everything" (Jolley, 1984:121). As exiles with a refugee mentality, they carry substantial mental baggage from the past along with the precious household goods they keep locked away in trunks—"It is vulgar to display one's possessions" (Jolley, 1984:170). For them, Australia is merely a cultural wilderness. Leopold, himself a musician, expresses contempt for players in the local symphony orchestra.

> Leopold regarded the members of the orchestra as vulgar people. He told me once that some of the people just played to make a living and that they had no feeling for music at all. "They have no ear, they have nothing except a certain skill to manipulate their fingers and an instrument and so produce the required sounds." (57)

Yet maintaining the enclosed Heimbach world requires money, and Jacob's tuition fees help provide the milk and honey of relative prosperity, symbolised by regular supplies of real coffee, chicken livers, Polish cucumbers, and sesame bread (33). To ensure continuing abundance, the family tricks the thirteen-year-old Jacob into believing that, after a brief tussle, he has killed Waldemar, Leopold's idiot son. Waldemar has, in fact, been spirited upstairs to the attic (which Jacob has been told remains unused because the roof leaks badly), to be cared for by the aunts rather than being confined within an institution. Jacob, believing himself a murderer, accepts he is now bound irrevocably to the household—"I had no wish to be free" (36)—while the Heimbachs continue to treat him with loving devotion, fostering his musical career and accepting him as a substitute son. The family consider that their own victim status in Vienna justifies this deception, as Tante Heloise later explains, "I cannot describe what it is like to have one's home taken away and used by uninvited people and then we were not used to poverty" (120).

The Heimbachs' difficulties in coming to terms with Australia represent the conflict existing in many postcolonial societies where a newly evolving culture continues to be measured, often disparagingly, against that of the former imperial power. The ill effects of such conflict are most apparent in the life of their protégé Jacob. Just as the movement from Eden to the promised land may symbolise the forging of national identity, so it can represent the progress of an individual soul driven inexorably through the world by time. Jacob's attempts to capture an ideal existence, to reconcile the foreign and the familiar, are represented in terms of landscape where cultivated space like the Heimbachs' garden is set against, or linked with, a more spacious natural landscape. His father's vineyard, like Jacob himself, is located between the two. Although cultivated space, it is also part of the surrounding countryside. Initially, Jacob's lost paradise is his childhood innocence equated with the vineyard where he originally lived with his father and for which he continues to yearn as an adult. As a child the surrounding landscape inspired his reverence, evoking possibilities of a union between heaven and earth—"the vineyards crossing great space end in a quiet meeting with the sky" (10). Transition from childhood to the corrupt adult world is symbolised on Jacob's arrival at the Heimbachs' by an episode in their garden where Waldemar, crouched among the branches of a mulberry tree, holds out both clenched fists, asking in his strangely accented English, "Which hend you hev?" (12). When Jacob taps the left one, Waldemar lets fall a cockroach on his shirtfront, then pops a mulberry in his mouth. Jacob now eats from the tree of knowledge of good and evil and his mulberry-stained hands suggest the taint of original sin. On the first night in his new home, he runs away to the vineyard, only to be turned back by his Uncle Otto standing, like the angel with the fiery sword, in a square of light at the open door. There is no re-entry to the world of childhood, for time cannot be reversed.

When his father dies, Jacob, now a young man, agrees the vineyard be sold as prime real estate. Revisiting the district after this decision, he notes some vines in surrounding vineyards appear to kneel at prayer, while others have "arms lifted and hoisted over high posts" in an image suggesting both Israel's bondage in Egypt and Jacob's situation with the Heimbachs. "I thought again of them as I did when I was a child. I imagined them to be slaves with their shoulders lifted too high and lashed to posts" (46). Vineyards, which figure in the Bible as metaphors for God's relationship to his people and his disappointment with them, have affinity with narratives of the garden of Eden and the promised land. In Isaiah, the vineyard "planted with the choicest vine" produces only wild grapes (5:2). In the New Testament, where vineyards represent the kingdom of God, a son's loyalty to his father is tested by his readiness to work there (Matt 21:28–32), while in another parable (Mark 12:1–9), the owner's workers beat and kill the servants he sends to bring back the fruits of the grape harvest, eventually murdering even the owner's son in hopes of gaining his inheritance. While Jacob continues to be manipulated for the sake of his new wealth, he is now complicit in the situation, acquiescing in the destruction of childhood promise for material gain.

> I had not expected to see my father's vineyard burned. The whole way down to the river it was burned. Blackened spines of vines spread out on either side. Wooden pegs marked the sites for shops and houses. (47)

Like Eden, biblical vineyards are associated with judgment as well as abundance.

> And another angel came out from the altar, who had power over fire; and cried with a loud cry to him that had the sharp sickle, saying, Thrust in thy sharp sickle, and gather the clusters of the vine of the earth; for her grapes are fully ripe. And the angel thrust in his sickle into the earth, and gathered the vine of the earth, and cast it into the great winepress of the wrath of God. (Rev 14:18–19 KJV)

Surveying the burnt vineyard, Jacob notes that a pair of scales still hang in the old fig tree—corresponding to the Heimbach's mulberry tree—where

Jacob and his father used to weigh melons and grapes for sale. Everyone is eventually weighed in the balance and life's sweetness must be paid for.

Despite a sense of loss, Jacob, cosseted by the aunts with little treats of milk-sugar biscuits and sweet wine, chooses to remain in his comfortable new home, his land of milk and honey—the enclosed re-creation of European culture—even though he finds it all rather bland and stifling. Under Leopold's tutelage, he becomes a concert cellist performing frequently with the local orchestra and gradually finds himself drawn to Leopold's daughter Louise with whom, as his narration somewhat disingenuously implies, he is manipulated into betrothal and marriage, so his inherited wealth remains in the family. Sexual love is another variant of the paradise motif, and initially, for Jacob, desire focuses on Louise's room, a secluded flowery space—"A garden enclosed is my sister my spouse"—which can be reached only by traversing "the dark gulf which was Tante Rosa's room" (123) followed by Tante Heloise's room.

> Penetrating the two guarding rooms I felt excited. I looked with delight at her little room. It was small and framed in flowers for there were two little windows overhung with wisteria. Immediately outside were two trees grown together, the sweet scented chinese privet and a cape lilac. These were the enchantment pressing into the small maidenly room. (54)

But during his courtship and marriage to Louise, Jacob embarks on a love affair with Madge, who plays first violin in the local orchestra. Both women represent contrasting possibilities. Madge, married and considerably older than Jacob, is very Australian. Although something of a philistine—Jacob notes a lack of books and music in the intervals of their love-making—Madge shrewdly points out that, if local musical standards are provincial, Leopold's are equally so. Vulgar, slangy, and knowledgeable about sex, she is also warm-hearted and generous, associated with abundance and fulfilment. Louise, innocent and sexually inexperienced, embodies the refinement and enclosure of the little world her father and aunts have constructed, while Madge is linked to the spaciousness and promise of the Australian landscape. For Jacob, her body resembles the promised land: "It was like seeing the hint of the colour of petals in an unopened bud. There was always the promise of something more" (2).

Houses, frequently identified with the ideal of home and one of the principal marks made by colonists arriving in a new land, also serve as metaphors for attempts to construct a private world of personal harmony and delight: "our house is our corner of the world.... it is our first universe, a real cosmos in every sense of the word" (Bachelard: 4). Like Eden, however, they too are ambivalent places, providing a haven on the one hand, "a refuge from the impersonal open space of the landscape, or the disorienting space of the city" (Ferrier: 40), but, on the other, forming a possible prison from which occupants may long to escape. They can also be expressions of personal and national identity. Often, when establishing oneself in a new colony or migrating to a new country, "the act of building signifies the assertion of culture" (Ferrier: 42). In childhood, Jacob perceives the Heimbach house as romantic, if rather sinister, resembling a slightly decayed Austrian schloss. It is an attempt to re-create in some measure the family's beautiful old house, their home in Vienna, but "an entire past comes to dwell in a new house" (Bachelard: 5). Home, apparently so familiar and comfortable, is readily disrupted by the uncanny and unfamiliar, sometimes resembling a labyrinth with a monster at its heart (Salzman: 38). The Heimbachs' Australian house, its rooms mysteriously opening out of one another and its doorways heavily curtained as if to impede easy entrance or exit, is a nest of secrets concealing unmentionable episodes in the family's past, which a mildly tipsy Tante Heloise reveals one evening to the adult Jacob. Leopold's Jewish wife, whose frail mind gave way under the pressures of migration (her race the reason for their exodus), has been committed, at Tante Rosa's insistence, to the local mental hospital.

Waldemar's presence in the attic constitutes a still more explosive secret of which the growing Jacob receives hints and intimations he chooses to ignore. Although he realises that questioning the family might set him free, he remains silent even after Tante Heloise openly reveals the truth. A house may be "one of the greatest powers of integration for the thoughts, memories and dreams of mankind" (Bachelard: 6), but Jacob chooses to integrate with the contorted, labyrinthine house, which had originally seemed so foreign to him. When he looks for a house to rent as a love-nest for Madge and himself, the one he settles on is mysterious, romantic, sumptuously appointed, and very private, a suitable repository for family secrets. Standing well back from the road, thickly shrouded in dark trees, "it is protected by a battlement of balconies and verandahs" and surrounded by a high brick wall with wrought iron gates locked from the inside (Jolley, 1984:103). Jacob devises a fantastical plan of transporting the entire Heimbach family there to live on the first floor, with the top floor reserved for Waldemar and the ground floor for himself and Madge. His complicity in the family's deception is now so great he seeks to contrive ways they can transfer Waldemar without his official knowledge. For Jacob, the new house is merely an extension of the one he has lived in for so many years, with a special area to incorporate his own secret along with the rest. Madge, once associated with expansiveness and promise, is now to be secluded in a confined and secret place.

Jacob wants to maintain his comfortable existence by containing people important to his life within separate layers of the same structure, but inevitably his two worlds collide catastrophically. After Leopold's death from heart disease, he takes Tante Rosa to see the newly rented house while Madge unexpectedly visits the Heimbachs. On his return, Jacob discovers her body in the garden, brutally murdered, presumably by Waldemar who, having grown into a strong, enormous man since his incarceration in the attic, is given to violent outbursts. In a like spirit of mindless savagery, Jacob rushes indoors, demanding to know how Madge died, and in the face of the aunts' real or apparent incomprehension, hurls the kerosene heater across the room, enveloping Tante Rosa in Flames. The initial deception of the young Jacob into believing he had committed murder reaches its terrible conclusion with the fire that destroys everything the family sought to preserve. Jacob is now a murderer in earnest, for Tante Rosa dies horribly of her burns. Waldemar is removed to a mental hospital. Tante Heloise's mind gives way under the strain, and she spends her remaining years senile in a geriatric ward.

The consequences for Jacob and Louise are equally devastating, since Jacob's money, kept by the aunts wrapped in parcels, is destroyed along with other family treasures. Once he agreed to burning his childhood home and vineyard so he could invest the resulting wealth in the Heimbach household and the values it embodies, only to burn that down as well. Because his attempts to extinguish the fire leave Jacob with a crippled claw for a hand, he must now exist without either love or music since he has lost his touch for both. Louise, stripped of her family's support, lives the rest of her life in a loveless, poverty-stricken marriage exiled to the wilderness in a "cold little house" bordering an industrial wasteland with her young daughter Elise who, like Waldemar, is severely retarded. Her factory work maintains the family, since Jacob's efforts as a door-to-door salesman are largely ineffectual. Now a permanent outsider with other people's doors continually shut in his face, the case of products he always carries, like the luggage so many migrants keep ready packed, symbolises his state of exile. Louise's eventual death, from overwork and despair, precipitates the final crisis in Jacob's life.

In Genesis, the story of Cain murdering his brother Abel follows immediately on the account of their parents' expulsion from Eden and also prefigures the later rivalry between Isaac's twin sons Jacob and Esau, when one brother cheats another of his birthright, each going on to found rival nations, Israel and Edom (Gen 27:1–14). Regina Schwartz claims these ancestral myths of kinship demonstrate a tragic requirement of collective identity, "that other peoples must be identified as objects to be abhorred" (80).

> According to the biblical myth, the origins of hatred and violence among brothers is scarcity. If there is not enough to go round, then Jacob must literally impersonate Esau to get what is his, and Cain must destroy his rival to seek the favour that was Abel's. Scarcity, the assumption that someone can only prosper when someone else does not, proliferates murderous brothers and murderous peoples. (Schwartz: 83)

To preserve their family and cultural identity, the Heimbachs cast Jacob in the role of Cain to substitute him for Waldemar, whom they cannot bear to expel from the household, although publicly they deny his continuing existence. Jacob, through his gradual awareness and acquiescence, appropriates Waldemar's birthright. Jolley draws several analogies between her character and his biblical namesake. Each is manoeuvred into marrying one woman while in love with another (Gen 29:15–28). The biblical Jacob wrestles all night with an angel who touches his thigh: "and the hollow of Jacob's thigh was out of joint, as he wrestled with him" (Gen 32:25 KJV). After Louise's death in *Milk and Honey*, Jacob, unable to face returning home, books into a motel. Baffled by complicated and unfamiliar taps in the shower, he slips and falls badly scalded, injuring his groin. After a night of hallucinatory pain, he begins to confront his past actions, deciding he must now seek out Waldemar.

Imprisoned in the Heimbachs' attic, Waldemar represents the wildness, barbarism, and coarseness his family cannot incorporate psychologically into their refined, cultivated vision of the world. Repressing such characteristics intensifies their power, so their eventual eruption becomes highly dangerous. Waldemar functions as Jacob's double, a projection of his destructive impulses. Both are the same age and have been raised in European families. Jacob hungers after the sweetness of existence, and Waldemar is greedy for sweet food. Both are imprisoned, Waldemar in "this terrible room" (49) and Jacob in a snare of emotional blackmail. In manhood, Waldemar's corpulence reflects Jacob's moral grossness, and his violent behaviour corresponds to the increasing destructiveness of Jacob's nature. Jacob implies his marriage is unconsummated, suggesting Elise is Waldemar's child, but this may be wishful thinking, and his frenzied vision, shortly before setting fire to the house, of brother and sister copulating in the attic, may well be a nightmare perception of his own relationship with Louise.

To meet Waldemar again, Jacob revisits the mental hospital where he and Leopold once taught some of the patients singing. At first he fails to find him and returns to the car where he discovers Elise distributing his entire salesman's stock to a group of patients, Waldemar among them. Divested at last of the baggage he has been carrying around, Jacob feels a sudden release, freed into a new way of life and receiving the possibility of a new start as Waldemar asks once more "Which hend you hev?" In a gesture of love and reconciliation, Jacob takes Elise's hand and places it in Waldemar's, himself taking Waldemar's other hand. Once again an Old Testament story is re-enacted, where Jacob meets the brother he has wronged offering him munificent gifts and presenting him to his wives and children: "And Esau ran to meet him, and embraced him, and fell on his neck and kissed him: and they wept" (Gen 33:4 KJV). Waldemar out in the open, his violence controlled by medication, is very different from the prisoner in the attic who haunted Jacob's imagination. In taking Waldemar's hand, Jacob acknowledges and accepts the animal impulses in his own nature, with all their destructive possibilities, so rendering them harmless.

The hospital gathers up many of the novel's principal motifs—paradise, wilderness, home, exile, and the promised land. Visiting in the past involved crossing a stretch of waste ground—a place resembling the burnt vineyard—where there was a tip ringed with smouldering fires and a tractor ploughed "bottles and tins, old clothes and unwanted furniture into the sour ground" (132). But, driving to the hospital with Elise, Jacob finds the wasteland transformed into a park and realises burnt flesh can heal.

> Perhaps the rubbish in a person's life could be pushed somewhere beneath a smooth skin. Perhaps a shining and elastic skin could grow and, in place of a decrepit human being, there could be something radiant and glowing. (175)

Like the Heimbach house and the one Jacob rents for himself and Madge, the hospital "is ringed with trees," many characteristically found in Australia: "Norfolk Island pines, kurrajong trees, jacarandas and flame trees" (182). Initially, on his visits with Leopold, Jacob finds the hospital alienating and disturbing. But he is impressed by the building itself with its cool hall and marble mosaic floor inlaid with green and blue flowers, though questioning the appropriateness of its handsome staircase, to which Leopold responds, "it is right that there is something extravagant and beautiful for the people in here" (177). Ultimately, however, the hospital becomes home for Jacob, Waldemar, and Elise, all of whom find occupation there, Jacob as a cleaner, Waldemar as the shave orderly, and Elise carrying patients their meals. The once dreaded place is now an image of the kingdom of heaven as the staircase and white-robed nuns evoke the biblical Jacob's vision when he dreamt of a ladder reaching from earth to heaven, with "the angels of God ascending and descending on it" (Gen 28:12).

For Jolley, paradise and its negation are regions people create in their minds and imagination. Along with the verse from Exodus, she includes as an epigram Blake's poem:

> Love seeketh not itself to please,
> Nor for itself hath any care,
> But for another gives its ease,
> And builds a Heaven in Hell's despair.
>
> Love seeketh only self to please
> To bind another to its delight,
> Joys in another's loss of ease,
> And builds a Hell in Heaven's despair.

Human inadequacy and imperfection, against which paradise appears a refuge, taint all attempts to envision or create it in actuality. Jacob eventually wins through to a measure of self-knowledge and understanding, perhaps the only paradise anyone can hope to attain. Paul Salzman claims that, in the hospital, Jacob and Waldemar reflect "the foreign that has been contained" (39). For Jolley, however, the hospital is an image of inclusion as opposed to all the images of exclusion earlier in the novel. The only haven which comes close to being satisfactory in the novel is one which incorporates otherness, all those traditionally marginalised by society—"foreigners," sinners, the intellectually handicapped, and the mentally ill. With all its limitations, the hospital is an image of plenitude as opposed to the state of scarcity Regina Schwartz refers to where "someone can only prosper when someone else does not." In *Milk and Honey*, the promised land represents a "new" country, Australia, where exiles seek a home but remain blind to the abundance and possibilities it offers. Milk and honey flow only for those who cease clinging to the past and forego the treasures they believe are rightly theirs.

WORKS CONSULTED

Bachelard, Gaston
    1969   *The Poetics of Space*. Trans. Maria Jolas. Boston: Beacon. (Orig. 1958)

Bird Rose, Deborah
    1996   "Rupture and the Ethics of Care in Colonized Space." Pp. 190–215 in *Prehistory to Politics*. Ed. Tim Bonyhady and Tom Griffiths. Melbourne: Melbourne University Press.

Curnow, Allen
    1982   *Selected Poems*. Auckland: Penguin Books N.Z.

Curthoys, Ann
    2000   "Mythologies." Pp. 11–41 in *The Australian Legend and Its Discontents*. Ed. Richard Nile. St. Lucia: University of Queensland Press.

Ferrier, Elizabeth
    1987   "From Pleasure Domes to Bark Huts: Architectural Metaphors in Recent Australian Fiction." *Australian Literary Studies* 13/1:40–53.

George, Rosemary Marangoly
    1996   *The Politics of Home: Postcolonial Relocations and Twentieth-Century Fiction*. Cambridge: Cambridge University Press.

Giammatti, A. Bartlett
    1966   *The Earthly Paradise and the Renaissance Epic*. Princeton: Princeton University Press.

Gibson, Ross
   1984   *The Diminishing Paradise: Changing Literary Perceptions of Australia.* Sydney: Angus & Robertson.

   1992   *South of the West: Postcolonialism and the Narrative Construction of Australia.* Bloomington and Indianapolis: Indiana University Press.

Hughes, Robert
   1968   *Heaven and Hell in Western Art.* London: Weidenfeld & Nicolson.

Jolley, Elizabeth
   1984   *Milk and Honey.* Fremantle: Fremantle Arts Centre Press

   1992   *Central Mischief.* Ringwood Victoria: Viking.

Lansbury, Coral
   1970   *Arcady in Australia: The Evocation of Australia in Nineteenth Century English Literature.* Melbourne: Melbourne University Press.

Moodie, Susanna
   1996   *Roughing It in the Bush.* London: Virago. (Orig. 1852)

Muir, Edwin
   1960   *Collected Poems.* London: Faber & Faber.

Prest, John
   1981   *The Garden of Eden: The Botanic Garden and the Re-Creation of Paradise.* New Haven and London: Yale University Press.

Salzman, Paul
   1993   *Helplessly Tangled in Female Arms and Legs: Elizabeth Jolley's Fictions.* St. Lucia: University of Queensland Press.

Schwartz, Regina
   1997   *The Curse of Cain. The Violent Legacy of Monotheism.* Chicago and London: University of Chicago Press.

Stephen, James
   1953   "Colonization As a Branch of Social Economy." Pp. 281–91 in *James Stephen and the British Colonial System 1814–1847.* Ed. Paul Knaplund. Madison: University of Wisconsin Press. (Orig. 1858)

 New and Recent Titles

Other Ways of Reading
African Women and the Bible
Musa W. Dube, editor

This volume of essays, the first of its kind, highlights some of the unique ways in which African women read and interpret the Bible in their diverse historical and cultural contexts. Featured methods include storytelling, postcolonial feminist reading, womanhood/ *bosadi* and womanist reading, divination, and reading from and with grassroots communities. Responses locate the collection along a spectrum of scholarship including that of Western feminists, African women theologians, and African male theologians. This book, originating from the Circle of Concerned African Women Theologians, is a significant contribution to global biblical scholarship and hermeneutical reflection.

Code: 060807   264 pages 2001
Paper: $24.95 ISBN: 1-58983-009-1

The Labour of Reading
Desire, Alienation, and Biblical Interpretation
Fiona C. Black, Roland Boer, and Erin Runions, editors

How might the task of reading the Bible be regarded as labor? What happens when biblical texts are read in ways that highlight the work of interpretation? *The Labour of Reading* provides a collection of new and distinct readings of biblical texts. Gathered to honor the scholarship and teaching of Robert Culley, these essays seek to carry on his legacy. Covering both the Hebrew and Greek Bibles, they range through cultural and literary studies, philosophy, sociology and feminism, among other disciplines. The unifying motif is the need to work hard at and labor with the text: the legacy of Robert Culley.

Code: 060636   336 pages 1999
Paper: $30.00 ISBN: 0-88414-011-3

Society of Biblical Literature • P.O. Box 2243 • Williston, VT 05495-2243
Phone: 877-725-3334 (toll-free) or 802-864-6185 • Fax: 802-864-7626
Online catalog: http://sbl-site.org/Publications/catalog
Shipping and handling extra

WHICH GOOD BOOK? MISSIONARY EDUCATION AND CONVERSION IN COLONIAL INDIA

Sanjay Seth
La Trobe University

ABSTRACT

The following essay in postcolonial criticism narrates the tale of how an attempt to accommodate to colonial "difference" led to a slippage of meaning, which in turn produced an outcome altogether different from that which had been intended. Though the history of Europe is frequently narrated as one in which science came into conflict with and triumphed over religion, in colonial India it was missionaries themselves who came to see Western science as an ally in their proselytising efforts. Given the "natives" stubborn attachment to his own religions, they concluded that here the prelude to conversion would have to be the introduction of Western science and learning, which would serve as a solvent of Hindu and Islamic belief, thus paving the way for the introduction of the true Word of God. This view yielded a corresponding strategy, namely, the extensive involvement of Christian missionaries in education. However, missionary efforts to educate the native led, not to a weakening of old values and their replacement by new ones, but (in the view of some) to a nihilism so alarming that it led many colonial officials to advocate as a solution the introduction of instruction in the religions of India into the very schools and colleges that, it was once hoped, would be the solvents of such false religions.

Colonialism was always more than the ruthless exploitation of natural resources, labour, and captive markets, though it was always that. It was also a process of "export" (of peoples, of social processes, and of technologies, even of viruses and diseases) and exchange, albeit highly unequal exchange undertaken in coercive circumstances. In this process, that which was exchanged assumed new forms and meanings in changed circumstances. It has often been observed that economic and social forms that were part of the history of Europe, when introduced to the colonies, often had entirely different and unexpected consequences; for instance, the long debate within the colonial administration in Bengal on the system of land ownership and revenue collection to be instituted in Bengal did not result in measures that facilitated the emergence of a class of improving landlords and a yeoman peasantry, as desired, but rather produced a *rentier* feudal landlord class and rack-rented peasantry. The significance of widely cited examples such as this, however, is sometimes misunderstood. It was not that in the colonies things had unexpected consequences simply because the different (colonial) "conditions" meant certain processes were bound to have different effects, in the same way that light travels at different velocities in different media. In this example, it is not just that the permanent settlement in Bengal had the results it did because systems of land tenure were very different in India, thus frustrating and falsifying the intentions of the authors of the permanent settlement. Such an understanding of history treats "event" and "process" as lying outside of "meaning" and "language." In fact, the enactment of changes in land ownership, the introduction of technology, the despotic nature of colonial rule—these were never simply events or processes that existed independent of the significations and meanings they carried and that were ascribed to them. For the transfer of institutions, structures, and processes, and the enactment of intentions and desires in the colonies, required that they be cast in the "idiom" (in the linguistic as well as extralinguistic sense) of the colonial theatre. This always created the possibility of a slippage of meaning, of a sign coming to signify something other than, or in excess of, its intended meaning; and such misreadings were characteristic, even constitutive, of the colonial encounter. The colonial theatre was not where the intentions of the colonized were calmly enacted (civilization exported, capitalism transplanted), nor where the "cunning of history" did its work, with the dialectic producing outcomes opposite to those intended by the rulers. Rather, it was the site where dissemination and displacement occurred, where processes and tales of Western provenance were enacted with a slippage.

An essay in postcolonial criticism, this essay examines one such displacement. One of the artefacts that Europe sought to export to the colonies was Christianity. Here there was no question but that what was being introduced was a matter of meanings, ideas, and belief. As this essay seeks to document, the agencies responsible decided that in India the revelation of God's word would follow a distinct trajectory; for it to be heard and embraced the recipients of it had first to be remade so that they were in a position to appreciate it. Education was to be the means of this. Such education was not, however, to be entirely or even principally religious. In the "special conditions" of India, secular learning, the relation of which to religion was a matter of debate in Europe, was unambiguously seen as an ally of Christianity, indeed, as an essential preparatory phase for the reception of Christianity. In India science and enlightenment came to be seen as the handmaidens of true religion. But India proved to be even more "different" than missionaries had allowed for; Western education paved the way, not for conversion to Christianity, but rather—or so at least missionaries and many others came to believe—to scepticism and impiety. The hoped-for outcome was deflected because the meaning and significance of Western learning was absorbed in an unauthorized, "mistaken" way. Western education, the answer to the riddle of how to spread the message of Christianity in India, came to seen as part of a new problem, that of educated Indians losing their moral bearings, to which problem instruction in their own religions was, ironically, advocated as a solution.

Christian Leavening

Apart from a few Christian communities in south India, left behind from contacts with Christianity in earlier centuries, the progress of Christianity in India was intimately tied up with the activities of its British rulers. British rule facilitated Christian and missionary activity indirectly in a host of ways, and directly through the sometimes sympathetic intervention of colonial officials. Yet it was one of the peculiarities of the Raj that in its official capacity the British Indian government resolutely refused to champion Christianity. From the mid-eighteenth century, when the East India Company went from being a trading monopoly to also becoming ruler over a large and growing territory, it pronounced a policy of religious neutrality and social noninterference—it sought the obedience of its subjects, but not any transformation in their beliefs or practices. Even if on occasion the colonial authorities—usually with great reluctance—could be prevailed upon to outlaw certain practices, such as *sati* or widow-burning, they repeatedly professed their religious neutrality. After the Mutiny, when the British Parliament took over direct administration of India, the Queen's proclamation assured her subjects that their faiths would continue to be respected. As long as her subjects paid and obeyed, those subjects could profess whatever they chose; even the civil law under which they were administered was for a long time Hindu and Muslim law, as interpreted by British-established courts.

Indeed, until 1813 missionaries could only operate on Company-controlled territory with Company permission, and subject to many constraints. One of the earliest missionary bodies, the Baptist Missionary Society, active in India since 1793, chose to found its chief mission at Serampur, then under the control of the more welcoming Danish authorities, rather than in British India. It is true that the powers Company officials had to limit and if need be prohibit missionary activity were not always vigorously exercised; in fact, many a devout colonial official assisted those propagating the faith. But at other times the prohibitions were strictly enforced, as for instance after the mutiny of native troops stationed in the southern Indian city of Vellore in 1806, a mutiny widely attributed to a reaction against overzealous and insensitive missionary activity.

The charter of the East India Company was renewed—and revised—by Parliament at twenty-year intervals. In 1793 efforts by the Clapham sect evangelists to insert a "pious clause" requiring Company support for missionary activity was rebuffed, but the renewal of the charter in 1813 was accompanied by missionary bodies being given a free hand to carry out their activities, as well as the establishment of a bishopric and of archdeacons for the three presidency towns of Calcutta, Madras, and Bombay. The revised charter also committed the Company to accept some responsibility for the education of its Indian subjects, even if initially only to the tune of a miserly one lakh (sc. 100,000) of rupees a year. Both measures in their different ways marked the advance of the idea that British rule was to be justified not just for its economic benefits to Britain, nor even for the peace and law and order allegedly provided to Indians, but that the ultimate and "providential" reason why Britain had been granted India was to ensure the "moral and material progress" of India, soon to be charted in annual "Moral and Material Progress" reports.

The changes wrought in 1813 marked increased tolerance and even a limited measure of support for missionary activity, but not, the government avowed, a retreat from its policy of religious neutrality. Government now allowed missonaries to operate freely, but government itself remained neutral. For instance, the schools it established after the revision of its charter did not permit religious instruction, and it continued to resist all efforts to make state-supported education a vehicle for the propagation of Christianity, as when the Court of Directors in London disallowed a proposal from Madras to permit the use of the Bible in class in government schools, declaring, "We cannot consider it either expedient or prudent to introduce any branch of study which can in any way interfere with the religious feelings and opinion of the people."[1]

In missionary ranks the idea that education would be a powerful and even predominant aspect of the mission to win over souls was taking firm root. By the early decades of the nineteenth century conversions had been few, and those overwhelmingly among low castes, outcastes, and tribal groups; the "heartlands" of Hinduism remained not simply unconquered, but almost untouched. Caste in particular seemed to be an insuperable barrier to conversion, for conversion meant placing oneself outside of caste and thus severing most social ties and forms of social intercourse. Time and again missionaries complained that the institution of caste, and a stubborn attachment to their own "superstitions," made the work of winning over natives all but impossible. Thus, the Abbé Dubois, who had spent a lifetime in India, went so far as to

---

[1] *Selections from the Records of the Madras Government,* no. 2 ("Papers relating to Public Instruction") Madras 1855, Appendix VV.

declare that if the Hindus went to Europe to win converts to Siva and Visnu they were more likely of success than missionaries in India (73). Even those who had not, like the Abbé, despaired of success, found that street preaching, "exposing" the fallacies of Hinduism and Islam, and engaging in controversies with votaries of these religions—among the standard forms of proselytising activity[2]—succeeded in drawing audiences, but they were largely ineffective in securing converts. The Herculean efforts of the Serampur missionaries in translating the Bible into Indian languages—it was fully translated into six (including Sanskrit), and partly translated into another twenty-nine—was widely admired in England and seen as proof of the advance of the Christian cause. However, in India the quality of the translations was much criticized (Bryce, 1839:100–103), and more importantly, scepticism was widely voiced over the efficacy of such means in spreading the Word. The Abbé Dubois, for instance, prophesied that "these *soi disant* translations will soon find their way to bazaar streets, to be sold there, as waste paper, to the country grocers, for the purpose of wrapping their drugs in them" (112).

It was because a measure of disenchantment with prevailing methods had manifested itself that the idea of education as a means to conversion came to be accorded greater importance. This did not derive from the commonplace idea of "getting them young," for most champions of Christian education agreed that its potential did not principally lie in the prospect of numerous individual students converting. Rather, the importance accorded to education derived from the conviction that because Hindu society was particularly resistant to conversion, in India the saving of souls might have to proceed along a more time-consuming, and circuitous, path. The first bishop of India, T. F. Middleton, wrote in 1818, "The minds of the people are not generally in a state to be impressed by the force of argument, still less to be awakened to reflection by appeals to their feelings and to their fears.... [W]hat is further required seems to be a preparation of the native mind to comprehend the importance and truth of the doctrines proposed to them; and this must be the effect of education " (qtd. in Neill: 206). In a somewhat similar vein Bishop Cotton pronounced in 1860: "The general clearing away of ignorance, folly and superstition effected by education are as likely to pave the way for Christ's spirit as the plan of hurrying from village to village, preaching for a day or two, and not reappearing" (qtd. in Metcalf: 131).

---

[2] For a discussion of the experiences of street preaching of the Serampur missionaries based on their diaries, see Mani (ch. 3). For the Hindu responses in some of these early controversies, see Young. In a letter (30 July 1833), Duff said of the crowds which gathered to hear street preachers, "Those who attend are, for the most part, stragglers of the lowest orders of natives.... They come ... solely for the purpose of scoffing and blaspheming" (Church of Scotland Foreign Mission Papers, Ms. 7530, National Library of Scotland).

The Reverend Miller, Principal of Madras Christian College, itself an outcome of this emphasis on education, went even further and told the Allahabad Missionary Conference of 1872 that conversions were not the measure of the success of Christian education, nor even what it principally aimed at: such education sought instead "a change of thought and feeling, a modification of character and formation of principles tending in a Christian direction ... to leaven the whole lump of Hinduism," aiming "not directly to save souls, but to make the work of saving them more speedy and more certain than it would be without it" (qtd. in Mathew: 56).

Most missionaries involved in the provision of education *did* hope to effect individual conversions; but, like Miller, they saw the chief value of education as lying in the fact that it served as a "leaven," acting upon Hindu society so as to gradually, in a molecular fashion as it were, transform it and *"prepare* the people at large, for the general ultimate reception of Christianity" (Duff, 1839:351) There was opposition as well—mission societies back home were wont to wonder why their emissaries were expending so much energy and resources on teaching rather than preaching—but from roughly the 1830s on many of the missions in India came to see the provision of education as one their chief tasks, especially in urban areas. The notion had taken hold that educating the young was necessary to prepare the minds of Hindus for later receptiveness to the Word of God—that education was, in a phrase often used at the time, a *"praeparatio evangelica."*

Science As Solvent

The Scottish Church was especially active in educational work, and none more so than its first Indian missionary, Alexander Duff. Duff's General Assembly Institution opened in Calcutta in 1830, aiming to provide the boys of native gentlemen with religious instruction as well as with a grounding, through the medium of the English language, in Western arts and sciences. Duff was emphatic that education had to be at advanced rather than elementary levels, and in English rather than the vernaculars, if it was to have the desired transformative effect; and it had to be directed at the upper classes of native society if its impact were to flow through Hindu society as a whole, rather than be confined to its immediate recipients. His school began with much fanfare, with more applicants for admission than it could accommodate, and in subsequent years, as it expanded, it never experienced difficulty in filling new vacancies.

A demand for English education was developing among metropolitan elites in this period, a demand that grew at a rapid rate after 1835 when the British Indian government decided to patronize English over Oriental education and also began to make government employment increasingly dependent upon possession of educational qualifications. In

1854 the government announced that it would make government funds available to private (including missionary) schools and colleges, and thereafter there was a rapid growth in the numbers of schools and colleges offering Western education. The prestige attached to the conqueror's language, the access it gave one to the emerging colonial public sphere of courts, local and provincial councils, and the like, and, not least, the fact that it aided in what was many an urban middle-class colonial subject's highest aspiration—a goverment job—all combined to make English education a highly sought after commodity.

Mission schools and colleges provided this commodity, and some of them were thought to provide it exceedingly well. Such institutions were sought out by parents despite, rather than because of, the religious instruction they provided. Of course, missionaries were well aware of this, as the Scottish Church's James Bryce acknowledged of Duff's school:

> The native youths do not come to it to obtain religious or Christian instruction, nor is that the object for which their parents send them there. What they are seeking is that education which is best to qualify them for earning a future livelihood; and they only do not refuse to take at the same time the instruction which you offer them, or rather, which you make an express condition of their receiving, in order to get the secular education which they want. (Bryce, 1856:23–24).

Thus there followed a cat-and-mouse game in which the missionary institution offered the bait of an English education, while the student and his parents sought to take the bait without swallowing the hook. Lal Behari Day, a Brahmin who had attended Duff's school, reported that his father answered friends who urged him against sending his son to a missionary school by saying that "he did not intend to make of me a learned man, but to give me so much knowledge of English as would enable me to obtain a decent situation; and that long before I was able to understand lectures on the Christian religion, he would withdraw me from the Institution, and put me into an Office" (Day: 474). Occasionally conversions did occur—Lal Behari Day was one such—but when "a conversion does occur," as a colonial official observed in 1859, "it is well known that the school is at once emptied, and only by slow and painful degrees that it attains anything like its former condition."[3] More often, parents succeeded in getting their sons an education without the disaster of conversion befalling them.

The secular education provided by mission schools and colleges was not included in the curriculum simply as a carrot dangled in front of Indian

---

[3] *Correspondence Relating to the System of Education in the Bombay Presidency:* 65.

parents. It was seen as having a critical role to play in preparing the minds of India's elites for the ultimate reception of Christianity. Alexander Duff provides an enthusiastic and revealing description in his mammoth *India and India Missions* of how he came to the important discovery that the "truths of modern literature and science" could function as "the handmaid of true religion." He recounts how soon after the opening of his school he was conducting a junior class in which he asked, "What is rain?" A student replied that it came from the trunk of the elephant of the god Indra. Pressed for his source, he replied that he learnt this from his guru, whose authority in turn was a *Shastra,* a Hindu text. Instead of directly contradicting the student, Duff describes how he led his students through the everyday example of rice boiling in a pot: the rising of steam, condensation, the re-formation of water—at each point explaining the process and gaining the assent of students for the explanation. Assent is spontaneously given—heat causes the evaporation of water in the form of steam, and so on—until suddenly one boy, "as if ... finding that he had ... gone too far" manifests alarm and exclaims, "Ah! What have I been thinking? *If your account be the true one, what becomes of our Shastra?"* (560). The explanation, Duff writes, introduced the first doubt, the first suspicion, regarding the truth of the Hindu faith, and thus was the first step in "a mental struggle, which, though painfully protracted ... only terminated in the case of some, with the entire overthrow of Hinduism" (560). If this encounter with Western scientific knowledge was a revelation for his student, the incident was also, Duff declares, something of a revelation for himself. Literature and science were taught at his school because they were adjudged as "indispensable to an enlarged and liberal education." But this incident revealed to Duff a further, and more compelling, reason: "It now seemed as if geography, general history, and natural philosophy,—from their direct effect in destroying Hinduism,—had been divested of their secularity, and stamped with an impress of sacredness. In this view of the case, the teaching of these branches seemed no longer an indirect, secondary, ambiguous part of missionary labour,—but, in a sense, as direct, primary, and indubitable as the teaching of religion itself" (563).

This was close to the view of senior English officials like Macaulay and Trevelyan, who had been responsible for the introduction of Western education in India and had thought that it would ultimately pave the way for the triumph of Christianity. Western science—and English literature, as Gauri Viswanathan notes and argues in an important study—would, it was thought, be corrosive of Hinduism and thus would serve to disseminate and secure not only the colonial power's hegemony and legitimacy but also its religion. Here too it was recognized that India was different from Europe, and thus by undermining faith in Hinduism Western education might initially lead to scepticism, or the embrace of deism or various forms of "reformed" or

Protestantized Hinduism, rather than a direct embrace of Christianity. Some thirty years after Macaulay penned his famous Minute, his nephew and biographer, Sir George Otto Trevelyan, judged that while very few educated Hindus had become Christians, his uncle's expectations had not been falsified, for "an educated Hindoo almost inevitably becomes a Deist" (202), and once sufficient numbers of Hindus had forsaken "Brahminism" for deism, "we may trust that the majority of cultivated Hindoos will not be averse to accept the creed of their rulers" (204).

There was, however, an important difference between this and the position of Duff and most other missionaries, for to accept the legitimacy of the secular education provided in government schools was to accept a very secondary role for missions and missionaries, and moreover was directly counter to debates that were to rage in Britain over denominational education. Most missionaries were critics of what they described as the "godless" education provided in government schools, and they campaigned to overturn the exclusion of religious instruction from such schools. In a related manner, they insisted that even if it were the case that Western education led to some form of deism or to scepticism, the decoupling of loss of faith from discovery of another, or of "destruction" from "construction," was a danger rather than something to be welcomed. As Duff told a House of Lords Committee in 1853, "it is certainly not good simply to destroy," and thus his institution aimed "to combine as it were together, in close, inseparable and harmonious union, what has been called a useful secular, with a decidedly religious education" (Mahmood: 72). Western science and literature were negative and preparatory, for they destroyed Hinduism and paved the way for the true faith. Christian teaching was positive; it replaced what had been destroyed. Secular knowledge on its own could be harmful; religious preaching to those unprepared for the gospel could never be harmful, but it could prove inefficacious. They were joined together in a properly Christian education, where each could do its work simultaneously with the other and act upon the youth of the educated and influential classes, whose example and influence might then act as a "leaven" upon Indian society.

Duff and others found confirmation in this view of things in the controversy surrounding Hindu College. The college was established in 1817 by some of the leading upper-caste Brahmins in Calcutta as a nondenominational centre for the teaching of the new, European knowledge. It was to become the home of a rationalist and sceptical "movement" led by a young and charismatic teacher, Derozio. Although it never had more than a handful of students, "Young Bengal" scandalized Calcutta society by its mocking of established convention (including through the eating of beef and consumption of alcohol) and religious beliefs, and its espousal of agnostic and atheistic doctrines. The commotion caused in respectable Calcutta society and the resultant dismissal of Derozio from the college staff led to endless speculation and denunciation of the immoral and "sceptical" effects of Western education or, at least, of secular education. Missionaries were often to use the example of Hindu College as an example of the "dangers" of secular education, and Duff very often presented his Institution as an alternative model to that provided by Hindu College, and even as a measure to "reclaim these wanderers, whose education and worldly cirumstances invest them with such mighty influence among their fellow-country-men."[4] But while Hindu College provided missionaries with a useful example of the dangers of secular education, and an opportunity to extol the virtues of their own schools and colleges, nonetheless there was still a very real sense in which government secular education was seen as an ally in their struggle (Viswanathan: 62), even if one much inferior to the desired alternative of Bible-teaching government schools. Reverend Summers told an international conference of Protestant missions in London that "90 per cent of the Hindu youth trained in Government colleges have ceased to believe in Hinduism and have become sceptics.... God be praised for such a beneficient result and [may] he lead them on through scepticism to a reasonable faith in Christ" (qtd. in Mathew: 68). James Bryce wrote indulgently, "'Young Bengal' ... are indulging the very silly, but not perhaps unnatural pride, that their 'little learning' is carrying them beyond ... priestcraft, as they designate all religious belief whatever. Teach them to drink a little deeper of the stream, and they may bend submissive to the apostles of the Cross" (1856:9). And even Duff approvingly quoted the editor of the *Inquirer* newspaper, a former student at Hindu College and a convert to Christianity, to the effect that "the Hindu college ... has ... destroyed many a native's belief in Hinduism.... No missionary ever taught us to forsake the religion of our fathers; it was Government that did us this service" (1850:88).

A Stalled Transition

The relative confidence of this earlier period—that Western education would eventually lead to more and more of the educated classes being weaned from their own religion and, perhaps via detours through reformed Hinduism such as the Arya Samaj or the Hindu-Christian eclecticism of the Brahmo Samaj, would be won over to Christianity—began to give way to concern in the latter part of the nineteenth century. The concern was fueled by a number of developments. One was simply that the hoped-for transition

---

[4] Letter 15 October 1830, Church of Scotland Foreign Mission Papers, Ms. 7530, National Library of Scotland.

to Christianity did not seem to be in the offing. Most of those who became dissatisfied with existing forms of Hinduism and joined reformed versions such as the Arya Samaj treated them not as staging posts in an onward journey, but as the terminus. Morever, from the latter half of the nineteenth century the Arya Samaj became more aggressively anti-Christian and even began to make efforts to reconvert Hindus who had converted to Islam or Christianity (Jordens). More importantly, however, the fear of "scepticism," initially raised partly as a bogey against "godless education," became part of a more generalized and widespread concern, and complaint, about educated Indians—that they were undisciplined, had lost faith and all the restraints that went with it, and that they were morally "adrift," with no strong sense of right and wrong.

The nature of this complaint was so broad and amorphous, and the evidence for it so general and varied—indiscipline in the form of nationalist protest and criticism, a decay in manners, alleged impiety, growing disrespect for parents and other elders[5]—that it was voiced by a range of sources, not only by missionaries, but often by government and by many Indians. (Indeed, so varied and vague is the complaint that it is best treated as evidence for the existence of a generalized anxiety, rather than as evidence for the existence of the phenomena said to be causing anxiety.) With some important differences in inflection, the complaint and the explanation generally offered for it took the following form: through their contact with Western learning, educated Indians, it was argued, had lost faith in their religion and traditions and customs, without having found substitutes that were not so alien to their (not wholly abandoned) traditions that they could be grafted onto them. The transition from idolatry to Christianity had dangerously stalled, the effect and symptoms of which were impiety, unrest, moral decay, and so on.

While addressing a conference, Governor Sir George Clark of Bombay adverted to "certain evils" to which the introduction of Western education had given rise, among them that "The restraining forces of ancient India have lost some of their power; the restraining forces of the West are inoperative in India. There has thus been a certain moral loss without any corresponding gain."[6] Keshab Chunder Sen warned that "In times of transition ... we always find that men for a while become reckless. The old faith is gone, and no new

---

5 One gets a flavour of this from a letter (17 June 1908) of the Inspector General of Education in the princely state of Mysore: "Irreverence of all kinds and disrespect for authority have been on the increase. Modesty, self-restraint and good sense are largely at a discount, while presumption, vanity and unrestrained aggressiveness appear to be increasing" (Home Education, August 1910, 1–3[A], National Archives of India).

6 *Report of the Proceedings of a Conference on Moral, Civic and Sanitary Instruction*: 2.

faith is established in its place. Society is unhinged and unsettled" (Murdoch: 3). By 1913 a Government "Resolution on Educational Policy" noted that "the most thoughtful minds in India lament the tendency of the existing system of education to develop the intellect at the expense of the moral and religious faculties" and described this as "unquestionably the most important educational problem of the day" (*Indian Education Policy 1913:* par. 5).

The density of this discourse on moral decline, and the relation of this idea of a "stalled transition" to one of the justifying premises of British rule—namely, that this rule would facilitate a transition from decay to dynamism, from backwardness to civilization—warrants separate treatment elsewhere. What is significant here is that the symptoms of this failed transition were seen to manifest themselves especially acutely in the form of a moral crisis, a loss of *moral* moorings; and that from there it was an easy step to ascribe this to the absence of religious instruction which might accompany and temper the effects of the new education. Even the British Indian Government came to embrace this conclusion, at least in part. However, bound by its policy of religious neutrality in government schools, the "correctives" it proposed took the form of advocating the introduction of special "moral textbooks," exhortations to teachers to seek to exercise a moral influence over their charges, schemes for housing students in hostels where good influences could be brought to bear and discipline instilled, and so on.

For others, not so constrained, the remedy was obvious—that religious instruction be a prominent feature of all schools, including government schools. The establishment of Hindu and Muslim "denominational" schools of a modern type, and the drive to establish colleges and universities that would combine Western learning with Hindu and Muslim religious instruction, made such arguments with great effect. For instance, Madan Mohan Malaviya, Congress politician and member of the (ultimately successful) movement to found a Hindu University in Benares, would refer to government acknowledgements that "moral education" was the Achilles heel of the educational system and suggest that "this is one of the strongest arguments in favour of a denominational university.... it will be able to make up an acknowledged deficiency in the present system of education" (29). Arguments of this type had of course long been used by missionaries to urge the teaching of Christianity in government schools; but now they were not the sole preserve of missionaries, but were being used more assertively and effectively by those urging education in the religions of India.

Difference

The missionary emphasis on the necessity of Western education as a *praeparatio evangelica* grew out of a recognition that India was "different" and that the manner in which the word of god was disseminated would have to be adapted to the specificities and peculiarities of India. Another measure of India's difference was that here, far more than in its European birthplace, secular learning was seen to be an ally of evangelization. But these attempts at adaptation and translation themselves underwent an unintended slippage. As we have seen, the Western education that was thought to be an aid in the dissemination of Christianity came to be widely seen as a source of irreligion and immorality. Nor was this by any means the only slip between intention and outcome, the only instance where a reproduction presented a distorted image of the original. Science itself never fully worked in the way that Alexander Duff anticipated, that is, to dispel "superstition" and undermine Hinduism. Gyan Prakash has powerfully argued that to wrest from Indians an acknowledgment of its authority, science had to be cast or staged in terms that made it accessible to the native, had to "dwell in the religious dispositions and literary writings of the 'natives'." But if this established science's authority, it was a "paradoxical legitimation," for Western scientific knowledge was thereby opened up to an indigenization, documented by Prakash, which assimilated it by finding its antecedents in an earlier, Hindu science—a curious case of "the establishment of science's power in its estrangement" (64). The mode by which Indians acquired Western knowledge through modern schools and education itself militated against the "proper" acquisition and absorption of this knowledge—for over a hundred years, virtually from the beginnings of Western education in India to Independence in 1947 (and beyond), it was to be a persistent lament that Indian students missed the point of and defeated the intent of the new knowledge by "learning" it in the "old" manner, namely, by committing it to memory.

These examples bring us back to the point with which this essay began. Colonialism, precisely because it could only function by presenting metropolitan processes and structures in a "native" idiom, invited "mis"-understanding, appropriation, and hybridization.That Western education did not prove to be as potent in spreading Christianity as had been expected, but instead led—or so some believed—to many educated Indians being deprived of the certainties of an old world and its moral code and yet without any replacements, is but one of many instances of this. The irony to be savoured lies, then, not in the fact of falsified intentions, for examples of this abound, but in the fact that even some missionaries came to find themselves sympathetic to the teaching of Hinduism in schools and colleges. As early as 1879 a critic of the missionaries observed that "complaint is made that somehow or other this 'Young-India' has lost the moral control of the old religions, and has not adopted that of the new," and went on to note the curious fact that "Regret seems to be felt for the extinction of the Hindu religion"(Cust: 14). And in 1910 H. W. Orange, Director General of Education for the Government of India, observed that "it is curious to find that there is among Christian missionaries some movement towards religious instruction in the faiths of this country."[7] The feeling was shared in government circles, which early in the new century relaxed the prohibition against religious instruction, allowing (optional) religious instruction, out of school hours, in government schools in the United Provinces and Punjab—in full recognition of the fact that in most cases this instruction would be in Hinduism and Islam. This policy was extended to Burma in 1910, where the Burma correspondent of *The Times* welcomed the new policy enthusiastically on the grounds that "The sanctions provided by Hinduism and Buddhism, though, as we believe, greatly inferior to those provided by Christianity, are immeasurably better than none at all."[8] And thus Western education, the "solution" to a problem—how to disseminate Christianity in India—itself became the problem of impiety and moral decline, to which one widely advocated solution came to be that instruction in the religions of India be introduced into the very schools and colleges which, it was once hoped, would be the solvents of such false religions.

---

[7] Education Department 74–76A, Sept. 1911, National Archives of India.
[8] Education Department 74–76A, Sept. 1911, National Archives of India.

WORKS CONSULTED

Bhabha, Homi
    1994   *The Location of Culture*. London: Routledge.

Bryce, James
    1839   *A Sketch of Native Education in India*. London: W. H. Allen.
    1856   *The Schoolmaster and the Missionary in India*. Edinburgh: n.p.

Cockburn, William
    1805   *A Dissertation on the Best Means of Civilizing the Subjects of the British Empire in India*. Cambridge: Cambridge University Press.

Correspondence Relating to the System of Education in the Bombay Presidency
    1860   Bombay: Education Society's Press.

Cunningham, J. W.
    1808   *Christianity in India*. London: Hatchard.

Cust, Robert Nedham
    1879   *Remarks on the Relation of Government to Education in India*. Hartford: Stephen Austin & Sons.

Day, Lal Behari
    1969   *Bengal Peasant Life, Folk Tales of Bengal, Recollections of My School-Days.* Ed. Mahadevprasad Saha. Calcutta: Editions Indian.

Dubois, Abbé J. A.
    1977   *Letters on the State of Christianity in India.* Ed. Sharda Paul. New Delhi: Associated Publishing House. (Orig. 1815–1821)

Duff, Alexander
    1839   *India and India Missions.* Edinburgh: John Johnstone.
    1850   *Missionary Addresses.* Edinburgh: Johnstone & Hunter.

Indian Educational Policy 1913
    1914   Calcutta: Superintendent of Government Printing.

Jordens, J. T. F.
    1991   "Reconversion to Hinduism: The Shuddhi of the Arya Samaj." Pp. 215–30 in *Religion in South Asia.* 2d ed. Ed. Geoff A. Oddie. New Delhi: Manohar.

Kaye, John William
    1859   *Christianity in India: An Historical Narrative.* London: Smith, Elder & Co.

Kuriakose, M. K., ed.
    1982   *History of Christianity in India: Source Materials.* Madras: Christian Literature Society.

Mahmood, Syed
    1981   *A History of English Education in India.* Delhi: Idarah-I Adabiyati-I Delli. (Orig. 1895)

Malaviya, Madan Mohan
    1911   *The Hindu University of Benares: Why It Is Wanted and What It Aims At.* Allahabad: Metcalf, Thomas.

Mani, Lata
    1998   *Contentious Traditions: The Debate on Sati in Colonial India.* Berkeley and Los Angeles: University of California Press.

Mathew, A.
    1988   *Christian Missions, Education and Nationalism.* Delhi: Anamika Prakashan.

Metcalf, Thomas
    1964   *The Aftermath of Revolt: India 1857–1870.* Princeton: Princeton University Press.

Murdoch, John
    1904   *India's Greatest Educational Need: The Adequate Recognition of Ethics in Her Present Transition State.* London and Madras: n.p.

Neill, Stephen
    1985   *A History of Christianity in India, 1707–1858.* Cambridge: Cambridge University Press.

Oddie, Geoff A., ed.
1991   *Religion in South Asia*. 2d rev. ed. New Delhi: Manohar.

Prakash, Gyan
1999   *Another Reason: Science and the Imagination of Modern India*. Princeton: Princeton University Press.

Report of the Proceedings of a Conference on Moral, Civic and Sanitary Instruction
1910   Bombay: Bombay Guardian Mission Press.

Sherring, Rev. M. A.
1875   *The History of Protestant Missions in India*. London: Trubner.

Stanley, Brian
1992   *The History of the Baptist Missionary Society 1792–1992*. Edinburgh: T&T Clark.

Trevelyan, George Otto
1991   *The Competition Wallah*. New Delhi: Indus. (First published in book form in 1864.)

Viswanathan, Gauri
1998   *Masks of Conquest*. New Delhi: Oxford University Press.

Young, Richard Fox
1981   *Resistant Hinduism*. Vienna: Institut für Indologie der Universität Wien.

A Pisgah Sight of Ireland: Religious Embodiment and Colonialism in *Ulysses*

Amardeep Singh
Lehigh University

ABSTRACT

This paper explores Joyce's use of biblical allegory in a postcolonial vein. Through a dense array of biblical citations in *Ulysses*, Joyce uses the ancient image of Jews in Egypt as a figure for colonial Ireland. At the broadest level, these citations serve not to instantiate a coherent theology but rather to create a symbolic language that emphasizes liberation through the intensified embodiment of daily life over a rhetoric of abstract, idealized nationalism. Through a creative and generally irreverent synthesis of religious symbols of the body, Joyce's characters can "decolonize their minds"—which is to say, they can break the epistemic crisis produced by an imperialism that is at once religious (alternately Catholic and Anglican) and political. The passage that crystallizes this interpretation of the novel is the tale Stephen Dedalus tells at the end of the "Aeolus" episode, "A Pisgah Sight of Palestine or The Parable of the Plums." The "Parable," which refers to passages in Deuteronomy, Exodus, and Numbers, is a lewd and satirical critique of both Irish nationalism and the British colonial presence in Ireland in the early twentieth century. Ireland is Palestine, the promised land for the Jews (Irish), as viewed by two elderly Irish ladies from the top of Nelson's pillar in Dublin. They look first at the surrounding Palestine (Ireland), and then up at the towering symbol of the empire, and finally reject both. Against the abstract logic of nation and church, the ladies prefer a sensual, bodily experience—the eating of plums. Through its visceral relationship to the problematic religious identities of its two main characters, the Bible serves as more than merely one among thousands of literary source texts incorporated into *Ulysses*. Expanding outward from the passage above, I explore several other direct biblical figures that pass through the consciousness of both Stephen Dedalus and Leopold Bloom, and attempt to figure the broad symbolic patterns of Joyce's novel in terms of its simultaneous biblicality and anticolonialism. Stephen is a Catholic rebelling against the priesthood and the Church, drifting toward a version of faith that more closely resembles Protestantism. The key image that remains under contestation for him is that of the body, specifically the body of his mother. Bloom, on the other hand, is by birth a Jew whose father converted to Protestantism, and who spends much of his day contemplating Zionism (a paracolonial enterprise), Catholic ritual, and his own Irish nationality. In developing this argument, I respond both to classic critical interpretations of the role of religion in *Ulysses* and to recent, postcolonial readings of Joyce's text, by critics such as Declan Kiberd, Ira Nadel, and Enda Duffy.

> *My beloved subjects, a new era is about to dawn. I, Bloom, tell you verily it is even now at hand. Yea, on the word of a Bloom, ye shall ere long enter into the golden city which is to be, the new Bloomusalem in the Nova Hibernia of the future.*
>
> Ulysses 15.1541–44[1]

> *If we do manage to leave Mizraim once more, we will not forget the fleshpots.*
>
> Theodor Herzl: 186

INTRODUCTION: DIASPORA AND *ULYSSES*

"Diaspora" is a secular term with religious roots. In its contemporary usage it is one of the keywords of postcolonial criticism, a discipline of profoundly secularist orientation. Though the Greek word "diaspora" is translated into English as "dispersion," in much postcolonial writing (both literary and critical), it has a more precise meaning: diaspora is the decentering of a territorially bounded idea of national culture through wide-ranging transnational migration. Importantly, these patterns of transnational migration, which were a major consequence of the colonial project, have not in fact resulted in the utter dissolution of the relationship between culture and territorial belonging. If anything, dispersed peoples have often tended to create an intensified longing for, and a clarified image of, "home." Dispersion, though it is essentially the narrative of a loss of home, seems to be an especially powerful way of motivating a desire for a home that is territorially grounded, an idealized image of place.

In contrast, the historical concept of "diaspora" refers to the dispersion of the Jews across Europe, which began nearly two thousand years ago. Importantly, the word came to have this association through both Jewish and Christian religious texts: though the threat of dispersion is present in the Hebrew Bible (or Torah), "diaspora" only comes to refer to Jews through its appearance in the Christian New Testament.[2] In its modern usage, the

---

[1] All citations from Joyce's *Ulysses* are taken from the Gabler text. I also make extensive use of Don Gifford's *Annotated Ulysses*.

[2] More specifically, the Greek word "diaspora" appears in the New Testament three times, two of which refer exclusively to Jews. But the origin of the New Testament *concept* of dispersion

OED locates the entry of "diaspora" into the English language in the 1870s specifically with reference to Jewish dispersion.[3] While a thorough history of the Judeo-Christian concept of "diaspora" is beyond the scope of this essay, what is apparent from this limited account of the religious etymology of the word is that the Judaic significance of diaspora is quite different from its postcolonial counterpart. For European Jews before the advent of Zionism, dispersion was a scriptural narrative and a spiritual condition, not specifically oriented toward a concept of nationalism centered on the production of modern nation-states.

However, in the latter half of the nineteenth century, a relationship between the two concepts of diaspora begins to be evident in the link between the biblical narrative of the "promised land" and the Zionist plan to colonize Palestine. It is not, however, a link that is immediately evident in much Zionist writing, where religious Judaism is seen as a hindrance to the progressive Jewish cause. Leaders of the Zionist movement such as Theodor Herzl were highly assimilated Jews, generally less interested in religious observance than in achieving social parity *as Europeans* through self-government; the Israel they had in mind was to be a "secular" nation-state.[4] Herzl, for instance, hardly refers to Jewish scripture in his extremely influential manifesto of Zionism, *Der Judenstaat* (*The Jew's State*). Rather than faith, Herzl specifically emphasizes modern industry and commerce in his imagining of the colonization of Palestine, devoting large sections of his manifesto to outlining the process of Europeanizing the proposed Jewish settlement. He makes the *derivative* quality[5] of his scheme clear by proposing

---

is rooted in the Hebrew Bible in the divine threat of dispersion that accompanies the inscription of the commandments (Deut 28:25). I should add that this scriptural reading of the origin of the term "diaspora" is further complicated by the fact that the historical event widely accepted as the moment that created the "Jewish diaspora" was in fact a nonscriptural (possibly even a *secular*) event, as it postdated the events of the Torah: the destruction of the Second Temple by the Romans in 70 C.E.

3 Coincidentally, the emergence of "diaspora" as an English word referring to Jewish dispersion was contemporaneous with the birth of the first phase of the Zionist movement in Germany.

[4] The evidence for this is manifold, but one very direct instance is a passage in *The Jew's State* where Herzl considers both Argentina and Palestine as possible locations for a Jewish state. He opts for Palestine not for reasons of divine sanction but for practical reasons— it will be easier to rally Jews who do believe in the "promised land" (Herzl: 148). For a fuller sense of the significance of Herzl in the context of the *fin de siècle* Zionist movement, see Berkowitz.

5 Here I am thinking of Chatterjee. Daniel Boyarin has made the connection between Zionism and anticolonial movements explicit in "The Colonial Drag: Zionism, Gender, and Mimicry," though Boyarin focuses on Zionism as specifically a form of "mimic" colonialism. Here, my reading of the movement aims to be somewhat more forgiving of Zionism in some ways, since critics such as Chatterjee have pointed to the ways in which a utilization of the rhetoric of the colonial authority (in the case of India) was a necessary, even a productive part of the

that a "Jewish Company" (modeled after the East India Company) be formed prior to the formal establishment of a Jewish state. When scripture does come up in Herzl's text, it is part of a rhetoric aimed to persuade Jewish readers *not to read it,* or at any rate, not to allow their relationship to the Gentile world to be dictated by unmodern adherence to divine commandments. It is in this spirit that Herzl comments, "If we do manage to leave Mizraim[6] once more, we will not forget the fleshpots." Though he here adopts the famous passage from the Exodus narrative of the Pentateuch (Exod 16:3), he completely reverses its meaning. The phrase "fleshpots of Egypt" has been widely interpreted by both Jewish and Christian readers of Exodus as a symbol of corruption in bondage: the Israelites, in their exile the desert, long to return to servitude in Egypt because of the material comfort it offered. Heedless of the dangers of the parallel, Herzl uses the same image of liberation from bondage (though here "Egypt" is actually Europe) to suggest that the colony he envisions will not be lacking for modern amenities.[7] In short, though it is structurally indebted to the scriptural concept of "Eretz Yisrael," the divine sanction for the Jewish return to Palestine, Herzl's reference to scripture enters his argument as a sardonic disavowal of any identification with beleaguered Israelites or other biblical figures. Though Zionism is now generally understood as an exemplary instance of religious nationalism,[8] in its original manifestation Zionism was a discourse that aimed to distance itself from religious Judaism.

The ambivalent relationship to religious texts and practice that characterize Herzl's Zionism is widely present in the character of Leopold Bloom

---

anticolonial struggle. Applied to Zionism, it therefore seems possible to read the movement as *simultaneously* paracolonial and anticolonial.

6 "Mizraim" is Hebrew for "Egypt."

7 The paragraph that immediately precedes the passage I quote is as follows: "Those who have seen something of the world will know at the present time that little everyday customs are transplanted quite easily to all sorts of places. Indeed, the technical achievements of our time, which this plan would like to put to use for all humanity, have been used up to now mainly in the context of these little things. There are English hotels in Egypt and on the mountain peaks in Switzerland, Viennese cafes in South Africa, French theaters in Russia, German opera houses in America and the best Bavarian beer in Paris. If we do manage to leave Mizraim once more, we will not forget the fleshpots" (Herzl: 186).

8 I define "religious nationalism" as a variant of nationalism as a collective imagining of shared space that derives its warrant from sacred texts, specifically the earthly geography described in those texts. This clearly has had a significant influence on Zionism and has much to do with the entrenchment of Israeli nationalism in the present day. But it also has been a factor in India, where the Vedas are used by the Hindu right to justify everything from high-caste privilege to the 1991 razing of Babri Masjid in Ayodhya. The dependence of specifically *modern* religious nationalism on sacred texts is linked to the mass circulation of versions of those texts in print culture, as well as the circulation of an interpretive symbology of those texts through electronic media.

in *Ulysses*. Leopold Bloom repeatedly engages the problem of Zionism, where it is closely tied to the discourses of colonialism, racial others, and the images of the Orient that enter Bloom's consciousness through an extremely heterogeneous range of stimuli. In *Ulysses*, however, Zionism's alignment with colonialism is dramatically reversed; for Bloom, Zionism may be less the colonial enterprise envisioned by Herzl than an anticolonial struggle. As such, it has close parallels to the quite different anticolonial movement that is Irish nationalism, which is profoundly important to both Bloom and Stephen Dedalus. In the messianic language of the passage from the "Circe" episode quoted at the beginning of this essay, both discourses are present. In the midst of a long series of impersonations, Bloom announces the fulfillment of Jewish prophecy in distinctly New Testament tones ("My beloved subjects, a new era is about to dawn. I, Bloom, tell you verily it is at hand"). What is striking is that Bloom uses biblical rhetoric (as much derived from the Gospels as it is from the Pentateuch) to lead his audience not to Palestine but to "Nova Hibernia"—New Ireland. A diasporic image of return, in other words, inflects the liberation ideology of Bloom's Irish nationalism, which as an anticolonial movement would seem to differ from Zionism because it is already geographically grounded (in Ireland). Irish nationalism, one assumes, is already at "home."

There is, nonetheless, an Irish diaspora with both religious and secular dimensions operating in *Ulysses,* in at least three ways. First, as a nationalist text written by Joyce in exile, *Ulysses* itself may be an Irish diasporic artifact. Aside from the fact that it was written entirely abroad, the deep commitment to the details of Dublin's street geography and the close, affectionate memory of the material and sensual experience of the city are classic marks of a diasporic construction of home. The Irish diaspora is also present in the myriad references in the text to Republican militants and other Irish nationalists forced to operate abroad (such as the Fenians Stephen Dedalus meets in Paris), as well as the frequent references to Dublin residents who have moved to America. Finally, the central thematic of wandering, figured in the two characters' wandering around Dublin, allegorizes the inability to return to a national and cultural home that characterizes the diasporic plots of numerous diasporic narratives.

Both Ireland and Palestine are versions of the "promised land" in *Ulysses.* Only, which "promised land" is to be Bloom's, Palestine or Dublin? Where in geographical space will "Bloomusalem" flower? In what follows, I examine in greater detail the mutual dependence of scriptural and secular images of the "promised land" in diasporic nationalisms that are sometimes Jewish/Zionist, sometimes Irish-Catholic/Republican, and sometimes both at once. More generally, I intend to consider the interaction of religious discourse with a secular form of nationalism in a postcolonial framework. For while the marginalization of scriptural textuality and religious practice in the writing of Theodor Herzl and others is a fact that many Jewish cultural critics have noted, the role of religion in modern narratives of national liberation has not been discussed sufficiently in postcolonial criticism to date.

Joyce's *Ulysses* was written at a critical moment in the historical development of both nationalist movements,[9] so it is not unreasonable that Joyce would think to marry Zionism and Irish nationalism. On the Jewish side, *Ulysses* presents in Leopold Bloom an image of a Jew who yearns for a version of "home" defined partly by his straightforward (and secular) desire for the revitalization of his family life, and partly by a desire (that may be transhistorical) for spiritual protection in the fold of Judaism. While the precise content of Bloom's "faith" remains elusive, there is no denying the lyricism of Jewish religious metaphors in Joyce's novel or the potential belonging to community they signify.

Though Joyce is commonly thought of as an ardent critic of both religious institutions and nationalism, recent critical biographies have suggested that his worldview was strongly and positively shaped by these discourses. There are, for instance, numerous connections in Joyce's personal and intellectual biography to Zionist thought. Neil Davison has pointed to Joyce's close involvement with European Jewry around the turn of the century, a moment when many European Jewish artists and intellectuals were attempting to forge a "national" consciousness. Both Davison and Ira Nadel give detailed accounts of Joyce's complex response to Zionism. It is known, for instance, that Joyce owned a copy of Herzl's *Der Judenstaat* as well as Sacher's *Zionism and the Jewish Future* as he wrote *Ulysses* (Davison: 129) and that he at times in his letters and conversations compared the plight of the Irish to that of the Jews (11). Davison argues that Joyce's book is actively involved in the Jewish creative process, even if the Jewish culture celebrated in *Ulysses* is a nationalism of eclecticism, hybridity, and cosmopolitan belonging rather than a monocultural adherence to "old wisdom" (128).

While European Jewish culture and national aspirations are certainly a prominent aspect of *Ulysses*, Irish nationalism is in fact more prevalent in terms of the sheer density of historical names and reference points given. Though *Ulysses* remembers Irish nationalism as it was before 1921, when the Irish Free State came into being, the book articulates a sophisticated critique of colonialism in line with those produced by much later authors from very different colonial contexts: authors like Chinua Achebe and Salman Rushdie. Particularly with regard to Irish nationalism, *Ulysses* is a postcolonial text, a

---

[9] The two decisive moments occurring as Joyce writes are (1) the Balfour Declaration of 1917, where the British Empire grants Jewish settlers certain privileges; and (2) in Ireland, the dramatic Easter Rising of 1916.

novel that foregrounds the experience of colonial subjects, expresses strong anticolonial sentiments, and yet is widely aware of the problems posed by dependence on a derivative form of nationalism to end English rule in Ireland. But the discourse of religion in colonialism also transforms the postcolonial narrative of struggle in key ways. For instance, in "James Joyce and Mythic Realism," Declan Kiberd powerfully describes Joyce's attention to the imposition of language as a tool of colonial management and, from the reverse perspective of the colonial subject, the deprivation of one's native tongue as the most oppressive violence of that form of subjugation (Kiberd: 327–55). In addition to language, the participation of the Anglican Church in political colonization adds the discrediting and prohibition of indigenous faiths (both pre-Christian and Catholic) to the list of Irish woes. Echoing the sentiments of Benjamin Disraeli, Joyce places the imposition of religion alongside the imposition of language among the most deeply tragic consequences of colonialism.[10] This is not a new theme: Irish critics such as Kiberd, Conor Cruise O'Brien, and many others are only too aware of the colonial nature of religion in Ireland. But while the deep (and perilous) attraction of the "master's" language has been widely discussed by postcolonial writers and critics all over the world, the consequences of the equally gripping set of desires represented by colonial religion (for Joyce, this is Anglican Protestantism) have not.

Bloom's invocation of both Irish nationalism and Zionism is highly idiosyncratic. His idea of "Bloomusalem" personalizes the political referent, spinning the allegories of religion and nationalism he alludes to away from the abstract entity of the nation and toward his personal feelings of inadequacy, alienation, and humiliation. Moreover, Bloom's juxtaposition of the two discourses is complicated by the location of the passage in a series of "trials" in the "Circe" episode of *Ulysses,* trials that Bloom repeatedly fails. Because of these factors, it would be easy enough to read *Ulysses* conventionally, as a polemic against both the church and the nation. Certainly Bloom's messianic pronouncement is ironic in the sense that it mocks his own delusions of grandeur, which are virtually indissociable from his many

---

[10] Other important postcolonial readings of *Ulysses* are Duffy and Cheng. Though Cheng's argument is the more straightforward, I find Duffy's deployment of Gramscian rhetoric of hegemony and contestation to be a particularly effective way of reading the novel's political ambivalence: "*Ulysses* ... is not a manifesto for postcolonial freedom, but rather a representation of the discourses and regimes of colonial power being attacked by counterhegemonic strategies that were either modeled on the oppressor's discourses or were only beginning to be enumerated in other forms.... We may ... discern in *Ulysses,* the novel read by metropolitan critics since its publication as the capstone-text of the western (and hence imperial) modernist tradition, rather a blueprint for the staging of the confrontations between the discourses and the material forces at odds in any anticolonial struggle" (Duffy: 21).

public humiliations and abjections in the text. But my intention is something other than a reading of Joyce as a writer who equates modernity with secularism, and nationalism with religion—while relegating all of these discourses to the scrap heap of history.

Religion and nationalism have a great deal of power over the paradigmatically "modern" subjects in Joyce's book, but this only becomes evident through a careful reading of the web of associations in which these discourses are situated in the text—their location in the novel's network of discourse: positions, people, ideas, events. An exciting aspect of reading a novel of intense heteroglossia such as this is that it is never a closed text. Dominant themes take shape not through Joyce's "grand design" but through careful mappings, the alignments and polarities that emerge through association to events in the text as well as its myriad intertexts. Irish nationalism and Zionism become parallel discourses not because of any strong (i.e., causal) historical connection, but through Joyce's articulation of them as linked in the figures of Bloom and Stephen (and sometimes in Bloom alone), defining each in terms of the other, relationally. This mutual dependence points to a concept of nationalism that is not circular so much as reciprocal.

The Promised Land

>[Bloom] *Brimstone they called it raining down: the cities of the plain: Sodom, Gomorrah, Edom. All dead names. A dead sea in a dead land, grey and old. Old now. It bore the oldest, the first race.*
>
>*Ulysses* 4.219–20

>[Stephen] *I call it* A Pisgah Sight of Palestine *or* The Parable of the Plums.
>
>*Ulysses* 7.1058

As a function of its status as a diasporic text, the discourse of nationalism in *Ulysses* is generally allegorical. But Joyce is sensitive both to the creative possibilities of allegory and to the ways in which the idealization allegory can also stretch the truth, sometimes with catastrophic effects. The most prominent allegory in the text, which alludes to both diasporicity and the territorial grounding of nationalism, is the biblical narrative of the "promised land." Interestingly, both Jewish and Irish nationalism are allegorized as the promised land, though the referents of the allegory are markedly different for Leopold Bloom and Stephen Dedalus. The "promised land" is for both characters a found image, deriving initially from a particular external stimulus, which in this case is a newspaper. Then, in response to triggers both external and internal, both Stephen and Bloom transform the image of the "promised land," producing narratives quite different from the ones they initially encounter.

Though the "promised land" has divergent referents and is expressed differently both in substance and in tone by each character, the split significance of the promised land transforms the discourses of both religion and nationalism in key ways. To begin with, however, as promised land, the Dublin (and Ireland) Joyce portrays does not appear especially promising. The available narratives of national liberation are narrow: both the rhetoric of Celtic revival and the linguistic revival of Gaelic are vexed projects. At its worst, Irish nationalism is represented by the militant rhetoric of "The Citizen" in "Cyclops," as utterly unwilling to allow the specter of religious difference to contaminate the nationalist narrative. In the Citizen, Joyce represents Irish nationalism as possessed by a violent monomania, with a dangerous and unproductive underpinning of anti-Semitism as well as anti-Protestantism. Stephen singles out this kind of extremism for mockery in his satirical *A Pisgah Sight of Palestine* or *The Parable of the Plums*. The fact that he and the newspapermen he converses with in "Aeolus" rely on the image of the "promised land" is especially important, as it is an example of the dependence of the Irish nationalist narrative on a religious allegory, an allegory that is neither precisely Catholic nor even properly Christian.

In contrast, the "promised land" narrative, as it is initially manifested in Bloom's mind in "Calypso," is triggered by his encounter with Jewish nationalism and is associated with the religious nationalism of the emerging Zionist movement. In a sense it is a simpler deployment of Palestine, as it refers, for Bloom, to actual Jews. Complications do enter in, however, as Bloom struggles with stereotypical images of both Jews and the Orient that are a part of his social conditioning as a European subject at the turn of the century. It is almost impossible for Bloom, though he is of Jewish descent, to eradicate the strong impulse to see Jews as "ancient" and the East as a land of the past. Rather like famously "self-hating" Jewish writers of early twentieth-century Europe (many of whom had also either been baptized or advocated it to encourage accelerated assimilation), Bloom sees the Jewish community through a mainstream lens[11] and resists placing himself within the frame.

The "promised land" first enters Bloom's mind in the novel through an advertisement for a Zionist settling scheme in a newspaper used by the butcher to wrap Bloom's pork kidney in "Calypso." In his internal response

---

11 Sander Gilman's essay, "Nietzsche's Jew," suggests that Nietzsche's image of European Jewry was "tripartite," constituted by (1) "the ancient Hebrew," (2) the "archetypical wandering Christian ... weak and destructive," and (3) "the Jew as contemporary, the antithesis of all decadence, self-sufficient and incorruptible" (cited in Davison, 125).

to it, Bloom turns it into a depressing image of decay, an image of the Jewish people stripped of productivity and vigor, struggling to remain intact. Stephen, on the other hand, invents a "Parable of the Plums" to satirize Irish nationalism using an image of two elderly Catholic nuns looking out on Dublin, metaphorically rendered as "Palestine." This language is inspired by Stephen's experience at the newspaper office, where he hears the recitation of an Irish nationalist speech that makes use of the Exodus metaphor as an argument for Irish independence. The two versions of the "promised land" could not be more different. One vision (Bloom's) concerns communities of Jews scattered across Europe, while the other (Stephen's) refers to Irishmen struggling with English colonialism. Bloom's vision is tragic and disturbed; Stephen's is cynical and bawdy. Bloom's imagery is decidedly literal (though it extends in numerous metaphoric dimensions in Bloom's mind), while Stephen's "Parable" is allegorical and entirely fictive. And yet, as the images echo throughout *Ulysses* (especially in "Circe" and "Ithaca") a set of correspondences emerges, aligning the two images toward each other—just as Bloom and Stephen seem to be oriented toward each other as displaced and wandering spirits.

Bloom's first musings on the "promised land" occur quite early in Calypso, his first appearance in *Ulysses*. He is at the pork butcher's, getting breakfast, and while waiting he begins to idly read one of the "cut sheets" there for wrapping meat. Although the exact name of the newspaper from which the sheets are derived is never specified, it seems to be a Jewish-themed paper.[12] The sections Bloom focuses on are the advertisements, Zionist advertisements in particular: "the model farm at Kinnereth on the lakeshore of Tiberias. Moses Montefiore. I thought he was" (*Ulysses* 4.156). The passing mention here of the prominent London Jewish advocate and proto-Zionist Moses Montefiore is troubled slightly by the absence of a predicate in the sentence that follows it: "I thought he was [what?]." Because Bloom never fills in the object, this moment of the indeterminacy of Moses Montefiore's identity only produces a further textual indeterminacy. One can surmise that the identity intended here is *Italian*, since "Montefiore" sounds Italian; Bloom is perhaps surprised to understand that Montefiore is not only Jewish, but also that he is involved in a planting scheme in Palestine.

---

[12] The centrality of the newspaper is particularly appropriate, given the importance of nationalism to *Ulysses*. Benedict Anderson's *Imagined Communities* posits a national print-culture as a major material precondition of a shared sense of national space. What's interesting about the role of the newspaper in Bloom's case is the fact that it appears to be a Jewish newspaper, with advertisements soliciting investment in colonizing schemes. Bloom may work for a major city paper, but the first thing he reads on this particular morning is a paper with an interest in a differently constructed national space—Israel.

Walking out of Dlugacz's Pork Butchery, Bloom glances at the wrapping of his pork kidney and reads the following advertisement:

> Agendath netaim: planters' company. To purchase waste sandy tracts from Turkish government and plant with eucalyptus trees. Excellent for shade, fuel and construction. Orangegroves and immense melonfields north of Jaffa. You pay eighty marks and they plant a dunam of land for you with olives, oranges, almonds or citrons. Olives cheaper: oranges need artificial irrigation. Every year you get a sending of the crop....
> Nothing doing. Still an idea behind it. (*Ulysses* 4.191–96)

The language of this passage is partly a citation from the advertisement ("Excellent for shade, fuel and construction"), and partly Bloom's impressionistic recreation of it. The images of bountiful crops ("immense melonfields") echo some of his mildly pornographic musings about the voluptuous woman he had been standing behind in the line at the pork butcher's (*Ulysses* 4.175–80) and are of a piece with the general thematic emphasis on fecundity that has been prevalent thus far in the episode. Bloom dismisses the planting scheme out of hand—"nothing doing"—but is nevertheless impressed by the "idea behind it."

Though it may be indirect, the "idea behind it" Bloom is thinking of here is none other than the principle guiding Jewish colonization in Palestine, which is to say, Zionism. Though Bloom's response to the commercial aspect of the planting scheme described here is dismissive, his mentality shares with Herzl's a strong emphasis on the mechanics of the project: how much money, how much labor—how much profit. Like Herzl, Bloom is a pragmatist, a planner, and a performer. Unlike Herzl, Bloom at this point in *Ulysses* has little room in his crowded mind for grand nation-building narratives. However, these narratives will play a role, as Bloom's performance in the "Circe" episode indicates.

For a few moments, Bloom continues to walk, his thoughts freely wandering: the speculative details of Mediterranean farming[13] are interspersed with snatches of real memories and images of people he knows in Dublin. But then a cloud begins to eat away at the sunlight, leading his thoughts also to cloud:

> A cloud began to cover the sun slowly, wholly. Grey. Far.
> No, not like that. A barren land, bare waste. Vulcanic lake, the dead sea: no fish, weedless, sunk deep in the earth. No wind could life those

---

[13] At this time, I have not been able to locate a reference to the probable source for the text of the newspaper clipping Bloom looks at. According to Berkowitz, however, it does seem likely that the appearance of such a clipping would have been not strictly chronologically accurate; Zionist agricultural ventures in Palestine did not begin to develop seriously until the 1910s.

waves, grey metal, poisonous foggy waters. Brimstone they called it raining down: the cities of the plain: Sodom, Gomorrah, Edom. All dead names. A dead sea in a dead land, grey and old. Old now. It bore the oldest, the first race. A bent hag crossed from Cassidy's, clutching a naggin bottle by the neck. The oldest people. Wandered far away over all the earth, captivity to captivity, multiplying, dying, being born everywhere. It lay there now. Now it could bear no more. Dead: an old woman's: the grey sunken cunt of the world.

Desolation. (*Ulysses* 4.218–25)

The cloud that triggers this spiral of despair is probably exactly the same cloud that depresses Stephen Dedalus as he looks out of the Martello Tower in "Telemachus," though it acts quite differently on Stephen.[14] That a minor metereological event such as the appearance of a cloud has a powerfully negative effect on Bloom in particular can be read as merely one among many instances in *Ulysses* of randomness. In particular, as a moment (among many) where Bloom is deeply emotionally affected by a very minor event, it may be simply an example of Bloom's celebrated, errant subjectivity. However, given the direct citations from both Genesis and Exodus in the passage, the appearance of the cloud may also be something more—something biblical. That is to say, the cloud may be read as a reference to the passages in Exodus where God appears to the Hebrews as "a pillar of cloud" (Exod 13:21) as he leads them out of Egypt and through a number of difficult circumstances before finally landing them in Canaan. But if the biblical cloud is a sign of God as a fixed point, an undeniable sign of divinity, the cloud in this passage seems to be the opposite. Joyce's cloud marks the diminishing of light (blocking access to that ancient, sometimes divine, source of truth and hope—the sun) and the onset of confusion. The reversal of the function of the cloud on Bloom in this way is part of Joyce's widespread rebuttal of biblical textuality as a channel by which to access the divine.[15]

---

[14] Thanks to Ian Baucom for pointing this out to me. Besides the timing of the cloud's appearance (shortly after eight in the morning), the fact that the same language appears in both Stephen's and Bloom's minds as the cloud appears may be the strongest evidence of this. Here is Stephen's version of this: "A cloud began to cover the sun, slowly, wholly, shadowing the bay in deeper green. It lay beneath him, a bowl of bitter waters. Fergus' song: I sang it alone in the house, holding down the long dark chords. Her door was open: she wanted to hear my music. Silent with awe and pity I went to her bedside. She was crying in her wretched bed. For those words, Stephen: love's bitter mystery" (1.248–53).

[15] Alternatively, it can be read as a metaliterary intervention similar to Salman Rushdie's cameo as "God" in *The Satanic Verses*. There, Rushdie poses himself as "God," the creator of the universe that is his novel, and demands that his protagonist "stop fooling around with some flatfoot blonde" and instead begin earnestly pursuing his divine/angelic mission. Transferred to the universe that is *Ulysses*, the cloud then becomes Joyce, intervening in the uncomplicated "morning" thoughts of his protagonists (both of them), redirecting them.

As Bloom ponders Palestine, the contemporary trigger ("Agendath Netaim") switches registers, becoming historical and textual. In his clouded thoughts, the precise geographical region of the Middle East Bloom thinks of as so horrifyingly barren becomes less important than language describing the sites in question in the Pentateuch. Much of Bloom's language here derives particularly from Genesis, especially the references to Sodom, Gomorrah, and Edom. The negative, punitive image of decimation that dominates certain episodes of Genesis overwhelms Bloom, detached from any moral or narrative trajectory. When his thoughts begin to move toward the people who live in the "dead land," Bloom's recall of the biblical images turns toward Exodus. Here, Bloom's revulsion at the idea of a dead land leads him to begin to reject an apparently dead people: "The oldest people. Wandered far away over all the earth, captivity to captivity." But the reference to the Israelites is fleeting; Bloom's thoughts return almost irresistibly to images of a mixed fruitfulness and multiplication: "multiplying, dying, being born everywhere." This is the other Exodus—the Israelites prospering and multiplying despite the punishments of Pharaoh and despite the hardships of the desert.[16]

The distinction between the people who belonged to the dead land—the Jews—and the land itself is an important moment of bifurcation in Bloom's consciousness. If this distinction is to grow in force in Bloom's mind as the novel progresses, he will have to come to terms with the prevailing image of Jews as an ancient, persecuted people. The direction it seems to lead in is an image of the Jewish people that is largely "diasporist," defined as a community by the experience of exile. Ultimately, in this passage, the image of life is not enough to restore buoyancy—the sequence ends as he hits rock bottom, with the most extreme image to appear in Bloom's thoughts in this part of the novel: "the grey sunken cunt of the world." How to read this image? On the one hand, Bloom's image of decay embodied in women—specifically, in a slang term for female genitalia—has an associative connection to Stephen's volatile, disturbing images of female sexuality, some of which appear in response to his "cloud" experience in "Telemachus." As importantly, it can be read as a "feminization" of the Jewish people. Neil Davison, for instance, suggests that Joyce's skepticism about Zionism is filtered through his exposure to the Austrian Zionist Otto Weininger, who has been described by many Jewish critics as a classic "self-hating Jew."[17]

---

16 Bloom reconsiders these images later in *Ulysses*, to much happier effect: "High voices. Sunwarm silk. Jingling harnesses. All for a woman, home and houses, silkwebs, silver, rich fruits spicy from Jaffa. Agendath Netaim. Wealth of the world" (8.635-36).

17 "Bloom's 'old woman' metaphor represents the womanliness of the Jews through an allusion not only female, but of female decrepitude—'grey sunken cunt of the world.' It would

Stephen construes an image of the promised land in the "Aeolus" episode that in many ways mirrors Bloom's image in the passage above. However, to a lesser extent, Stephen's "Pisgah Sight of Palestine" also echoes a quite different recollection of Exodus from Bloom's, which is important because it also appears in "Aeolus." In contrast to the passage cited above, here Bloom seems to have only a minimum of affect associated either with his identification as a Jew or with the pain recorded in the Exodus narrative. If the earlier Bloom was susceptible to a dramatic mood shift because of the appearance of a cloud, this is the ruminating Bloom, chewing through a prodigious amount of material. Bloom's citation of Exodus is triggered by the sight of a typesetter at work:

> He stayed in his walk to watch a typesetter neatly distributing type. Reads it backwards first. Quickly he does it. Must require some practice that. maNgiD kcitraP. Poor papa with his hagadah book, reading backwards with his finger to me. Pessach. Next year in Jerusalem. Dear, O dear! All that long business about that brought us out of the land of Egypt and into the house of bondage *alleluia. Shema Israel Adonai Elohenu*. No, that's the other. Then the twelve brothers, Jacob's sons. And then the lamb and the cat and the dog and the stick and the water and the butcher. And then the angel of death kills the butcher and he kills the ox and the dog kills the cat. Sounds a bit silly till you come to look into it well. Justice it means but it's everybody eating everyone else. That's what life is after all. How quickly he does that job. (*Ulysses* 7.205–13)

It's significant that Bloom begins this train of thought because he associates the typesetter's backwards reading with Hebrew, particularly because Hebrew orthography will play an important part in the cultural exchange between Stephen and Bloom in the "Ithaca" episode. Here, the particular context that "Hebrew" invokes for Bloom is his memory of his father's reading of Hebrew from the *Haggadah* at Passover. Bloom's memory is, notably, erratic; he remembers the Hebrew for the Shema prayer before realizing ("No, that's the other") that it actually does not appear in that prayer. He does, of course, remember directly from the Haggadah a line that comes from Exodus ("out of the land of Egypt and into the house of bondage"; compare to Exod 13:3–4). Bloom's train of thought closes with his recall of the *Chad Gadya* chant that closes the second seder of the Passover ritual, followed by a quick moral

---

thus appear that Joyce perceived Weininger's own self-hatred as a Jew, and built a similar attitude into Bloom's own 'Jewishness.' But this is not the case. Rather, the implication throughout *Ulysses* is that Bloom's self-deprecation comes not from a 'Jewish nature,' but from a lack of a strong, unified identity, which pivots on his denial of his own Jewish identity" (Davison: 145).

interpretation: "Justice it means but it's everybody eating everyone else. That's what life is after all."

Stephen's image of the promised land is triggered by a more direct invocation of it. Professor MacHugh recites from memory a speech delivered by John F. Taylor, an Irish barrister. Taylor's speech[18] was a response to Gerald Fitzgibbon, over the subject of the revival of Gaelic then being proposed:

> Mr chairman, ladies and gentlemen: Great was my admiration in listening to the remarks addressed to the youth of Ireland a moment since by my learned friend. It seemed to me that I had been transported into a country far away from this country, into an age remote from this age, that I stood in ancient Egypt and that I was listening to the speech of some highpriest of that land addressed to the youthful Moses.... And it seemed to me that I heard the voice of that Egyptian highpriest raised in a tone of like haughtiness and like pride. I heard his words and their meaning was revealed to me.... Why will you jews not accept our culture, our religion and our language? You are a tribe of nomad herdsmen: we are a mighty people. You have no cities nor no wealth: our cities are hives of humanity and our galleys, trireme and quadrireme, laden with all manner merchandise furrow the waters of the known globe. You have but emerged from primitive conditions: we have a literature, a priesthood, an agelong history and a polity. (*Ulysses* 7.828–850)

This is part of a debate about language, but Taylor's melodramatic rhetoric makes it clear that the stakes are much higher—the general relationship of Ireland to English colonial power. The reference to the Exodus narrative is quite direct and extensive (in contrast to the "Agendath Netaim" advertisement that triggered Bloom's first recollection of the language of Exodus). However, Taylor maps the conflict between Pharaoh and the Israelites to a contemporary setting, honing in on the discourse of imperialism in a way the Exodus narrative does not ("our cities are hives of humanity and our galleys ... furrow the waters of the known globe"). The particular invocation of modern events—urbanization, expanding commerce, globality—fundamentally transforms the Exodus narrative from a display of divine might and absolutist morality to the new moralism of capital.

When he satirizes Taylor's speech with his own vision of the Irish "promised land," Stephen twists the allegory to his own taste, inventing two fifty-three-year-old Dublin women ("Dublin vestals"), who take plums up to the top of Nelson's pillar (i.e., Mt. Pisgah). The pillar in question is topped by a statue of Admiral Horatio Nelson, a shining symbol of English naval power. Through indirect association, Nelson has already been referred to by

---

[18] According to Gifford, this (actual) speech was delivered in 1901.

the professor because of his part in ensuring the collapse of "the catholic chivalry of Europe" in the naval defeat of Napoleon at Trafalgar (*Ulysses* 7.566). Although Stephen's satire is partly an attempt to mock the inflated anticolonial rhetoric of Taylor's "Exodus" speech, the choice of Nelson as one object of derision certainly fits the professor's view of things. Perhaps more surprisingly, for all the bare arrogance of his blatant reversal of Professor MacHugh's breathless national allegory, Stephen in fact barely manages to make his point. At first, Stephen's narrative is preoccupied with the monetary details of the vestals' picnic—probably reflecting a financial obsession stemming from his own dire penury. Then, Stephen's "Parable" is interrupted by a bored-seeming professor ("Vestal virgins. I can see them. What's keeping our friend?"). Finally, Stephen gets to the point of his story, his Dublin vestals eating plums at the top of the pillar:

> -When they have eaten the brawn and the bread and wiped their twenty fingers in the paper the bread was wrapped in they go nearer the railings....
> -But they are afraid the pillar will fall, Stephen went on. They see the roofs and argue about where the different churches are: Rathmines' blue dome, Adam and Eve's, saint Laurence O'Toole's. But it makes them giddy to look so they pull up their skirts....
> ...
> -And settled down on their striped petticoats, peering up at the statue of the onehandled adulterer.
> -It gives them a crick in their necks, Stephen said, and they are too tired to look up or down so to speak. They put the bag of plums between them and eat the plums out of it, one after another, wiping off with their handkerchiefs, the plumjuice that dribbles out of their mouths and spitting the plumstones slowly out between the railings. (*Ulysses* 7.1000–1030)

Three things happen: they look down but it makes them giddy; they look up but it hurts their necks; and finally they give up on taking in the scene, and simply eat plums. Looking down, the two women have a strategic perspective on Dublin—rather like the bird's-eye view of a map. In contrast to their day-to-day perception of the city, from the top of Nelson's pillar the city is at once at somewhat of a distance and widely accessible in all directions. It is the unmediated Dublin, the "promised land" of the Irish nationalist dream. Importantly, the main landmarks the "vestals" identify are the surrounding Catholic churches—signifying an Irish Catholic difference.

Of course, they cannot look for long, because the view "makes them giddy." They sit, and instead look upward at the statue of Nelson, the supreme symbol of British superiority—over both Ireland and Europe. It's unclear what part of the statue they can actually see, however, and the awkwardness of their perspective on Nelson is represented in Stephen's verb, "peering." Here Stephen also throws in a note of insult directed at Nelson, "the onehandled adulterer," referring to an aspect of the history that the two women probably do not know. Ultimately, they have as little interest in hurting their necks for a view of the symbol of power—as seen from below—as they do in looking down at the city below.

Though he turns away from Nelson, in the final gesture Stephen takes the sexually provocative reference to adultery and redirects it onto the women themselves. Utterly disregarding either narrative available to them at the top of the pillar, they seem to simply eat plums. In the language in which he describes their eating, Stephen redoubles the casually insulting language he has used to describe the women throughout his story: the plumjuice "dribbles" out of their mouths (earlier, they "waddled" up the stairs of the pillar). In the *coup de grâce,* Stephen marks how they "spit the plumstones slowly out between the railings." Through the sexual connotation of plumstones (testicles) and a general sense of postcoital satiety, this image is as lurid as it is packed: the scene alternately invokes homoeroticism, fellatio, autoeroticism, and cannibalism. Unlike many of Stephen's other visions of female sexuality, however, this image is remarkably peaceful. The dominant sexuality represented here is, if anything, autoerotic, as the women seem to be completely satisfied by the consumption of their plums. Neither the imperial "adulterer" nor the domes of Irish Catholic saints interest them beyond an idle flirtation.

The meaning of Stephen's satire is obscure to his audience until he finally names the satire, or rather, double-names it: "*A Pisgah Sight of Palestine* or *The Parable of the Plums.*" The dual naming of the story is an important indicator of its multiple targets—Catholic Church, the British Empire, and the Irish "nation." The first title is from the episode in Deuteronomy (34:1–5), where Moses climbs Mount Pisgah and views the land promised to his ancestors and to him, only to be told by God that he will not be permitted to enter. A "Pisgah Sight of Palestine" in Joyce's anticolonial reading becomes the sight of a land—specifically, a nation space—which the viewer will never get to own. The second title points to the general parody of Christian themes in Stephen's story, present in the identification of the women, who are clearly substandard Catholic subjects, as "vestals," as well as in the naming of Nelson as an "adulterer."

In general, a parody such as this one might in fact "skip" all reference to the Jews, much in the way the Exodus narrative was historically "Protestantized," for instance, by the Puritans in early New England (J. Boyarin). However, the fact that Bloom has invoked Exodus, both in this episode and in an earlier episode, with Jews and Judaism as the specific referent in his thought, complicates the narrowly textual reading. Stephen's image of Palestine strongly connotes Bloom, whom we may think of in much the same position as the two women atop Nelson's pillar, although not entirely by choice. That is to say, Bloom is neither English nor comfortably Irish, though he certainly aspires toward the latter identity. Like the women in Stephen's Parable, his mind is distracted from the two idealizations by sensual matters.

Conclusion: Diaspora, The Promised Land, and Postcolonial Criticism

The intersection between the two images of the "promised land" is a powerful crystallization of the many different discourses being juxtaposed in Joyce's novel. It is, first and foremost, the intersection of Stephen Dedalus and Leopold Bloom. As such, the "promised land" is the intersection of a bitter satire (Stephen) and a tragic feeling of displacement and desolation (Bloom). It is also the intersection of archaic religious orthodoxy with omnivorous, irreverent, and modernist eclecticism. Thirdly, the "promised land" is the ground on which a member of a dominant, global religious hierarchy (the Catholic Church) can meet a partial member of a marginal and extremely maligned one (the Jews). The ground of the intersection is also the ground of the intersection between "Greek" (Stephen Dedalus) and "Jew" (Leopold Bloom).

The image of the "promised land" has been invoked in social struggles throughout the world, from diaspora Jews in Europe, to African American civil-rights activists, to advocates of Palestinian rights in the present day. But the utilization of the "promised land" as a universal image of liberation, as with the narrative of "Exodus" more generally, is by no means uncontroversial. The public debate between Michael Walzer and Edward Said, for instance, on the ethics of universalizing the term has been an important example of the dangers of interpreting Exodus as a "universal" allegory. Indeed, following Jonathan Boyarin's critique of the debate, my intent here has been neither to prescribe "Exodus" as a postcolonial redemption narrative nor to deny its historical importance as a metaphor, even an imprecise one. In spite of its limitations, the metaphor of the "promised land" continues to be important to a postcolonial mode of reading because of its emphasis on liberation and space, on the centrality of territorialization in the struggle against colonial authority.

Works Cited

Anderson, Benedict
 1991 *Imagined Communities.* New York: Verso.

Berkowitz, Michael
 1995 *Zionist Culture and West European Jewry Before the First World War.* Chapel Hill: University of North Carolina Press.

Boyarin, Daniel
    2000   "The Colonial Drag: Zionism, Gender, and Mimicry." Pp. 234–65 in *The Pre-occupation of Postcolonial Studies.* Ed. Fawzia Azfal-Khan and Kaplana Seshadri Crooks. Durhan, N.C.: Duke University Press.

Boyarin, Jonathan
    1992   "Reading Exodus into History." *New Literary History* 23:523–44.

Chatterjee, Partha
    1986   *Nationalist Thought and the Colonial World: A Derivative Discourse?* London: Zed Books.

Cheng, Vincent
    1995   *Joyce, Race, and Empire.* Cambridge: Cambridge University Press.

Davison, Neil
    1998   *James Joyce,* Ulysses, *and the Construction of Jewish Identity.* Cambridge: Cambridge University Press.

Duffy, Enda
    1994   *Subaltern Ulysses.* Minneapolis: University of Minnesota Press.

Gifford, Don
    1988   *Annotated Ulysses.* Berkeley and Los Angeles: University of California Press.

Herzl, Theodor
    1997   *The Jew's State: A Critical English Translation.* Trans. Henk Overberg. Northvale, N.J.: Aronson.

Kiberd, Declan
    1995   *Inventing Ireland.* Cambridge, Mass.: Harvard University Press.

Nadel, Ira
    1996   *Joyce and the Jews.* Gainesville: University of Florida Press.

Walzer, Michael
    1985   *Exodus and Revolution.* New York: Basic Books.

 New and Recent Titles

Dynamics of Diselection
Ambiguity in Genesis 12–36 and Ethnic Boundaries in Post-Exilic Judah
R. Christopher Heard
Code: 060639   224 pages   2001
Paper: $29.95 ISBN: 1-58983-001-6

Knowing Kings
Knowledge, Power, and Narcissism in the Hebrew Bible
Stuart Lasine
"Stuart Lasine skillfully guides his readers through the labyrinthine and largely unexplored tunnel system connecting the courts of the biblical kings and their heavenly counterpart, Yahweh, with those of a dizzying array of other monarchs across a broad range of cultures and historical epochs. In the process, our understanding of biblical kings, both human and divine, is deepened and thoroughly defamiliarized. This is a consummately literate and erudite study that richly repays reading and rereading."—*Stephen D. Moore, The Theological School, Drew University*
Code: 060640   360 pages   2001
Paper: $39.95 ISBN: 1-58983-004-0

Mikhail Bakhtin and Biblical Scholarship
An Introduction
Barbara Green
Code: 060638   216 pages   2000
Paper: $24.95 ISBN: 0-88414-020-2

Society of Biblical Literature • P.O. Box 2243 • Williston, VT 05495-2243
Phone: 877-725-3334 (toll-free) or 802-864-6185 • Fax: 802-864-7626
Online catalog: http://sbl-site.org/Publications/catalog
Shipping and handling extra

IN PRAISE OF POLYTHEISM

John Docker
Australian National University

ABSTRACT

How much is Western intellectual work, in philosophy, psychoanalysis, political theory, inspired and energised by creation stories? In this essay, I explore Freud's famously idiosyncratic *Moses and Monotheism*, where the great psychoanalyst, fearing death in late 1930s Vienna, speculates that Moses was actually an Egyptian, who brought to the ancient Israelites the rational monotheistic religion of the heretical Pharaoh Akhenaten. Thus did reason, ethics, and the idea of a single unknowable God survive in history, thriving in Judaism and then Christianity and in Western thought to the present. I approach *Moses and Monotheism* as a kind of novel, a "Family Romance" in Freud's own terms, joining a long history of Egyptophilia in archaeology, film, and fiction. I question Freud's heroising of Moses. And I vigorously oppose Freud's attack on Egyptian polytheism, which endorses one of Christianity's crimes against humanity, its destruction of paganism.

Whether the offspring of Kronos or the blessed son of Jove or of the great Rhea,
Hail to thee, Attis, sad message of Rhea.
The Assyrians call thee thrice desired Adonis,
All Egypt calls thee Osiris,
Greek wisdom the heavenly horn of the moon,
The Samothracians "dignified Adamna,"
The Haemonians Korybas,
The Phrygians now Papas, then Tot or God,
Or "Without-Fear," goat-herd, mown ear,
Or man, born by the almond with many fruits, flute-player.
                                    Gnostic text quoted in Assmann: 52

And Moses was learned in all the wisdom of the Egyptians, and was mighty in words and in deeds.
                                    Acts 7:22

... the theological conviction that the hieroglyphs of the Egyptians contain a hereditary wisdom, which illuminates every obscurity of nature ...
                                    Benjamin: 170

> When I use Biblical tradition here in such an autocratic and arbitrary way, draw on it for confirmation whenever it is convenient, and dismiss its evidence without scruple when it contradicts my conclusions, I know full well that I am exposing myself to severe criticism concerning my method and that I weaken the force of my proofs.... Certainty is not to be gained in any case, and, moreover, we may say that all other authors have acted likewise.
>
> Freud, 1967:30n

> The wanton destruction of our Pagan heritage is the greatest tragedy in the history of the Western world.
>
> Freke and Gandy: 304

In this essay I wish to stage a conversation between two "historical novels," Freud's famously refractory not to say exquisitely perverse *Moses and Monotheism*, written at the edge of catastrophe, and Timothy Freke and Peter Gandy's sprightly *The Jesus Mysteries: Was the Original Jesus a Pagan God?*, a manifesto urging drastically revised foundations for religious thinking in the new millennium. Freke and Gandy offer their book as a popular intervention rather than as an academic text. Through this conversation I hope to contemplate one of the great conflicts in world history, between polytheism and monotheism as they clash in the contrast between Egyptology and the biblical story of Exodus. Egyptology and Exodus seek and romance competing creation stories, yet where "Egypt" is central to both as point of origin.

In praising polytheism, I am not advocating an impossible return to the ancient polytheistic world of Mesopotomia, Egypt, Greece, Rome. I will entertain polytheism as a philosophical idea, a monad, for as Walter Benjamin reminds us in the prologue to his *The Origin of German Tragic Drama*, Leibniz's notion of monad limns the One and the Many, that every single monad contains, in an indistinct way, all the others (Benjamin: 30).

I will be bringing the Benjamin of *The Origin of German Tragic Drama* into the conversation, especially when a contrast between monotheism and polytheism is cast in terms of relative advantages or disadvantages for theories of knowledge. I will also be invoking the Egyptologist Jan Assmann's *Moses the Egyptian*.

I will throughout be attempting to bring biblical narratives into conversation with postcolonial perspectives, yet with provisos: that I feel that the frame stories of postcolonial and contemporary cultural theory more generally are not only too determinedly secular but also blindly and contentedly recent-minded, as if all that is really significant in world history belongs to the last couple of centuries of modern empires and their aftermaths and dissolutions. Postcolonial theory has everything to gain from considering far, far longer time frames, to keep in mind that a thousand or two thousand years are eras quite short in humanity's long and bizarre histories. Another concern throughout this essay will be to question the claims to historicity of Western theology; in particular, figures like Moses and Jesus will be assumed to be cultural figures, characters in texts, myths, creation stories, tellings and retellings, dubious genealogies.

Creation Story

I'll first tell the creation story of this essay. For most of the 1990s I'd made curious voyages into ethnic and cultural identities for my book *1492: The Poetics of Diaspora;* in 1999 I'd sent the manuscript off to the publisher in London. Early in 2000, as I was drifting listlessly about in a state of post-writing-of-large-project tristesse, appeared the political theorist William E. Connolly, a visiting fellow to the Humanities Research Centre, Australian National University, Canberra, where I work. He suggested a miraculous solution to tristesse and ennui. In conversation we had recognised a common interest in the importance of religious narratives, especially the Old Testament stories, as foundational in European and Western history, an interest we idly called "post-secularist" (Connolly). He said that because of the work he was now doing on layered, dissonant conceptions of consciousness and perception, thinking and culture, he had become interested in Freud's discussion of deep memory in *Moses and Monotheism.* He said his HRC work-in-progress seminar would proceed by playing riffs off Freud's book, his paper to be entitled "Memory Traces, Mystical States and Deep Pluralism" (entertainingly performed 29 February 2000). He pointed out that another visiting scholar at the HRC, the film theorist E. Ann Kaplan, was also interested in *Moses and Monotheism* for its conceptions of delayed trauma, and she would be giving a paper soon as well ("Trauma, Cinema, Witnessing," 21 March 2000). Why don't you, he proposed, also deliver a paper on *Moses and Monotheism,* so there would be an absorbing series of three papers on a protean text that was becoming increasingly attractive to international scholarship. I acquiesced. I read and read. I gave a paper, "Creation Stories—Moses, Spinoza and Freud," on 4 April 2000. Professor Connolly had been very shrewd. Tristesse was forgotten; I was now possessed by a new interest, monotheism and polytheism. I wished, still wish, to do more work on it, extend it in different directions (Docker, 2001b).

In June of 2000 I travelled with my son Ned Curthoys on a research-and-conference visit to England. We would both do research during that month, and I would accompany him to a cultural studies conference in Birmingham in the final week of June where he was to give a paper. I wanted to pursue research in the British Library (which I first had to find in London—I remembered only the old British Museum) on the early eighteenth-century theological writings of John Toland, a reputed follower in England of Spinoza. Near the end of June, after returning to London from the Birmingham conference, my son and I visited the Freud Museum in 20 Maresfield Gardens, in Hampstead. It was my suggestion. I said we—Ann Curthoys and Ned and I—had visited the Freud Museum in Vienna in 1991 (Docker, 1995:418–22). Now I'd like to visit the London Freud Museum, Freud's home of 1938–1939, where I understood most of his household possessions from Vienna had been transferred, including the famous couch. Ned said, fine, his memories of Vienna were a little dim, but he'd certainly like to see the London museum. (My own dim memory is that there were some objects still to be seen in the Vienna museum, including various droll Priapic figurines.)

It was Monday, 26 June 2000, so a diary entry informs me. We made an appointment on the phone, were kindly allowed to visit out of usual visiting days, made our way to 20 Maresfield Gardens NW3, a short walk from Finchley Road Tube, got let in by a side door on the left of the museum, and, with no other visitors there, could stare at leisure at the various displays. Freud's Viennese consulting room, study, and library had been recreated. We moved slowly, trying to store memories and impressions. My memory is probably completely wrong, but I was struck by mention of Freud's daughter Anna's bedroom, its walls unadorned except for a photo of her father above her bed. Very odd, one thought to oneself. I especially tried to concentrate in the room where Freud's consulting couch was on spectacular display; I attempted to imprint into memory the large array of Near Eastern, Egyptian, and ancient Greek and Roman antiques he'd apparently picked up scouring secondhand shops when he was young. What to make of this lifelong interest of Freud's?

I don't wish to suggest superiority to it. For many years, off and on, more off than on unfortunately, Ann Curthoys and I (and now we've enlisted the help of British historian Iain McCalman) have been researching and writing a book to be called *Sheer Folly and Derangement,* a phrase taken from an Edward Said essay, "Raymond Schwab and the Romance of Ideas": "A peculiar feature of Schwab's scholarship ... is that he does not take explicit note of the sheer folly and derangement stirred up by the Orient in Europe" (Said, 1991:253). We are tracing the journey of this idea from the early eighteenth century, in translations of *The Thousand and One Nights,* Montesquieu's *Persian Letters,* and Lady Mary Wortley Montagu's Turkish Embassy letters; through various maverick figures like Beckford and Isabelle Eberhardt; to the twentieth century's rich pickings, in *The Sheik* as novel and Valentino film, Graham Greene's *Stamboul Train* and *The Quiet American,* and Mills and Boon popular romances of the 1980s and 1990s set in the Middle East. I also have to confess to my own lifelong passion for oriental cuisine and delusory desire to be descended from the Sephardim, expelled from Spain early in 1492 (Docker, 1998:181–200; 2001a).

Can Freud—can we Europeans all—be placed in the bizarre annals of orientalist thought, musings, imaginings, follies, dreams, disorientations, and derangements?

I came to the Freud Museum shop, at the back of the house next to the garden, and pondered at length over what postcards to buy, finally settling on five. I chose a photo of Freud and daughter Anna in 1920, sitting outdoors at a restaurant with wine glasses and decanter and wine bottles spread before them, Freud smoking a cigar and looking at the camera, Anna gazing elsewhere. I also chose a sketch of Freud drawn by Salvador Dali in 1938. Then I picked up and decided on a card featuring Eros, the information on the back saying: "One of six statues of the god of love in Freud's collection of antiquities." Then I chose a card, the back of it saying: "Baboon of the God Thoth.... A favourite object from Freud's collection, which stands on his desk." Then, the card I really wanted, a colour photo of Freud's couch. I paid my money and the visit was over. We were let out. We began to walk towards Hampstead Heath, working out directions from our *London A–Z*. My son said he would like to see the house in Tanza Road next to the Heath where we had rented a tiny apartment and stayed for several months in the early eighties, and he had gone to a primary school nearby, a school he had fond memories of. Curiously, I became over-confident, declaring I didn't have to look at the *London A–Z*; I could find Tanza Road from memory. My memory failed me miserably. I insisted we set off through the Heath, in entirely the wrong direction, often through tortuous bypaths (I had visions of being attacked); footsore, weary, assaulted by hayfever in the June heat, we ended up near Highgate, coughing, sniffling, exhausted. I'm haunted by this: I'd denied my son the revisiting of a treasured memory. I'd been utterly stupid. It was an appalling end to the visit to the London Freud Museum; and two days later we were on a flight back to Sydney. I would have to make it up to my son another time. How cunning Freud had been. He had died in 20 Maresfield Gardens on September 23, 1939, shortly after the outbreak of war. He wasn't going to allow any future visitor there to leave undisturbed. A little deranged, off to commit folly. To get lost in Hampstead Heath.

Now I sit here, in Canberra, at ANU, in October/November 2000, with summer coming reluctantly, near the sedate grey lake, turning over the Freud postcards. I stare at the card of the couch, and it and its setting really is remarkable. On the floor in front is a long narrow Persian carpet, a runner; on the wall behind is another richly decorated Persian carpet, impressively worn with age. And in the centre of the card is featured the couch covered with a massive Persian carpet, on which presumably the patient sat, with legs outstretched, alongside large sumptuous cushions that pick up colours from the carpets, ochre red, burgundy, brown, yellow. This surely could not ever have been a sober setting for psychoanalytic reflection.

How strangely sensuous it appeared. Perhaps, I sit here now thinking, Freud wasn't so different from Jung after all. If Jung wished to explain dreams and eros and the unconscious in terms of mythological archetypes, so Freud—perhaps—could interpret his patients' dreams, desires, traumas, as they talked and he sat unseen behind them on an armchair, by way of the fragments and icons of Egyptian and Mesopotamian and classical mythologies he daily, hourly, observed. He was so close to them; he was surrounded by them (the "couch" postcard also shows figurines on a shelf behind where Freud would sit); they were near at hand, signs of distant mysterious pasts speaking somehow to the present, to modernity.

But how? What dreams of interpretation were excited by Freud's lifelong fascination with the ancient land of the pharaohs? In *Freud: A Life for Our Time*, Peter Gay tells us of Freud's delight in ancient Mediterranean and Near Eastern statuary even from his early days as a researcher in Paris, arriving there in 1885, visiting the Louvre and lingering over the antiquities. Back in Vienna, established at Berggasse 19, Freud's collection once he had money to purchase and with gifts from friends, began to crowd the house. Wolf Man is reported as observing that Freud's consulting room reminded him not of a doctor's office but of an archaeologist's study; Wolf Man particularly noticed the Egyptian antiquities. Freud would himself compare psychoanalysis to archaeology, the exciting detecting within the patient's consciousness and unconsciousness of deep, long-buried fragments and layers; he was a great admirer and envied the life of Heinrich Schliemann, the discoverer of Troy's myth-laden antiquities, even seeing himself as the Schliemann of the mind. Freud also felt that his passion for antiquities related to his enigmatic sense of Jewishness, that the statuettes and plaques he surrounded himself with reminded him of a part of the world he would never visit, yet thought was somehow mysteriously his own. It was also, Gay feels, an addiction, like his smoking cigars. Freud told Fliess in 1897 that addictions like those to cigarettes and cigars are only substitutes for masturbation, the primal addiction. In full psychoanalytic mode, Gay himself ventures, perhaps rather playfully: "If Freud's helpless love for cigars attests to the survival of primitive oral needs, his collecting of antiquities reveals residues in adult life of no less primitive anal enjoyments" (Gay: 47–48, cf. 170–73, 326, 602).

The interest in Egypt so evident in the London Freud Museum intrigued me for quite nonpsychoanalytical reasons. It was not long before, in April 2000, that I had given the seminar paper focussing on Freud's *Moses and Monotheism*, the paper which had turned me into a monotheism-polytheism obsessive. Whether such obsession qualifies as an addiction in Freud's terms, and hence is a substitute for masturbation, apparently the primal addiction, I don't know.

Freud and Egyptophilia

Let's quickly reprise the context and theses of *Moses and Monotheism*; to his delight, Freud lived to see the English translation published (Gay: 643).

In January of 1935 Freud wrote to Lou Andreas-Salomé that he was investigating questions that had harried him through his life: what events, happenings, and personalities in the long past had created the particular character of the Jew; and how might we explain the very origin of religion. In the letter Freud sketched in his main idea: the Jews were in effect created by "the man Moses," Moses being not of Jewish birth but a high-ranking Egyptian and a follower and perhaps associate of the pharaoh Amenhotep IV, somewhere around the time of 1350 B.C.E. Freud says he will relate the development of Jewish religion and indeed religions in general to his psychoanalytical notions of the return of the repressed. He wished to explore the view that the strength of religion lies in its historical truth (Bernstein: 117–18).

Eccentrically, Freud placed two prefaces at the centre, or just off-centre, of the book. In the first preface Freud confides, apparently to himself, that while he had published in *Imago* the book's opening essays on Moses and the Jews, he could see no way of publishing the much longer last section, with its provocative material about the origins of religion, because it would endanger the position of psychoanalysis in Catholic Austria, whose practitioners might then be forbidden their work. "So," Freud mournfully notes, "I shall not publish this essay." The book was perhaps never to be seen in its whole form, or perhaps would be discovered long afterwards. This first preface was dated, "Written before March 1938." The second preface following immediately after is dated London, June 1938. Freud now reports to his readers that, because of the German invasion, he had had to leave "the city which from early childhood, through seventy-eight years, had been a home to me." He was now in "beautiful, free, generous England," where he found the kindliest welcome and a security that would permit him to at last make public the third essay. The only slightly baffling aspect for a foreigner of being in England was, Freud reports, frequently receiving letters expressing concern for the welfare of his soul and anxious to point him the way to Christ as well as to enlighten him about the future of Israel (Freud, 1967:66–71).

In his 1935 letter to Andreas-Salomé, Freud says his book will be a kind of "historical novel" (Bernstein: 117; see also de Certeau: ch. 9, "The Fiction of History: The Writing of *Moses and Monotheism*"; cf. Boer, 1999). *Moses and Monotheism* is a fantasia of creation stories, a text that creates characters, enigmas, riddles, delayed narrative effects, mysterious journeys of an idea. The narrator is engagingly self-reflexive, as if an archaeologist commenting to himself on how his dig is going, what is it revealing or not revealing, is it going in a wrong direction, are his tentative speculations on what has so far been found fruitful or dead ends or wrong. Occasionally he pauses for a rest, reviewing what he feels he has established as truth, repeating himself.

Exodus is a foundational story that is increasingly perceived as politically problematic, as ethically contradictory, not least in recent postcolonial theory inspired by Edward Said's wonderful essay "Michael Walzer's *Exodus and Revolution:* A Canaanite Reading," an essay that suggests the lineaments of a new, alternative creation story. Said points out that the narrative of Exodus has a vision of freedom for one people that is yet premised on defeat and even extermination for another, the Canaanites, those who are already in the promised land, a land which by divine injunction and sanction is to be conquered and occupied. Said sees the displaced and dispossessed Palestinians as the present-day Canaanites of the Middle East, part of a world history where Exodus has unfortunately proven all too influential, inspiring Puritans in New England to slay Native Americans or the Boers in South Africa to lay claim to huge areas of formerly held African lands (Said, 1988).

Said's view of Exodus as a frame-story for settler colonialism has been taken up and developed in relation to Israel, the United States, and Australia by a growing number of postcolonial theorists, in the work of Ella Shohat, Regina Schwartz, Deborah Bird Rose, Ann Curthoys, and Roland Boer (2001). Such readings relate the beginning of Exodus, with the Israelites fleeing bondage in Egypt, to the proposed end of their journey, enjoined by God to possess the lands of the Canaanites. As Regina Schwartz argues in *The Curse of Cain,* the Exodus story authorises a victimological narrative, the belief in world history that earlier bondage and persecution and suffering justifies later conquest, violence, and destruction; that if one has been a victim, one can never be a victimizer, and even if one victimizes others one somehow remains a victim (Schwartz: 55–62; see also Shohat: 140–41; Rose: 199–200, 203–5; Curthoys; Boer, 2001; Docker, 2001a: ch. 7).

Unlike such recent postcolonial theory, Freud is almost wholly admiring of the ethico-political legacy of Moses and Exodus for Judeo-Christian civilization. Yet Freud's conception of his hero and his rewriting of Exodus are also curiously Egyptological. In admiring Egypt, *Moses and Monotheism* questions a key aspect of the legacy of Exodus, that "Egypt" is the enemy of history, truth, progress, enlightenment, and civilization.

An Egyptocentric Monotheism

Let's recall the bold new creation story of Western civilisation, civilisation as Western, that the narrator of *Moses and Monotheism* sketches for us.

Freud's historical novel wavers between the polyphonic and the monologic, between an attractive uncertainty or at least seeming uncertainty and a rather absurd positivist certitude and authorial omniscience, asserting that Moses did indeed "live and that the exodus from Egypt, led by him, did in fact take place" (Freud, 1967:4).[1]

Freud suggests a new beginning for the story of Exodus, where Jahve is not present. In this new beginning we find that Moses is a noble and distinguished Egyptian, perhaps a prince, priest, or high official, a man of great abilities, ambitious, and energetic; he lives at the time of the pharaoh Amenhotep IV, whom Freud calls Ikhnaton. The young pharaoh, ruling only for seventeen years, believes in monotheism, the Aton religion, the first of its kind in the history of the world, the belief in one God. Very soon after his death in 1358 B.C.E., the new religion is, however, swept away and the memory of the monotheistic king is proscribed. Moses, a convinced adherent, is devastated. He decides to travel with his retainers, scribes, servants—his followers who will become known as the Levites—to a border region, perhaps Goshen, where certain Semitic tribes reside, tribes Freud refers to as a "throng of culturally inferior immigrants." He adopts the people as their leader, transferring to them Ikhnaton's Egyptian monotheism. The Semites can now carry forward Ikhnaton's aborted historic mission, as they journey "peacefully and without pursuit" away from Egypt toward Canaan (Freud, 1967:18, 24, 30–35, 38, 46).

Moses, this "great man," had heard that in Canaan "a capable people could seize new land." Later, however, the "savage Semites" decide to kill Moses, finding the strict monotheism he forces on them to be irksome. They abandon for a while the Egyptian Aton religion and meet up with other Jewish tribes who have adopted from the "Arabic tribe of Midianites" a volcano god, Jahve, originally, says Freud, an "uncanny, bloodthirsty demon who walks by night and shuns the light of day," the kind of god the people need to make them feel "strong enough to undertake the invasion of Canaan," "to conquer new lands by violence" (Freud, 1967:33, 38, 43–44, 58, 61, 78).

It's interesting how much Freud's text, however unwittingly, can be seen here, in its calling attention to the violence of the Jewish conquest of the land of Canaan, anticipating contemporary postcolonial critique of Exodus.

Gradually, the narrator of *Moses and Monotheism* feels sure, because of the productive effects of guilt, the people ethically work on themselves to

---

[1] The Egyptologist Jan Assmann (2, 163) writes that Moses might conceivably have historically existed, but there is no evidence that he ever did exist; his being is entirely legendary and mythological. Cf. Thompson: ch. 13.

re-adopt and internalise Moses' religion, and furthermore work on their conceptions of God so that finally Jahve is recreated in the image of Moses. Freud establishes for history a pattern of murder, guilt, resurrection, where Moses' death repeats the murder by the sons of the primal father. Moses becomes the figure of the Redeemer, which Christ will later also be. Freud himself, facing death in Vienna, unable to publish the vital last part of the argument, will perhaps one day also be a Redeemer, as he turns out to be in London, where he can bring to the world the vital knowledge of the true source of Judaism, Christianity, and European monotheistic civilization. Such knowledge will counter the ethnocentrism of the children of Israel, who will have to stop repressing that their lawgiver was a "great stranger," as indeed Jahve had been a stranger, originally an Arab Midianite god (Freud, 1967:46–47, 62–63, 77–78).[2]

Such knowledge will also counter the ethnocentrism of Europe in general, which will have to cease being hostile toward those it considers non-European, for Jews and Christians and indeed Muslims all should recognise together that in their monotheism they possess a common Egyptian religious and intellectual origin (Freud, 1967:118).

Freud tells us that the pharaoh Ikhnaton developed in his short reign the "idea of a universal god." Ikhnaton stressed the "ethical aspects" of the sun god, Aton, all-loving as he was all-powerful. Ikhnaton described himself in his inscriptions as always "living in Maat," that is, truth and justice, and he set humanity as its highest aim a life of truth and justice. The new religion elevated the god Aton as an abstraction, suggesting a historically new spiritualisation. Mosaic religion, Freud feels, then developed Ikhnaton's precepts into an even more rigorous monotheism. In prohibiting the making of any image of God, Mosaic religion "signified subordinating sense perception to an abstract idea"; it was and is a "triumph of spirituality over the senses." In compelling the Jews to worship an invisible God, a God who would have neither a name nor a countenance, the Mosaic prohibition created the Jews as a people of the book; a scattered people were held together by the study of written records, as in the Torah. Spiritual endeavour, instinctual renunciation, and respect for intellectual work became their ideals. By such "moral asceticism," a "constantly increasing instinctual renunciation," the Jews were able to reach "ethical heights that had remained inaccessible to the other peoples of antiquity." And the beneficiaries of this advance are not only the Jews in their life to the present but also Christianity and civilization (Freud, 1967:19, 22, 23n2, 26, 58, 61–62, 73, 144, 147, 158, 164).

---

[2] Cf. Gay (607, 646). Assmann (159) notes that Freud persisted with his claim that Moses was killed even though the Old Testament scholar Ernst Sellin, his historical source, had "given up his theory."

Freud's antiocular claims here, conventional as they are, are highly contestable, including within Jewish tradition itself, in rabbinic Judaism, in Kabbalistic mysticism, by Spinoza, and in contemporary hermeneutics like that of the theologian Daniel Boyarin (Spinoza: 63, 70–72, 228, 233; Boyarin: 534–43; Docker, 2001b).

Contra Polytheism?

Freud's exaltation of monotheism is accompanied by loud contempt—perhaps rather too loud—for its presumed opposite. Yet we have to append a large query mark over Freud's antipolytheism.

Let's return to the opening scene in *Moses and Monotheism* where Freud violently attacks ancient Egyptian religion, which he refers to as an "unlimited polytheism." Freud complains of a "bewildering mass of deities." Some are personifications of great natural powers like heaven and earth, sun and moon. We find an important power such as Maat alongside a "grotesque creature like the dwarfish Bes." Most of them are local gods that have not yet overcome their origin in totem animals. The names of these gods and the hymns in their praise identify them with one another in ways that are hopelessly confusing. Magic and ceremonial, amulets and formulas dominated the service of the deities, as they did the daily life of the Egyptians. The Egyptian had an insatiable zest for making images of his gods in clay, stone, and metal. Such a religion, Freud disdains, is very near to "the primitive" in terms of its "intellectual level" compared to monotheism, which has soared to the heights of sublime abstraction (Freud, 1967:18–20, 22).

Freud's late contempt for polytheism is surprising, if we think biographically of Freud the working psychoanalyst in his rooms in Vienna and London. Peter Gay says that Freud's "antique objects gave him sheer visual and tactile pleasure; Freud caressed them with his eyes or fondled them as he sat at his desk." Freud at times, Gay notes, would take a new acquisition to the dining room to study and handle it there (Gay: 171).

In these terms, Freud appears very much like the polytheistic Egyptian he despises in *Moses and Monotheism:* the psychoanalyst treats the almost unlimited and confusing number of statues that crowd his rooms in highly ceremonial ways, as if they have magical significance; the statues are made from a variety of tactile materials; the psychoanalyst is fond of fondling them, caressing them, with an insatiable zest for taking visual pleasure in their presence and ubiquity. Freud the psychoanalyst as archaeologist felt that the antiquities assisted his speculations and explanations, particularly when most puzzled by a patient. Gay tells us that, bewildered by Rat Man's thoughts and revelations, Freud asked Rat Man to observe and think about the antiquities in the consulting room (Gay: 264). Further, Freud associates his antique statuary with food, as in his habit of introducing new acquisitions to the dining room. In his daily life, then, Freud himself did not construct a hierarchy of faculties; he did not subordinate sense perception to abstraction; he did not divorce intellectual work from the visual, the tactile, or the olfactory as with food and the places where food is enjoyed. On the contrary, he associated thinking through problems and arriving at new ideas and perspectives with an *interaction* of abstraction and the senses; thought and images and the body; sight, touch, smell, taste. His rooms were a sensorium. And in analysing the obsessions and fetishes of others, he was surely always sharply aware as he caressed and fondled his beloved pagan idols of his own obsessions and fetishes.

In *Downcast Eyes*, Martin Jay has evoked the contradictoriness and inconsistencies of attitudes in the Western intellectual tradition to the relationship between knowledge and vision; sometimes vision is celebrated as illuminating, at other times suspected of being dangerously complicit with political and social oppression. I think such inconsistency and contradictoriness is evident in Freud, and not only in Freud.

Freud's daily valuing of sensuous vision and touch in his rooms as stimulants to reflection, contemplation, and interpretation—of the confusing, puzzling, bewildering, that which appears to resist comprehension and explanation—has striking similarities with strands of twentieth-century cultural theory, not least (working backwards) in Derrida, Bakhtin, and Benjamin. We might fancifully think here of Derrida's creation story of deconstruction as a desire to contest Freud's narrowing view of polytheism in *Moses and Monotheism,* where Freud praises monotheism for associating knowledge with writing as words on the page; monotheism is to be prized because it denies images and representations. In *Of Grammatology* Derrida desires to see "writing" as evident in a variety of textual forms, including the visual: in everything that gives rise to inscription, past and present, as in the pictographic, the ideographic, the hieroglyphic, the cuneiform, in choreography, cinematography, music, sculpture. Writing can be articulated in graphic substances, in materials such as wood, wax, stone, ink, metal, vegetables, and with instruments like points and brushes (Derrida, 1980:3, 9, 68, 87, 89, 129; Docker, 1994:136).

We might also think of Bakhtin's argument in *Rabelais and His World* that in the Renaissance the complex philosophy and cosmology of carnival and carnivalesque were produced in the continuous interactions of humanist knowledge, science, worldly political experience, and advanced literary techniques with folk traditions of the ludic and grotesque body, in marketplace drama, feasting, spectacle, festivals, processions (Bakhtin: 72–74).

We might also think of *The Origin of German Tragic Drama*, where Benjamin produces complex approaches to knowledge from his study of seventeenth-century German mourning plays and baroque art. Benjamin sees in such baroque visuality in art and theatre an allegorical mode where there is a teasing tension between the apparent clarity of an idea expressed in emblematic form and the multitude of accompanying illustrative examples, images, representations, which multiply meanings so that they become increasingly multivalent. Benjamin refers us to the doubleness of allegory, which is at once "convention and expression; and both are inherently contradictory." Allegory, says Benjamin firmly in reply to neoclassical, some romantic, and modernist dismissal of it, "is not a playful illustrative technique, but a form of expression, just as speech is expression, and, indeed, just as writing is." And in baroque allegory, says Benjamin, even the "written word tends towards the visual" (Benjamin: 162, 175–76).

The "perspective of allegory," says Benjamin, is a "development of myth." In defending allegory against its frequent devaluation in literary and cultural history, Benjamin is also I think concerned to evoke the strengths of polytheism and polytheistic mythology, given that allegory arose as polytheistic mythology's accompanying mode of interpretation. Especially in the section "Allegory and Trauerspiel," Benjamin wishes to draw attention to the philosophical importance of the allegorical tradition, in particular the ways the "false appearance of totality is extinguished" by the baroque interest in ruins, fragments, remnants, dispersal, death, corpses, decay. Benjamin contrasts medieval allegory, Christian and simply didactic, with Renaissance allegory, which drew on Egyptian and Greek antiquity. Benjamin draws our attention to the Renaissance allegorical tradition of female figures as in Ripa's *Iconologia* (1603). He refers us to the interest of the Renaissance humanist scholars in an allegorical exegesis of hieroglyphs, especially the enigmatic pictorial signs on obelisks, medallions, columns, triumphal arches. In seventeenth-century baroque drama and art the Renaissance interest in Egyptian and Greek allegory and polytheistic myth is entwined as well with Christian "pictorial languages." Baroque allegory's stock of "visual requisites" became "unlimited" : "With every idea the moment of expression coincides with a veritable eruption of images, which gives rise to a chaotic mass of metaphors." The many obscurities in the connection between meaning and sign, where one and the same object can just as easily signify a virtue as a vice and therefore more or less anything, were held in the baroque tradition to surpass even the Egyptians with new subtleties (Benjamin: 163, 166, 168–69, 171–78, 247n21; cf. Curthoys and Docker, 1999).

The individual, independent fragments of speech in baroque theatre, says Benjamin, acquire "a dignity equal to that of gods, rivers, virtues and similar natural forms which fuse into the allegorical" (Benjamin: 208). Perhaps Freud's rooms, where their curious topography of multiple gods was the scene of his patients' often bewildering speech fragments, were also a kind of baroque allegorical theatre; a theatre of ruins, psychoanalytic, archaeological, mythic, which he hoped might surpass even the Egyptians with new subtleties in the figuration of origins, history, mind, body, world, and cosmos.

To clarify this sequence of my argument: Freud in my view was a polytheist in his life and works (as in *Civilization and Its Discontents*), whose psychoanalytic insight and speculations gained much from diurnal sensuous contact with images and representations of Egyptian (and other ancient) deities. It was such lifelong wisdom that he attempted to suppress and deny in his last testament, but even in *Moses and Monotheism* there are interesting contradictory moments.

The Disaster of Monotheism

In occasional asides in *Moses and Monotheism* Freud evokes the new monotheism as a religion of prohibition and enforcement, brought to its new adherents from the top down. With its entry into the world, the belief in one God, Freud concedes, gave birth to "religious intolerance, which was foreign to antiquity long before this and for long after." Ikhnaton effaced the word *god* whenever it was used in the plural. He ignored the death-god Osiris and the concern for the realm of the dead that was so important in popular Egyptian religion. And, like Ikhnaton, the man Moses was an enlightened despot, giving commands and forcing his religion on the Jews. Freud notes that from its first appearance monotheism was a kind of reaction-formation, defining itself against that which it forebade or prohibited or persecuted or attempted to erase from history (Freud, 1967:24–26, 28–29, 31, 35, 41, 82).

Where Freud nonetheless is willing to overlook the violence of repudiation in monotheism, Jan Assmann in *Moses the Egyptian* regards the advent of the notion of counterreligion as a continuing disaster for Western history. Assmann argues that Akhenaten introduced into the ancient world what he calls the Mosaic Distinction, the monotheistic presumption of true and false religion, and that such a "murderous distinction" worked its destructive way forward in terms of ever more distinctions and subdistinctions, between Jews and Gentiles, Old and New Testaments, Christians and pagans, Muslims and unbelievers, Catholics and Protestants, Calvinists and Lutherans. Monotheism introduced the notion that true religion lived by rejecting everything as paganism that went before and which is outside of itself. The Mosaic Distinction found enduring narrative form and discursive normative power in Exodus, where Egypt and all it represented, especially the worship of images of multiple gods, is to be henceforth regarded as the religiously wrong, as horror, falsehood, idolatry, and apostasy. Monotheism also introduced the notion of canonization, of certain texts as canonical and others as heresy (Assmann: 1–7, 12, 170, 211).

Yet, Assmann suggests, there have been periodic attempts to overcome the Mosaic Distinction that Exodus creates between "Egypt" and "Israel," especially in the Enlightenment, and particularly in the thought of Spinoza.

When Spinoza, Assmann says, abolished the distinction between God and Nature, he was interpreted as opposing the Mosaic Distinction between Israel as Truth and Egypt as Error. Egypt could be positively evaluated for its notions of the One and the Many, the invisible creator god and the many visible gods of creation. Such notions could permit recognition within Egyptian religion of continuities between polytheism and monotheism, a fruitful tension, a wealth of paradoxicality, treasures of ambiguity. Through Spinoza's concepts there could be a rediscovery of one of the great cultural and historical achievements of ancient Egyptian and Mesopotamian polytheism, their practices and modes of cosmopolitanism and translatability. Assmann refers us to the international character of the religions of the ancient Near East, where, by means of mythical narratives and theocosmological speculation and beautiful verse, the names of gods could be translated from one society to another (Assmann: 8, 20, 45–54, 136, 168, 193, 217).

Jesus in Egyptology

> ... *may you visit many Egyptian cities*
> *to gather stores of knowledge from their scholars.*
> "Ithaka" (Cavafy: 36)

Moses and Monotheism is an Egyptophilic novel: the Jews are indeed a chosen people, but they were chosen by the "magnificent" Moses, who gave to the Jewish people an Egyptian religion though not *the* Egyptian religion (Freud, 1967:21, 76). For Freud, it was ancient monotheistic Egypt that created the wisdom of the ages, however much for long periods hidden or suppressed or displaced. *Moses and Monotheism* contests the more usual epistemological desire of Egyptology, to recognise that it was ancient polytheistic Egypt that created the wisdom of the ages, however much for long periods hidden or suppressed or displaced (think of that remarkable romancing of Egypt, Martin Bernal's *Black Athena*).

If for Freud Moses was an Egyptian, could it be that Jesus is also of Egyptian origin? In this creation story, Jesus will emerge not as a historical figure but as entirely mythological, his beginnings in polytheistic Egypt, in the figure of Osiris, the great death-god ignored and suppressed by the monotheistic Pharaoh Akhenaten.

In the near-millennial year of 1999 appeared Timothy Freke and Peter Gandy's *The Jesus Mysteries: Was the Original Jesus a Pagan God?*, whose authors embark on a dangerous Odyssean journey around the Mediterranean ancient and modern, facing entrenched institutional power and orthodoxy, armed only with the delight of speculation, with controversial and provocative questions, their ship of knowledge tossed by riddle and enigma, lured by disinformation, decoys, traps. Everywhere was darkness and mist created by accretions of obfuscation. In the millenarian traditions of apocalypse, Freke and Gandy wish to rectify a mighty wrong, to rescue humanity from disaster. What they call Literalist Christianity, proclaiming itself the only true faith, has violently destroyed societies, religions, and civilizations across the world. Yet the central claim of Literalist Christianity, that paganism and Christianity, polytheism and monotheism, are in absolute opposition, may be dramatically less than true. "Our desire," Freke and Gandy affirm, "is not to attack Christianity, but to point to the possibility of it regaining something it has lost—the Inner Mysteries which reveal the secrets of Gnosis" (Freke and Gandy: 95, 254, 304, 307–9).

Freke and Gandy see themselves as "detectives," on the verge of cracking a whodunnit, about to uncover one of history's great miscarriages of justice. Like tricksters, they "dare to think the unthinkable." They will search out the profane secrets of institutional *historia sacra*. From their reading in new scholarship and their own researches, they realize that they are stumbling onto what has been only rarely recognised since Mediterranean paganism as a geocultural system was savaged by Literalist Christianity over a millennium and a half before: that there are astonishing similarities even unto tiny details between the story of Jesus and pagan myths of godmen and redeemers—similarities such as baptism as rebirth in water; the sign of the fish; a purifying flood; sacred geometry as in the figure of seven or twelve; divine communion, the rite of eating the body and drinking the blood of a revered god; the Madonna and child, and the three Marys; the notion of an afterlife; the divination of an ineffable one God who cannot be represented; the intuition of a holy trinity, the sacred One which is yet Three; the concept of Logos, the One Soul of the Universe, the Daemon which is within each one of us (Freke and Gandy: 1–3, 13, 44, 49, 51, 59–60, 70–72, 87–90, 94–97, 100–103, 141, 205, 256).

Their text will unfold for us this "process of discovery," stories that involve an intricate "continuum" of paganism and Egyptology, Gnosticism and Christianity. As each door opens and light pours in, they rush to the next, not without personal misgivings and fear, for they admit that they were "brought up in a culture which portrays paganism and Christianity as entirely antagonistic religious perspectives." They are often stunned and shocked themselves, as well as intrigued and surprised, by what they find (Freke and Gandy: 2–3, 12, 308).

They hope (as, in its way, Freud's project in *Moses and Monotheism*) to release into modernity repressed knowledge of what goes back to humanity's very beginnings and is "the very source of civilization." Above all they wish to recover the historical greatness of the ancient pagan Mystery religions and of Gnosticism, which was closely associated with these religions. The Mystery religions, they work out, were composed of exoteric Outer Mysteries, consisting of myths which were common knowledge to the populace and rituals that were open to anyone who wished to participate in them. There were also esoteric Inner Mysteries, which contained sacred mystical secrets known only to those who had undergone powerful processes of initiation, processes which could bring about personal transformation and spiritual enlightenment. It was the philosophers who were the spiritual masters of the Inner Mysteries, for the pagan Mystery religions inspired the finest minds of the ancient world (Freke and Gandy: 4, 27).

It was the philosophers as well who maintained and passed on the vital knowledge throughout the Mediterranean and classical world; and such philosophers were at once sages, scientists, magicians, miracle workers, healers, and priests, often suspected and persecuted by power and authority. Pythagoras, travelling to Egypt in the sixth century B.C.E., spent twenty-two years in the temples becoming an initiate of the Egyptian Mysteries. Returning to Greece he preached all the wisdom of Egypt, attracting followers who set about creating a Greek Mystery religion modelled on the Egyptian Mysteries. The indigenous wine god Dionysus, a minor deity in Hesiod and Homer, was transformed into a Greek embodiment of Osiris the preeminent godman of the Egyptian Mysteries. This historical transformation achieved by Pythagoras and his followers would be confirmed by Herodotus when he travelled to Egypt nearly five centuries before him who would became known as Christ. In Egypt Herodotus observed a huge festival held annually on the shores of a sacred lake in the Nile Delta, enacting a drama, a passion play, the death and resurrection of Osiris. Herodotus perceived that the Passion of Osiris was the very same drama that initiates could see enacted for them at Eleusis as the Passion of Dionysus: "The Egyptian myth of Osiris," Freke and Gandy decide, "is the primal myth of the Mystery godman and reaches back to prehistory," establishing its "perennial philosophy" (Freke and Gandy: 27–28, 36, 77, 228).

Freke and Gandy admire what they perceive as the internationalism and cosmopolitanism of the ancient world. In this world the figure whose collective identity was referred to as Osiris-Dionysus could be and was easily translated into other Mediterranean cultures, becoming Attis, Adonis, Bacchus, Mithras. Such figures were important in both the Outer and Inner Mysteries. Such figures were, like Osiris, both men and gods. Like Osiris they might experience cruel persecution, death, and mutilation, and hence could sympathize with human beings in their sickness and suffering; like Osiris they could conquer death, and so hold out the hope for humanity that it too could overcome death in a desired afterlife. The initiates of Osiris-Dionysus in the Inner Mysteries could go further. For such initiates, these great godmen could be interpreted in complex allegorical ways. In identifying with the death and resurrection of Osiris-Dionysus, the initiates could symbolically die to their lower earthly nature and be reborn; they could be resurrected into a higher ethical and spiritual life in this life (Freke and Gandy: 28, 30–31, 232).

Freke and Gandy wish also to uncover the fateful historical process by which Literalist Christianity helped destroy the pagan world and its Mystery religions. In their recreation, a key if unwitting part is played by the Gnostics, who should nevertheless be reestablished as revered figures in religious history. Freke and Gandy realize that the early Christian community was for centuries not unified, but composed of a whole spectrum of different and competing schools. In particular the Gnostics came to be opposed by the Literalists, who insisted that the Jesus story is a record of historical events, and whose beliefs were adopted by the Roman Empire in the fourth century C.E. The Literalist and narrowly authoritarian Roman Church would persecute out of existence, memory, and textual knowledge the Gnostics. Yet it was the Gnostics, Freke and Gandy feel, who had had the imagination and learning to create the figure of Jesus in the first place. As "mystics and creative freethinkers," anarchic and egalitarian, tolerant and individualistic, bold and subtle, literary and poetic, they were hated by the bishops of the Literalist Church, and their many fascinating gospels were deliberately excluded from the narrow canon of the New Testament, until that remarkable event in modern history, the chance discovery in 1945 of a whole library of Gnostic texts, in a cave near Nag Hammadi in Egypt (Freke and Gandy: 8–9, 13, 109, 252, 259–60).

The Gnostics emerge for Freke and Gandy as cosmopolitan hellenized Jewish intellectuals (they particularly mention Philo of Alexandria), who were concerned by the crisis of Judaism brought on by failed nationalist revolts and their disastrous aftermath. In this time of peril for their religion (the Romans having in 70 C.E. laid waste Jerusalem), the Gnostics crafted a Jesus figure, a redeemer, who was a Jewish version of the pagan godman Osiris-Dionysus. They hoped that their fellow Jews would cease to pursue a political strategy for independence from Empire that was leading to their violent destruction. Rather, they might revere a godman whose death and resurrection was allegorical and who could hold out the hope for all Jews that spiritual transformation was possible in the present, within themselves where Jesus could be found, in self-knowledge. The Gnostics were profoundly versed in and attracted to many aspects of pagan knowledge, including its valorisation of powerful female figures and wisdom; they shared with the pagan world an admiration for the goddess Sophia, and women were important in Gnostic religious practice, including as priests. Gnostics drew from the pagans a twofold division of Outer and Inner Mysteries. Some Gnostics believed that their Outer Mysteries concerned the godman Jesus, but their secret Inner Mysteries focussed on the passion and suffering of the goddess Sophia, a tragic figure who, just as Isis sought Osiris, searched desperately for Jesus. Gnostics imagined that all watery substances were tears shed by Sophia. For the

Gnostics, the Mysteries of Jesus, a synthesis of pagan and Jewish mythologies and teachings, superseded the Law of the Jewish God Jehovah (Freke and Gandy: 10–14, 110–15, 119–21, 162, 207–9, 222–23, 251, 256, 260–61, 266–67, 276).

Freke and Gandy mourn what they see as one of history's least fortunate ironies, that the Gnostic creation of a Jewish godman was taken up not by the mass of Jews, who indeed rejected the idea of such a redeemer, but by non-Jewish Literalists who more and more strongly believed that Jesus actually existed, that he had a biography, was known in history by his disciples, had a habitation and a name. Further, Freke and Gandy suggest that while the Gnostics believed that the Jesus story was to be interpreted allegorically and mystically, there was a powerful historicist logic in Judaism, a belief that its founding sacred stories like Genesis and Exodus were historically true. This logic came to possess the Literalist Christians, who moreover knew nothing of the Inner Mysteries. The Literalist Christians accepted as orthodoxy and dogma literal versions of the Outer Mysteries that were concerned with the rituals, mythical acts, and miracles of a godman. While the Gnostics flourished for a long while where they had originated, in Alexandria, until violently suppressed in the fourth and fifth centuries, Literalism gathered strength in those areas of the empire that were cut off from the masters of Gnosis in the East, eventually becoming centred in autocratic, tyrannical Rome itself. Where Gnosticism had been pluralistic, Literalist Christianity triumphed in the fourth century as a religion of obedience and terror, and even today, Freke and Gandy feel, while modern Christianity is composed of countless diverse sects and schisms, they nearly all of them, Catholics, Orthodox, Protestants, Non-Conformists, are fundamentally formed by the Literalism that took historical shape in the fourth century. Still today most Christians base their faith on the historical existence of Jesus. The historical disaster of Christianity in world history is that if Jesus is taken as the one and only Son of God who requires the faithful to acknowledge his being as unique historical event, then Christianity must be in ceaselessly destructive opposition to all other religions who do not observe this claim to historicity (Freke and Gandy: 121, 242, 249–52, 266, 301, 303, 308).

Freke and Gandy look forward in utopian spirit to a time in the new millennium when the ancient-world conversations between paganism and Gnostic Christianity can be revived, reanimated, recreated.

Conclusions

Clearly in this essay I prefer the creation stories of Jan Assmann's *Moses the Egyptian* and Freke and Gandy's *The Jesus Mysteries*. Certainly I enjoy and have been stimulated to new thinking by the exhilarating quirkiness of

Freud's *Moses and Monotheism*. But Freud increasingly in this "historical novel" came to claim absolute historical truth for his wonderful tales, his hunches, guesses, leaps, conjectures, and inventions. In this sense, Freud in *Moses and Monotheism* becomes part of and lends his authority to a potent combination of positivism and Literalist Christianity. He also lends his authority to support a Western mythos, that thinking through and with myths must be an inferior mode of knowledge compared to the (claimed) purity of abstract reason. In this creation story, Western Judeo-Christian civilization advanced when it recognised that to think through and with myths is a primitive childhood stage of its civilization, fortunately left behind when Greece developed philosophy separate from mythology, and when Judeo-Christianity established that its faith is based on history, not myth.

I prefer the creation stories of Freke and Gandy's *The Jesus Mysteries* because their "historical novel," in a carnivalesque gesture, turns around these foundational Western propositions—still foundational despite the many persuasive critiques in cultural and political theory (see Benjamin: 27–29, 31–32, 43, 46; De Man; Derrida, 1982; Connolly, 1993; Sandywell; Curthoys and Docker, 1997; Chakrabarty; Bennett). Freke and Gandy suggest that Jesus is not a historical figure, and that to conceive of him and the stories about him as historical is absurd and fantastical. They further suggest that the pagan philosophers were far more sophisticated and worldly than the Literalist Christians because they always recognised that religious figures like Osiris, Dionysus, Attis, Adonis, Bacchus, Mithras, are mythological and that the stories surrounding them were to be interpreted with allegorical subtlety. The pagan philosophers were rightly disdainful of literalism and the canonical cast of mind as naïve, credulous, bizarre, simple-minded, primitive, ridiculous, narrow, small-minded, superficial. The pagan philosophers saw myths as a fertile poetics, as stories that could be endlessly and daringly and adventurously reworked, recombined, changed, adapted; they were to be reinterpreted in individual, surprising ways. And so too did the Gnostics in relation to their poetics of a pagan-Judaic mythological figure they called Jesus (Freke and Gandy: 5, 10–11, 31, 61–62, 70, 76, 97–99, 136–39, 190, 288–89).

Clearly also I savour the portrait, in Assmann's *Moses the Egyptian* as in *The Jesus Mysteries*, of the ancient pagan Mediterranean world as enacting principles of cosmopolitanism and translatability. Such cosmopolitanism—such antinationalism—relates to Jewish history both ancient and contemporary. If the Gnostics were indeed hellenized, cosmopolitan antinationalists, then I admire them, for I think nationalist revolts, carried out by a few in the name of all, including the Jewish revolts against the Roman Empire, inevitably bring down disaster, destruction, and atrocity upon their peoples. (I think the same of twentieth-century Irish history, that the nationalism of the republican movement, in the revolting actions of the

IRA, has brought down only misery, suffering, and atrocity on the Irish people.) The Zionist movement, drawing its discursive and ideological sources from nineteenth-century European nationalism as well as appealing to the pathos of the ancient revolts, is an apparently successful contemporary nationalist movement that secured a state, claimed to be in the name of all Jews. The Zionist state of Israel carries out nationalist principles of ethnic purity, the appallingly destructive desire to make of a society one people, one religion, one ethnicity, in full exclusive ownership of one land. In these terms, I prefer the cosmopolitanism of Jewish intellectuals of the ancient Mediterranean world like Philo and Josephus, living in a time of great empires.

To defend empires in contemporary cultural theory is to risk heresy. It's worth noting that Freud in his polytheistic text *Civilization and Its Discontents* wrote: "To the Romans ... religious intolerance was something foreign" (Freud, 1989:73). And Assmann refers to the "kind of cosmopolitanism and its belief in the translatability of religious ideas and denominations which flourished in the Roman Empire" (136).

I very much admire Assmann's overall creation story whereby humanity could recognise not only cosmopolitanism and translatability but also the notion of the One and the Many as gifts of the ancient polytheistic world to modernity (34, 193, 217).

Yes, I have misgivings about Freke and Gandy's *The Jesus Mysteries* as creation story and historical novel. I think it too much unifies the pagan world, as if there are no discontinuities, conflicts, oppositions, in approaches to knowledge between its key philosophers and philosophical schools. *The Jesus Mysteries* presents ancient knowledge as if it coheres around a Platonic distinction between body and mind. In presenting the pagan Mysteries within an Egyptological frame, it offers a story of humanity whereby its true philosophy, its perennial wisdom, emerges from the one part of the world; this is Egyptocentrism, or Middle Eastcentrism, or Mediterraneancentrism (as it were), a quite conventional narrative of world history. In this sense, *The Jesus Mysteries* is insufficiently catholic toward polytheism and animism in all the world's histories and cultures, through space and time.

Works Consulted

Assmann, Jan
  1997   *Moses the Egyptian: The Memory of Egypt in Western Monotheism*. Cambridge, Mass.: Harvard University Press.

Bakhtin, Mikhail
  1984   *Rabelais and His World*. Bloomington: Indiana University Press.

Benjamin, Walter
1996 *The Origin of German Tragic Drama.* Trans. John Osborne. London: Verso.

Bennett, Jane
2001 *The Enchantment of Modern Life: Attachments, Crossings, and Ethics.* Princeton: Princeton University Press.

Bernstein, Richard J.
1998 *Freud and the Legacy of Moses.* Cambridge: Cambridge University Press.

Boer, Roland
1999 "The Resurrection Engine of Michel de Certeau." *Paragraph* 22:199–212.

2001 *Last Stop Before Antarctica: The Bible and Postcolonialism in Australia.* Sheffield: Sheffield Academic Press.

Boyarin, Daniel
1990 "The Eye in the Torah: Ocular Desire in Midrashic Hermeneutic." *Critical Inquiry* 16:532–50.

Cavafy, C. P.
1992 *Collected Poems.* Rev. ed. Trans. Edmund Keeley and Philip Sherrard. Princeton: Princeton University Press.

Certeau, Michel de
1988 *The Writing of History.* Trans. Tom Conley. New York: Columbia University Press.

Chakrabarty, Dipesh
2000 *Provincializing Europe: Postcolonial Thought and Historical Difference.* Princeton: Princeton University Press.

Connolly, William E.
1993 *The Augustinian Imperative: A Reflection on the Politics of Morality.* London: Sage.

1999 *Why I Am Not a Secularist.* Minneapolis: University of Minnesota Press.

Curthoys, Ann
1999 "Expulsion, Exodus and Exile in White Australian Historical Mythology." Pp. 1–18 in *Imaginary Homelands.* Ed. Richard Nile and Michael Williams. St. Lucia: University of Queensland Press.

Curthoys, Ann, and John Docker
1997 "The Two Histories: Metaphor in English Historiographical Writing." *Rethinking History* 1:259–73.

1999 "Time, Eternity, Truth, and Death: History As Allegory." *Humanities Research* 1:5–26.

De Man, Paul
1979 "The Epistemology of Metaphor." Pp.11–28 in *On Metaphor.* Ed. Sheldon Sacks. Chicago: University of Chicago Press.

Derrida, Jacques
    1980   *Of Grammatology.* Baltimore: Johns Hopkins University Press.

    1982   "White Mythology: Metaphor in the Text of Philosophy." Pp. 207–71 in *Margins of Philosophy.* Chicago: University of Chicago Press.

Docker, John
    1994   *Postmodernism and Popular Culture: A Cultural History.* Melbourne: Cambridge University Press.

    1995   "Rethinking Postcolonialism and Multiculturalism in the *fin de siècle.*" *Cultural Studies* 9:409–26.

    1998   "His Slave, My Tattoo: Romancing a Lost World." Pp. 181–200 in *Unfinished Journeys: India File from Canberra.* Ed. Debjani Ganguly and Kavita Nandan. Adelaide: Centre for Research for New Literatures in English.

    2001a   *1492: The Poetics of Diaspora.* London: Continuum.

    2001b   "Softening Monotheism, Exploring Polytheism—Moses, Spinoza, and Freud." In *Demoralizing Theory!* Ed. Jane Bennett and Michael J. Shapiro. Forthcoming.

Freke, Timothy, and Peter Gandy
    2000   *The Jesus Mysteries: Was the Original Jesus a Pagan God?* London: Thorsons.

Freud, Sigmund
    1967   *Moses and Monotheism.* New York: Vintage Books.

    1989   *Civilization and Its Discontents.* Trans. James Strachey. Intro. Peter Gay. New York: Norton.

Gay, Peter
    1988   *Freud: A Life for Our Time.* London: Dent.

Jay, Martin
    1993   *Downcast Eyes: The Denigration of Vision in Twentieth-Century French Thought.* Berkeley and Los Angeles: University of California Press.

Rose, Deborah Bird
    1996   "Rupture and the Ethics of Care in Colonized Space." Pp. 190–215 in *Prehistory to Politics: John Mulvaney, the Humanities and the Public Intellectual.* Ed. Tim Bonyhady and Tom Griffiths. Melbourne: Melbourne University Press.

Said, Edward W.
    1988   "Michael Walzer's *Exodus and Revolution:* A Canaanite Reading." Pp. 161–78 in *Blaming the Victims: Spurious Scholarship and the Palestinian Question.* Ed. Edward W. Said and Christopher Hitchens. London: Verso.

    1991   *The World, the Text, and the Critic.* London: Vintage.

Sandywell, Barry
    1996   *Presocratic Reflexivity: The Construction of Philosophical Discourse c. 600–450 BC.* London and New York: Routledge.

Schwartz, Regina M.
    1997   *The Curse of Cain: The Violent Legacy of Monotheism.* Chicago: University of Chicago Press.

Shohat, Ella
    1992   "Antinomies of Exile: Said at the Frontiers of National Narrations." Pp. 121–43 in *Edward Said: A Critical Reader.* Ed. Michael Sprinker. Oxford: Blackwell.

Spinoza, Baruch
    1989   *Tractatus Theologico-Politicus.* Trans. Samuel Shirley. Leiden: Brill.

Thompson, Thomas L.
    1999   *The Bible in History: How Writers Create a Past.* London: Jonathan Cape.

THE WORD SET IN BLOOD AND STONE: THE BOOK OF GOD FROM TRIBES TO KINGDOMS AND NATIONS

Paul James
Monash University

ABSTRACT

Evocation of the Bible has always played a role in nation formation and continues even in these late-modern secular times. On the return of the Stone of Destiny to postcolonial Scotland on St. Andrew's Day, 1996, a ceremony was held at St. Giles Cathedral to celebrate the national occasion. Crossing the fields of sacred liturgy to nationalist ideology, the Moderator of the General Assembly of the Church of Scotland addressed the congregation about the "long pilgrimage of years." Ironically, the Stone of Destiny, stolen exactly seven hundred years earlier by King Edward I, had lain all that time in another house of God, Westminster Abbey. Using the symbols of stone and the word as intersecting motifs, this article seeks to address the connection between the Bible and the process of nation formation. Attempting to include but go beyond the use of the content of liturgy in the invention of national tradition, the article examines the impact of the Bible as a central text in the changing form of association sustained in part by printing as a revolutionary mode of communication.

Evocation of the Bible has always played a role in nation formation and continues to do so even in these late-modern and postsacred times.[1] In the United States, the 2000 presidential election campaign was replete with references to the Book of God. Upon being selected by Al Gore as his presidential running mate, Joseph Lieberman called upon the Jewish Bible. "Dear friends," he said, "I am so full of gratitude at this moment. I ask you to allow me to let the spirit move me as it does to remember the words from Chronicles, which are to give thanks to God and to declare his name." In postcolonial Scotland on St. Andrew's Day, 1996, a service was held at St. Giles Cathedral to celebrate the return of the Stone of Destiny. It

---

[1] With thanks to Graeme James and Gary Bouma. The concept of "postsacred," like "postmodern," carries the prefix "post" in the sense of a formation that comes after and overlays prior formations without necessarily replacing them. The concepts *tribalism, traditionalism, modernism,* and *postmodernism* (and variations such as *late-modernism*) are used as the most general terms of a matrix of overlaying ontological formations.

was a national occasion through and through, a ritual occasion even more dramatic than the reopening of their Parliament after centuries of incorporation into Britain. At the service, a young person read in Gaelic from Genesis 28, telling the story of Jacob and his pillow of stone. Another youth read in Doric from John 1, describing the calling to faith of Saint Andrew, patron saint of Scotland, and his brother Simon Peter, *the rock*. The biblical-national connection, stone to stone, was intentional. Ironically, the Stone of Destiny, taken seven hundred years earlier by King Edward I, had lain all that time in another house of God—Westminster Abbey. There it had been used first as a symbol of the unity of the kingdom and then later the nation-state of Britain. It had been built into the gilt-wood chair used for the coronation of all its kings and queens, including the present Elizabeth II.

This stone—an extraordinary object which, as I will describe later, has its mythical origins in the Egypt of Exodus—is indicative of the way that religious iconography crosses the divide from traditional polity to modern nation-state. The Bible redounds with the lived metaphors of the word set in blood and stone, metaphors that modern nations will later take up. It exemplifies the overall argument of the essay that the nation formation involves *both* deep continuities and radical discontinuities with traditional (sacredly conceived) ways of life. This is easier to say than to theorise. Making this argument precise in its most general expression thus involves going in two simultaneous directions: first, that the discontinuity can be understood as a process of abstraction and reconstitution of prior ways of living in and understanding community and polity; second, running alongside the first but emphasising the continuity, that the nation as an abstract community of strangers—secular and horizontal—contradictorily *grounds* its subjectivities in the very categories that at another level of abstraction have been substantially reconstituted (James). Three such grounding categories are returned to throughout the essay: relations of embodied connection, times of sacred recollection, and places of enduring nature. The use of the concept of *grounding* here is intentional. It marks a clear distinction from the prominent modernist theorists of nationalism such as Ernest Gellner, Anthony Giddens, and even Benedict Anderson, who treat these categorical elements as the mere traditional *content*, refabricated for a modern context. By contrast, I am suggesting that these things still have categorical meaning as part of the contradictory form of the nation-state as abstract political community. This continuity has become clearer as the modern connection between nation and state has become problematised. In the contemporary world, I argue, embedded ontological categories have continuing significance for the nation, even as such evocations become less and less relevant to the state.

More particularly, drawing upon the symbols of the *word* and the *stone* as intersecting motifs, this essay seeks to address the connection between the Bible and the process of political formation from the kingdom to the nation. It argues that the Bible as one of the signifiers and practical expressions of the relationship between the sacred and the political-human has to be put right into the centre of understandings about the changing form of political community. It is not, however, that the Bible itself, or even practices projected in its name, are foundational for the formation of the nation and later nation-state. It is rather, by taking the (historically changing) place of the Bible seriously, that we can qualify the over-exuberant modernism of those who argue that the nation comes into being with the epochal translation of the sacred into the secular, that is, as the obliteration of the world of sacred nature-culture. The essay uses the Bible—in particular the motif of the communicable abstract Word—as a signifier of a broader argument that for traditional communities to become nations it is necessary that at one level they be abstracted from the cultural immediacies of place and face-to-face relations. It uses the second motif of the stone—in particular stones commemorating sacred ascension or transcendent mortality—to signify the intimately related argument that nation formation rests on a deep contradiction between the radical abstraction of social relations and a recalling of (culturally framed) "eternal" nature.

While Christianity finds a synthetic way of handling this ontological contradiction in the notion of the Word-Become-Flesh, the nation, I suggest, takes a different if apparently parallel path. The *modern* nation becomes an abstract community of strangers, but one that draws on the subjectivities and ideologies of abstract attachment to embodied others (blood-become-sacrifice) and actual places (soil-become-territory). Unlike Christianity, where Jesus is simultaneously God, God-Incarnate, and an embodied mortal man, no *one actual* person can stand in for the nation. National community, or more particularly each "ordinary person" within it, potentially carries that embodied connection. Certainly the nation throws up abstracted icons. Female figures lifted out of history were the most serious contenders for this role. Boadicea, Joan of Arc, or Marianne became iconic figures with their historical and particularised bodies left behind. However, it is indicative of the contradictory nature of the abstraction of the nation that its only lasting iconic representative is the "person" whose name we will "never" know—the Unknown Soldier. This abstracted soul, who like Jesus dies for us all, preferably has no remains, no bones to identify *him*. However, unlike Jesus with his body gone and the stone rolled away, the soul of the Unknown Soldier dwells beneath massive slabs of stones, firmly located in place. Even the postmodern versions of these cenotaphs depend on the symbolic stability of eternal nature.

The essay attempts to include but go beyond the use of the *content* and iconography of liturgy in the "invention" of national tradition. It thus briefly examines the impact of the Bible as a central text in the changing *form* of association sustained in part by printing as a revolutionary mode of communication. While the symbolic content of the Bible was important in the early modern period of Europe, I suggest that the printed word, including the Bible, as the outcome and indication of a changing dominant mode of communication was much more important. In particular, the Bible became the central and most ambiguous early "commodity" of print capitalism (Benedict Anderson's term). Martin Luther's sixteenth-century vernacular translations of the Bible, like its translations into Elizabethan English, marked a turning point in the process of nation formation. Much later, in nineteenth-century Africa, the Bible, by being translated into tribal languages, was an important catalyst for codification of the boundaries of the new community-polities. It was in the same century that the "Christian nation" of the United States was being proclaimed.

After this extended introduction, the essay divides into three sections, structured around the alternating themes of the form of the nation and the evocation of the nation. The first section emphasises questions of social form. It begins by examining the medieval formations of *natio* within the dominance of traditional forms of polity and community. This links into a concern to broaden and qualify Benedict Anderson's emphasis on print capitalism and what he misleadingly calls "the dusk of religious modes of thought" as the basis of the early stage of nation formation (Anderson: 11). The second section turns to evocation. It tracks the mythologies and commemorations of the nation from the medieval Stone of Scone to the modern chapels of the Fallen. The final section continues the emphasis on evocation and turns to the postcolonial United States as it breaks away from Britain to establish a republic and then a nation-state. Here my argument will be that by the nineteenth century the dominant culture of postcolonial America was using the Bible as a point of legitimation rather than as a sign of a covenant between nation and God.[2] This is not to suggest that the evocations became less intense. Quite the opposite. By the beginning of the twenty-first century the American Olympic basketball team could call a press conference to declare both their attachment to each other and their faith in the Bible. However, despite these nationalist evocations of the Book of God, it goes almost without saying that the new gods of Mammon,

---

2 Here sign is used in the Lévi-Straussian sense of a *lived sign* rather than as a reflexively understood *symbol*. A symbol in the present argument is more abstract in its reach than a sign. The nation is built on an increasingly self-conscious process of symbolic construction layered over a matrix of primordial signs.

Global Capitalism, and Liberal Freedom provided the dominant structural level of that rapidly changing national state as much as the others of the world.

The Form of the *Natio* and the Nation: Abstracting the Word

According to the classic theories in the field, it was not possible to think nationally before the emergence of modernity, whether it be through print capitalism and the demise of the hold of the sodalities of Christendom and the Islamic Ummah (Anderson) or through the uneven spread of capitalism (Nairn), industrialism (Gellner), institutional modernism (Giddens), or national politicisation (Hobsbawm). What all these modernist theories are right about is that it took a social upheaval of world-shattering proportions to *generalise* the possibility of thinking and acting nationally. However, what they systematically overlook are the lived references made to "nations" long before modernity. The use of the concept of *natio* goes back at least to the fourth-century *Vulgata Latina*. In that Latin translation of the Bible, Saint Jerome uses the concept to refer to the gentiles, and by the Middle Ages it becomes a term of self-naming. These were self-named *nationes* (the Latin term is used here intentionally to distinguish them from what came later) that are politically, historically, and culturally discontinuous with the much later modern nations. Notwithstanding this discontinuity, the way they came into being—the *form* of their constitution—has a level of continuity with the polity-communities of modernity.

When, for example, the medieval poet-cleric Petrarch writes *Italia Mia* (*My Italy*) he is writing centuries before Italy exists as a nation-state or even as an ethnically conceived community; nevertheless, his poem abstracts a "national" place for which he has a name. This is made possible, I suggest, because Petrarch—like Dante or Chaucer—is, at *one* level of his being, lifted out of traditionalism as the ontological frame of his dominant sense of space, time, and embodiment. It is not feasible here to pursue the many ways in which this intellectual distancing is overdetermined during the late-medieval period; however, most germane to our central theme, it was transcultural communities of scholars and clerics in places of learning and cloistered worship who first named *themselves* as *nationes*. At the University of Bologna, where Petrarch spent his student days, there was, almost from its inception toward the end of the twelfth century, a division of scholars into *nationes*. According to G. G. Coulton, the thirty-five *nationes* gradually coalesced into two groups—the Citramontanes and Ultramontanes, or those from the near- and other-side-of-the-mountain. A related, but distinct form of aggregation by *natio* was found in the meetings of the ecumenical church councils. The common thread between these two assertions of *natio* seems to be that they involved persons ambiguously abstracted from localised place. The process most often involved intellectuals or at least intellectually trained persons who, as clerics, transcribers of sacred texts, keepers of ledgers and the like, worked through techniques that allowed them in the capacity of their work to "transcend" time and space. In working through the word—that is, through writing as a medium of temporal storage and spatial crossing—they could address the dead and project forward to the future generations. Additionally, they were intellectually related groupings who in their living and working conditions, for example monasteries, were partially lifted out of the identity-conferring relations of kinship and familial *natus*. These were persons who found it important to distinguish between themselves and others, but were located in groups or settings where the distinguishing marks of old were insufficient or no longer available in the same way. For these persons, the concept of "this side of the mountain" or *Italia* came to be imbued with an ontological significance that drew upon but transcended face-to-face forms of social relations and subjectivity. Thus, even without a myth of common descent (*pace* Smith), strangers from this side of the Alps found common identity, named in contradistinction to those other strangers who came from elsewhere. This makes *traditional* national sentiment—if that is what we should call this subjectivity—qualitatively different in many fundamental respects from the *modern* nationalism of horizontal and generalised compatriotism. Nevertheless, despite this difference, is it a subjectivity that demands a broader explanation of nation formation than the modernist theorists currently allow? In the sense in which I am using these terms, modern nationalism is associated with a self-conscious politicization of the relation between community and polity, usually with the desire for a state for one's nation, whereas traditional national sentiment has no such associations. On the other hand, modern and traditional national subjectivities are related in that they both entail a process through which persons are, *at one level,* lifted out of the integral connections of face-to-face community and abstracted from messianic time and sacred place. It is this process that enables certain persons still living within the ontological formation of traditionalism—that is, intellectuals, clerics, poets—to name territorialised places or genealogically connected peoples as distinct and demarcated entities, bounded in territorial space and historical time and separable from other such similar entities.

One of the means by which this "lifting out" of identity occurs historically is through what can technically be described as the abstraction of the dominant mode of communication (see table 1). Put in a more down-to-earth way, we can say that as orality was overlaid by script as part of a more general change in the dominant modes of organising political community the nature of polity and community was transformed. Those persons who as scribes and interpreters of the word were at the centre of this emergent mode of practice were drawn into a new relationship to genealogical connection, sacred time and enduring nature. In this the Bible as both words of codified meaning and The Word of Truth gained a doubly powerful purchase on the literati, momentarily lifting them out of the here and now and enabling them to look back upon that world. This would explain how the Old Testament scholars find textual evidence to suggest that the Israelites were a *traditional* nation. Working on an even broader canvas, Jack Goody takes this point further. The technique of writing as a means of communication and storage of information is simultaneously a necessary condition of the formation of bureaucratic states and of the emergence of universalistic religions, namely those institutionalised religions such as Christianity, Islam, and Confucianism. It enabled a clear measure of separation of polity and religion from kinship as the dominant mode of organisation. I don't think that it is stretching this argument too far to say that just as religious and state institutions came into being through the same world-historical processes, so did the possibility of abstracting a community of people beyond the relative immediacy of face-to-face relations.

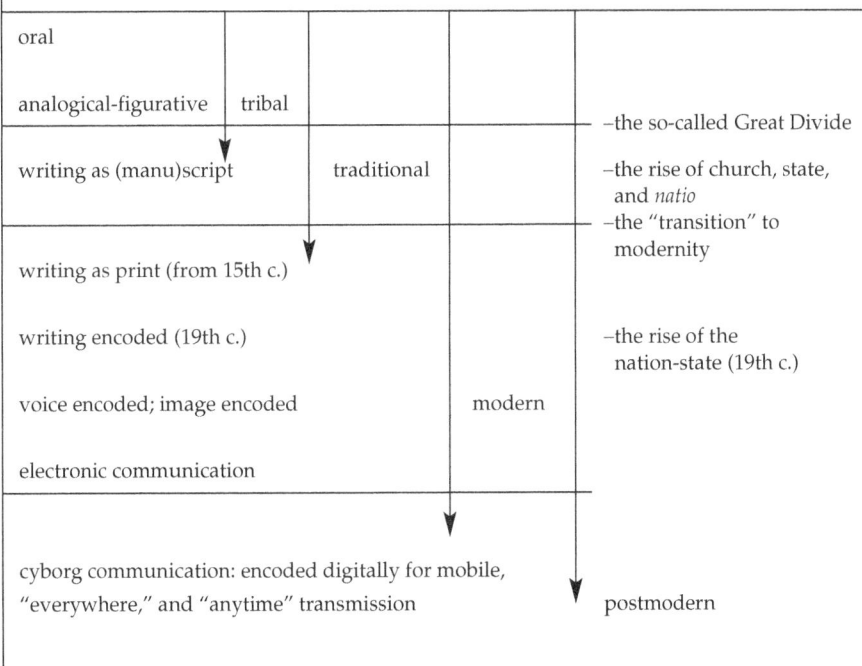

Table 1. Dominant forms of communication in different ontological formations.

(The modalities of communication are ordered here in terms of their formal abstraction of time, space, and embodiment. In practice, they are lived as levels-in-intersection, framed by the dominant mode of communication.)

All of this has the effect of qualifying Benedict Anderson's way of setting up his theory of the nation. While what I have been describing is a layered dialectic of continuity-and-discontinuity, a layering of ontological formations, he puts the pivotal emphasis on an epochal shift from traditionalism to modernism. Moreover, he focuses on a historically much later shift in the mode of communication—print—as it intersects with a new mode of production—capitalism. A fuller response to Anderson's path-breaking work would require working through the significance of other changing modes of practice beyond production and communication, including layers of transformations in the modes of exchange, organisation, and enquiry. However, for present purposes, all that I want to do is to qualify the epochal tone of his argument that the national consciousness becomes possible only when "three fundamental cultural conceptions, all of great antiquity, lost their axiomatic grip on men's minds" (Anderson: 36): firstly, the conception that a particular script-language such as Church Latin offered privileged access to the ontological truth; secondly, that monarchs ruled naturally as the divine legatees; and thirdly, that religious cosmology and history were indistinguishable. In beginning to qualifying this proposition, it is worth remembering that it was Church Latin that gave us the connected concepts of *natus* and *natio*. The Bible, for example, is replete with the naming of peoples, communities who at one level continued to live as twelve tribes long after they were named, but at a more abstract level as an interconnected whole. My argument, developed further in the next section, is firstly that none of Anderson's three conceptions was ever uncomplicatedly axiomatic even in traditional community-polities. Secondly, struggles over the (contingent) dominance of these conceptions continued long after the emergence of print-capitalism. As Benedict Anderson himself says, the Bible was at the centre of the printing and marketing furore associated with the sixteenth-century Reformation and Counter-Reformation. If Gutenberg's invention made the Bible into the first major print-commodity, it also extended the relationship between church and state. The less obvious point is that Martin Luther may have been challenging the sanctity of Latin, but his theology was based on a continuing sanctity of the word, albeit the word couched at a more abstract level as The Word of Communication Himself. God did not just express himself through a communicative language: he was Communication (Schulze: 129). Luther's point of departure was John 1: "In the beginning was the Word, and the Word was with God, and the Word was God." This is a remarkable statement of abstract universalism: words from the first century, returned to in the sixteenth century with a new technological drive.

For some time to come, we can add, the Bible, rather than disappearing, continued to sit comfortably in the hands of the monarchs as their power was projected into the indefinite future. An etching by William de Passe (c. 1598–1636) called "Triumphus Jacobi Regis," (c. 1623), depicts the extended family of the English king, James I. His seated wife Queen Anne of Denmark and eldest son Henry hold skulls to signify that they are dead; Charles, the heir to the united thrones, stands with hand resting on the Bible. The book sits in profile with the word "Biblia" inscribed on it to make sure that we know what we are looking at. In the same way that the skull motifs allow Anne of Denmark and Henry to be present to the contemporary viewer even though their bodies lie rotting in the ground, the Bible acts as a signifier of future sanctification. Henry will be king. The embodied king is yet to rule: long live the abstract king. We are actually not far from the coming of Cromwell and the English Revolution against the monarchy, but here again Cromwell offers the Bible as the sign and wonder of a new chosen people, the English. The English revolutionaries draw no genealogical continuity from the Israelites brought out of Egypt to themselves as the new chosen community of England. As we will see later in relation to the Puritans of New England, what connects this chosen people to those of Israel is the Abstract Word.

Liah Greenfeld (23) gets thoroughly carried away at this point, proclaiming incredibly that the birth of the English is not only the first of its kind but the "birth of all nations." Adrian Hastings (7) agrees and goes further: "Britain, for long the prototype of modernity, pioneered the nation-state, it also pioneered the non-national world empire." This is bizarre, but it has some strengths. In Hastings's writing, and keep in mind that he is Emeritus Professor of Theology at Leeds, the Bible becomes the central text of nation formation whether it be the original formation of the English nation or the coming to nationhood of the parts of its empire. Here, while I am sympathetic to his attempt to show the continuing relevance of religious sensibilities to nation formation, we have to question his one-dimensional overstating of the power of the Bible itself. It is simply reductionist to say as he does that "The specific root of [African] nationalism does not lie in the circumstances of post-Enlightenment modernity. On the contrary. It lies rather in the impact of the Bible, of vernacular literature and of the two combined in creating a politically stable ethnicity, effectively 'imagined' by its members across a unique mythology" (151). Much more was happening in Africa than the translation of the Bible, and that book as part of an emergent-dominant mode of communication—print—was only one edge of a general overlay of new modes of practice. There is much more that could be said about the empire itself and the importance of vernacular translations of the Bible in stabilising colonial boundaries, but I want to now turn back to discuss the deep history of one fractious imperial centre: the United Kingdom.

EVOCATION OF KINGDOM AND NATION:
CONNECTING THE WORD AND THE STONE

The word and the stone have historically been the intense markers of the power of the polity, from the earliest kingdoms to contemporary nation-states. The word and the stone act as signs of the contradictory embeddedness and ascension of embodied power. They are located at the point of crossover between what I have been suggesting is a contradictory relationship between the abstraction of social relations that makes a post-tribal polity possible and the continual practice of calling upon subjectivities of the "concrete" to sustain the depth of the nation. The following section turns to a discussion of the evocation of power to draw some connections between an Alice-in-Wonderland tea party of objects: crowns, precious jewels, lumps of old rough-hewn rock, and the testicles of young Christian boys. The underlying argument here is that their meanings vary across historically embedded frames and moments rather than being reducible to the objects *per se*. It is the very embeddedness of the objects that has a special relevance. The closer the objects are to what can be called *enduring nature-culture*, the more layers of meaning they can sustain. It is upon this ground that the nation as abstract community is subjectively defended and from which it structurally abstracted.

There is evidence to suggest that ritual seats or footprints in stone preceded crowns as markers of inauguration. In Scotland, but also Ireland and France, can be found footprints carved out of rock surfaces on the tops of hills. One example is found at Fort Dunadd, a single rocky massif rising above the Kilmartin Valley on the west coast of Scotland. On a rocky shelf at the top of the hill there is a stone-cut basin, large enough to act as a water receptacle for hand-washing, and two footprints, one shallow and one deep. In 1904, a detailed carving of what is thought by its characteristic double outline to be a Pictish boar was found on the rock behind, although when I went there in June 2000 I could not find it. Examples like Dunadd are believed to be the places that tribal kings stood for investiture ceremonies, and written records exist of later inauguration ceremonies, including those of the MacDonald Lords of the Isles in the late medieval period.[3] The full meaning of those events is, however, only available by archaeological inference, and the value of those places is now completely overshadowed by that of a single moveable stone, once used to invest the *traditional* Scots kings: the Stone of Scone. The first Scots' inauguration to be described in written detail

---

[3] Staff of the Royal Commission: 83–91. Entries for the seventh and eighth centuries C.E. in the *Annals of Ulster* kept in Iona record the presence of the kings of the Picts and the dynasty of the *Dál Riata* from Ireland (now known as the Dalriadic kingdom of North Britain).

is that of Alexander III, in 1249. In an account by an Aberdeen chantry priest, John of Fordoun, there was no crowning, but rather a churchyard ceremony presided over by the bishop of St. Andrews. The eight-year-old future king sits upon a "regal chair—that is the Stone—and the earls and the other nobles place vestments under his feet, with bent knees before the Stone."[4] The Stone was claimed in later texts to have been invested with *mana* and brought to Scone from the plain of Luz in Egypt via Sicily, Compostella in Spain,[5] the Hill of Tara in Ireland and Argyllshire in Scotland, the place of the footprints of Kilmartin. It was thus placed in a mythological kula ring that connected the Stone of Scone to the origins of the *Scoti* and back to the pillow of stone upon which Abraham's grandson Jacob had lain his head.

We could similarly trace the more recent history of the golden stool of the Ashanti, a gold-adorned wooden chair that descended from the clouds. This object was so sacred that it was not to be actually sat upon. On ceremonial occasions, the king would pretend to sit on it three times and then seat himself on his own stool, his arm resting on the sacred Stool. Edwin W. Smith relates the story of Governor Sir Frank Hodgson inadvertently beginning a war in March 1900 by telling King Prempeh that the Stool belonged to the Queen Victoria. As colonial governor of the Gold Coast and representative of the Queen, Hodgson said that he should be given the Stool to sit upon. Fighting began a week later, with 1,007 casualties on the British side and an unknown number on the Ashanti side. Writing a couple of decades after the event, Smith concludes that this is an "excellent example of the blunders that are made through ignorance of the African mind! The Governor regarded the Stool as a kind of Stone of Scone upon which the kings of Ashanti were seated at their accession" (Smith: 7).[6]

Writing a century later we can draw broader theoretical points out of these examples. Whether it be sacred stone or sacred stool, monarchical or tribal-colonial history, the object that supports the ascension of the embodied person into the sacred is contradictory. Kings, whether tribal or traditional, are elevated above the people into the realm of the sacred, but are at the same time still beholden to the embodied world. In one way, the

---

[4] Cited in Gerber (26). Gerber forgets to tell us that the account is based on oral legend and was first written down over a century after the event. However, for present purposes that does not matter.

[5] During my stay in Santiago de Compostella, I could find no reference to the Stone.

[6] Talking half a century later in 1953, Kwame Nkrumah says: "And so today we recall the birth of the Ashanti nation through Okomfe Anoykye and Osei Tutu and the symbolism entrenched in the Golden Stool; the valiant wars against the British, the banishment of Nana Prempeh the First to the Seychelle Islands; the temporary disintegration of the nation and its subsequent reunification" (cited in Manzo: 39).

form of this sociality of "being beholden" changes dramatically from tribal to traditional kingship, but there are still generalisations to be made. The elevated person is both from nature-culture and lifted beyond nature-culture. Kings, and less often queens, are lifted out as something special, chosen by God(s), elected by Holy Spirit(s), and called to sit on high thrones of stone or lifted up on shields of wood. Even in the case of imperial Japan, where the first emperor Jimmu (660 B.C.E.) was said to have descended from the Gods, subsequent emperors had to be inducted into office. However, for all the rituals of elevation—investiture, ascension, anointing, sanctification, veiling, and crowning—the early kings and emperors were still, in effect, confirmed in their position by the people around them.[7] Moreover, for all the sacring of kings they were still caught in a mediating position between culture and nature as a link in the various versions of the Great Chain of Being. If the theories about the footprints and swords in stone are right, then the king has simultaneously a threefold ontology: culturally framed by the community, anointed for ascension, and in the very act of ascension symbolically tied back into enduring nature. Those footsteps in the stone were *in* the stone, carved in enduring nature. These ambiguities meant that for all the anointings of their sanctified bodies, they could still be looked upon in moments of crisis and contradiction, in culture or nature, as persons embodied in mortal flesh and blood, and therefore could be brought down to earth. It is a reversal of the standing of Jesus as King of the Jews. His embodied mortality was accentuated by Gospel writers who took his transcendental power for granted. His anointing was to drag him down rather than to lift him up.

In the Christian West from the early medieval period, holy anointing became crucial to the ceremony of *lifting* a person to monarchical status. This simple statement has the effect of substantially qualifying the Weberian emphasis on the special charisma of the king. Charisma was substantially conferred, not a personality trait. The ceremony became at once genealogical and sacral-political, bestowing on the monarch an ecclesiastical sense of self, akin to papacy, and an elected power akin to that of emperor. This was to change subtly in the postmedieval period. In French this rite, called the *sacre*, was to become *sacre et couronnement.* In a similar secularising abstraction from the sacred, the English-language concept of *coronation* gradually took over from the concept of *consecration.* As C. A. Bouman points out, it was until well after Shakespeare's time that people asserted that, "Not all

---

[7] On the election of the king, see Taylor (book 1). On the simultaneously sacred and secular foundations of kingship, see Bendix (ch. 2). This classical book, although written with different themes of focus to the present study, provides an overview of the field of kingship with its empirical descriptions and careful generalisations providing an excellent counterpoint to my tendency to overgeneralise.

the water in the rough rude sea, can wash the balm off from an anointed king,"[8] but nevertheless a change was occurring. The sacred, like tradition itself, had increasingly to be defended. Bouman like others uses the concept of *sacring* to discuss the custom of regal anointing, with the first unequivocal European evidence of the process appearing in relation to the Visigoth king, Wamba (672 C.E.). By the ninth century, the rituals were becoming textually elaborate, and in the later Middle Ages, formularies on how it should be done crossed the boundaries of empire and kingdom. In Europe they travelled as interrelated manuscripts and manuals, circulating in a globalising field called Christendom. Writing had its own formalising effect on practical tradition as scribes copied down the rubrics and practices in as full a manner as possible, recording even antiquated and obsolete details of rituals that became again available for current use (Bouman: 71ff.). In other words, traditionalism already entailed a level of abstraction in order to "fix" regularities across time. By the time that we get to the famous example of Louis XIV (1643–1715) as absolutist ruler of France, the ritualistic splendour of the court has increased to an extraordinary level, but then so too has both the distance between the king and people, as has the tension between the king's two bodies—personal and sacred. If it was literally believed that the king of precolonial Rwanda should not bend his knees lest the kingdom shrink, by the time of Louis XIV it was only metaphorically true that if the king sneezed the whole country caught a cold. Ironically, it is at this point, as the power of the king is built on the apparently more solid foundation of modern military-bureaucratic dominance, that the absolutist state is about to fall over. Monarchy, at least in its manifestation in the sacred chain of being, is largely finished, and it becomes possible for national communities to constitute themselves as such.

The fall of monarchy (and the ascension of the nation) can be tracked through a short biography of crowns. Even more symbolically mobile than cumbrous rocks, crowns were regularly used in Europe from the eighth century to signify monarchical ascension. In the period of absolutism, they became objects of immense but ambiguously revered value. On the one hand, they accrued ambiguously sacred value as the objectified reality of the monarchy. In this "the crown" became the lived synecdoche of the body of

---

[8] William Shakespeare, *Richard II*, act 2, scene 2, cited in Bouman: ix. The assertions of that statement did not of course mean that the sacredness of the monarch was unambiguously unassailable, but such statements nevertheless did continue well into the twentieth century. See, for example, Perkins (15), where in describing the crowning of Edward VII in 1902, he says, "the tie uniting King Edward VII to the hearts of his subjects was something more enduring, more sacred than had ever existed before." However, keep in mind that at the time of writing he was the Sacristan of Westminster Abbey.

the monarch and, subsequently, institution of monarchy,[9] but more than that, each particular crown was afforded cultural depth in itself, carrying the meaning of the monarchs who wore it. There is evidence that those monarchs conceived of their crowns as gifts in the tribal-sacred sense.[10] However that may be, the meaning of being gifted a kingship—variously bestowed, conferred, and elected—changed dramatically across history. Crowns were loved, kissed, and looked upon in awe, particularly when they were dug up after being waylaid in some political struggle. On the other hand, out of context they became divisible objects able to be plundered for their valuable coloured stones. In early modern Britain, if the frame of a crown became old or weakened, the jewels were taken out and reset in a new frame. Much like the abstract body of the king—the body that in dying lives forever—the discarded frame either ceased to be part of the crown or was melted into the precious metal of the new, but the Crown always lived on.

Indicative of this practice of discarding the old frame, the oldest surviving English state-crown dates from as late as 1715. Although this is partly because Cromwell set out to destroy all prior signs of royalty, this simple fact qualifies Annette Weiner's argument that crowns as inalienable objects always had and have absolute transcendent value (37),[11] but more recent

---

[9] For a non-European example, see Godelier (201) quoting from an eighteenth-century Dutch traveler about the Japanese court of the Mikado. As a sacred personage, "In ancient times [the emperor] was obliged to sit on the throne for some hours every morning, with the imperial crown on his head, but to sit altogether like a statue, without stirring ... because it was thought by this means that he could preserve peace and tranquility in his empire.... But it having been afterwards discovered, that his imperial crown was the palladium, which by its immobility could preserve peace in the empire, it was thought expedient to deliver his imperial person ... from this burdensome duty, and therefore the crown is at present placed on the throne for some hours every morning."

[10] See, for example, Taylor on the "election" of the king. Taylor writes: "In the Will of king Ælfred is a clause which shows that he did not consider his crown as conferred by inheritance from his royal forefathers or by the pope's consecration, but that he held it as a gift which, to quote his own words, 'Dues et principes cum senioribus populi misericorditer ac benigne dederunt'." (13).

[11] Certainly most of the frames were melted down in 1649 to be sold off during the revolution, but the question remains how this mercenary act occurred if the objects were axiomatically sacred. How, for example, in a "True and Perfect Inventory" compiled by Parliamentary agents in that year could "King Alfred's crowne, or gould wyerworke sett with slight stones" be valued abstractly in terms of the number of ounces of gold in it (Perkins: 36)? Neither does the source that Weiner cites really support her contention. Clarke writes rather of precious objects of *status*, some discarded in favour of more glorious versions and some used as security for loans. It is indicative of the abstracted status of the monarchical crown that Joan Evans writes about many valuables—the rings of kings, the breastplates of high priests, amulets of gold, talismans of silver, and magical jewels galore, from those set with diamonds to those of beaver's teeth—but with nair a mention of crowns. The medieval Christian condemnation of engraved talismans that thus limited European crown-making to secular crafting is perhaps part of the explanation.

history calls it into question completely. The central stone in the monde on top of that oldest crown, once thought to be the real aquamarine, is a paste of the original that was removed in the early nineteenth century to be included in Queen Victoria's new crown. Because, until 1725, the only diamonds were mined in India and the few that made it to Europe were extraordinarily expensive, it became common practice in the eighteenth and nineteenth centuries to hire diamonds from jewel merchants to enhance the coronation crowns. The sense of the politico-sacred here continued while curiously being driven by commodity value. In the twentieth century, commodity capitalism made diamonds sufficiently available for crowns to be unique "authentic" things. However, by the end of the century and the beginning of the twenty-first, diamonds had become a girl's best friend, and crowns had become more a source of postmodern tourist curiosity than objects of sacred reverence. A Tower of London exhibition in the year 2000 notes, without further comment on the dour specificity, that George IV did not have the 12,314 diamonds "needed" for his coronation of 1821 so £65,250 worth were hired from commercial agents, "the Crown Jewellers." In the display case with the crown are 12,314 diamonds—not those diamonds, but any old diamonds—lent to represent the original hirelings by a globalising company out of the old African *empire*. Now that the abstract state is taxing the monarchy, and royal wealth is declining in relative terms, that globalising corporation De Beers is cheerfully thanked as a sponsor of the royal exhibition. Under these circumstances (and, against Benedict Anderson's argument, note how long this process has taken) the awe that attaches to the crown now becomes the awe of immense monetary value and perhaps the awe of historicity. It is no longer the awe of the politico-sacred. Crowns of state never had the quality of the crown of thorns—an ephemeral object that belied the earthly emphasis of monarchy on enduring nature—but by the twenty-first century, they lose any but a residual sense of the sacred. The crown becomes a postmodern commodity: one that cannot be exchanged and cannot be readily circulated out of the realm, but one that is nevertheless sold on a temporary and abstracted time-share basis.

It is paradoxically during the very period when the British crowns became unexchangeable commodities that we see a revival of the cultural fortunes of the Stone of Destiny (an object of nation rather than state). It is reinvested with ambiguous, fragile, but sustainable meaning: traditional *and* modern, religious *and* secular, national *and* civic. It also becomes a *postmodern* gift, the gift that is not actually given and that few true believers think is the real Stone anyway. Edinburgh Castle now houses not only the crown jewels of Scotland, but also a rough-hewn stone, believed to have been taken by Edward I of England in 1296 and returned seven hundred years later to Scotland by the Blair government in an act of prestation-hype. I call it prestation only in an ironic sense, because if you read the fine print the British *crown* (the state) still legally owns the Stone. In all of those "And Whereas" clauses prefacing the 1996 hand-calligraphed royal warrant for the "return" of the Stone, there is no clause enacting the giving. Prime Minister Tony Blair's speech of 3 July 1996 said it more directly: "The stone remains the property of the crown." It is a further irony that the *modern* legal document is given pseudo-authenticity by being hand-written in the traditional manner. The document is intended to take on the aura of the historically embedded Word. Reinforcing this point about the overlay of ontological formations, on the day of the return of the Stone to Scotland, deliberately chosen to be St. Andrew's Day, a religious ceremony was held at St. Giles Cathedral to celebrate the modern *national* (Scottish) and *state* (British) occasion. What we can say with certainty was that the words of the service were chosen carefully. Crossing the fields of sacred liturgy to nationalist ideology, the Moderator of the General Assembly of the Church of Scotland addressed the congregation: "During all the long pilgrimage of years, the ideal of Scottish nationhood and the reality of Scottish identity have never been obliterated from the hearts of the people. The recovery of this ancient symbol of the Stone cannot but strengthen the proud distinctiveness of the people of Scotland" (Breeze and Munro: 41). There you have it: even the man of the cloth did not say that *the* Stone had been given back.

The earlier reference to boys' testicles can now be related, but it is not just as whimsy that it is included here. Colloquial reference to the testicles as "the family jewels" is indicative of the contemporary ironical use of metaphor—even metaphors of once great power, now half-dead—to reinvest the body with meaning. More than that, we have only to read the tracts of religious fundamentalists to feel the continuing power of these embodied metaphors: the power of objects that take on sacred meaning, and meanings that become "flesh." Without a hint of irony, the Christian pamphleteer Harold Barrow writes in 1947 that the "old story of English history," the attempted stealing of the crown jewels in 1671, "suggests a parable about other crowns and jewels *far more precious* than the jewels in the king's regalia, for every boy has his own Castle of Manhood to defend, and within that Castle there are wonderful and marvellous possessions all of them bearing a sacred and symbolic meaning in the experience of Life" (Barrow: 7, emphasis added). Barrow is writing with religious certainty not so much about crown jewels, in either sense, as about the sanctity of *embodied life* and the religious meshing of the universal and the particular. He concludes:

> The Castle in the city of Edinburgh in which the Scottish regalia and jewels are safely stored is built firm upon the rock. So in your life there must be a sure and solid foundation. Then you will be able to say truly:
>
> "On Christ the solid rock I stand,
> All other ground is sinking sand." (8)

Poor poetics, but this is still the foundation of contemporary Christianity: that God *gave* to the world his only begotten son so that we may live. Over time, the foundation of the Kirk has been given metaphoric power in a multiple image. First, it comes as an image of *enduring nature*—the rock, continuous with the carved rocks used for the sacred investiture of kings, and connected to the reinvestment of national mythologies, for example, in the Stone of Scone as it is returned in 1996 across the Scottish border. Secondly, it comes in the form of *enduring culture*. In 1249 the bishop of St. Andrews consecrates the traditional ruler. In 1996 a ceremony is held at St. Giles Cathedral celebrating the national occasion and from the Old Testament, a young person reads the story of Jacob's pillow of stone. Thirdly, it comes in the image of an *enduring gift*—the blood of Christ as the kind of gift that, as Godelier rightly says, cannot be reciprocated. The point of this in terms of a theory of structural levels is that we have to remember that despite all the abstractions of exchange in a post-reciprocal, rationalised, commodified world there are still people who *at one level of their being* continue to live the enchantments of sacred keeping and exchanging. More generally, at a time of intense processes of abstraction, processes encapsulated in the concept of "globalisation," we are seeing a reaccentuation of the embodied and the sacred. Through all of this it is out of the loins of men, through the mothers of the nation, that the nation-state continues to be brought forth.

And so we are nearly at the end of a long journey involving some strangely connected things. The description only scratched the surface, but it was intended to show that however deeply the description was pursued, however richly textured the description was made, it depended upon concepts that described systemic patterns of both fundamental difference and deep continuity. In the period of the late-nineteenth and early-twentieth centuries, the nation as living community assumed the mantle once conferred on the person of the monarch. In other words, the community, both abstracted from any one individual yet grounded on the subjectivity of enduring embodiment, can no longer find its point of condensed signification in the One Individual. National communities build their identities on a different foundation while still reaching back into enduring nature and genealogical placement. A couple of examples will suffice.

The first example links the traditional and the modern. When the Scottish National War Memorial was built on the elevated grounds of the medieval Edinburgh castle in 1927, it was placed where once stood the Chapel of St. Mary, founded by King David I. It is no accident that that highest portion of "living rock" (a space of enduring nature) is left exposed in the shrine. On the lintel of the inner doorway are carved the words of the imperial poet Rudyard Kipling: "Lest we forget" (a temporality of sacred recollection). Books of Honour list the names of almost every single Scot who has died in war service from 1914 to the present (an abstract relation of embodied connection). In case somebody has been left out, around the walls of the shrine are carved words that recall the sentiments expressed in many cenotaphs: "And their names though lost to us are written in the book of God." In this the abstract Word connects all bodies, remembered and forgotten. Like most shrines, the Edinburgh Memorial resounds with biblical references. One author describes the inner sanctum thus:

> Eyes and feet turn instinctively to the central feature of the Shrine—the heart and core of the whole Memorial—the Stone of Remembrance and the Casket. The Stone is set upon and outcrop of the Rock itself, which here breaks through the flagged pavement as if eager to shoulder its burden.... Upon the face of the Stone, which is of green Corona marble, is cut the Cross of Sacrifice, surmounted by the inscription, Their Name Liveth. On the top, guarded by kneeling Angels like the Ark of the Covenant itself, stands the shining Casket.... It contains the Rolls of Honour which bear the names of Scotland's dead, deposited for the rest of time in the ineffable peace of this mystic, enchanted spot. (Hay: 100)

In this description the Word and the stone become mutually supportive. The second example links the traditional, modern and postmodern, the colonial and the postcolonial. In July 2000, to mark the hundredth anniversary of the passing of the Australian Constitutional Bill—the signing of Australian semi-independence as an imperial colony—five Australian prime ministers, past and present, attended a service at Westminster Cathedral, London. As part of the celebrations Tony Blair agreed to build an Australian war shrine in the heart of London in recognition of the sacrifice of Australian soldiers who died defending Britain. Addressing Parliament the next day and recounting the agreement, Prime Minister Blair by a slip of naming lauded not Australian but "American servicemen and women." It was a fitting finale to the ambiguously successful Australian attempt over the previous decade to make itself unique by revitalising its memory of those who had fallen in war. A central part of this process included belatedly following other countries of the world to find Australia's own unknown soldier. In the eulogy, Paul Keating spoke of a nation without modern nationalism:[12]

> This unknown soldier is not interred here to glorify war over peace; or to assert a soldier's character over a civilian's; or one race or one nation or one religion above another; or men above women; or the war in which he fought and died above any other war; or any one generation above any that has or will come later.

---

[12] Incidently, Paul Keating was the one immediate past Australian prime minister who refused to go to London to celebrate the anniversary of Federation.

Similarly, the sculptors of the tomb spoke self-consciously of the monument's abstract design as inviting dialogue across times and places. Standing behind the head of the red-marble slab they placed four ten-metre pillars representing the primordial elements of fire, water, earth, and air—the stuff of life and death. Here traditionalism met postmodernism. How do we know that the bones lying beneath the red marble, the person exhumed from a cemetery near the French village of Villers-Bretonneux, is an Australian rather than a German soldier? For some this is the question that cannot be asked, and for others it is an irrelevancy. Either way, the Word and the stone are still there helping to explain to us the power and immortality of the nation.

The Evocation of a Western Postcolonial Nation: "In God We Trust"

Throughout the essay I have been careful to treat the nation and state as different phenomena, analytically separable even during the time of the classic *modern* nation-state when in the late-nineteenth century the nation as community and the state as polity came into a taken-for-granted hyphenated union. This final section takes up this theme in relation to the United States of America as it broke away from British colonial rule. From Cromwell and the Puritan Revolution of Old England, discussed in the previous section, we move now to the Puritans of New England as they set out to establish a polity of the New Testament. In the period prior to the formal constituting of the United States in the eighteenth century, the Puritan "settlement" of the Americas was defended, in Perry Miller's phrase, as the act of a "Bible Commonwealth." They saw themselves as forging a covenant with God. Miller is worth quoting at length to compare with what comes later:

> Long before they came to America, [the New England theologians] had become members of a school of doctrine now known as the "federal" or "covenant" theology. They revised or amplified pure Calvinism by defining the relationship between the predestined elect and his God not merely as the passive recipient of grace, as did Calvin, but as an active covenant, after the model of that between Abraham and Jehovah in the Book of Genesis. According to this doctrine, the saint was redeemed not simply by an infusion of grace, but by being taken into a league with God, an explicit compact drawn up between two partners, wherein the saint promised to obey God's will and God promised infallibly to grant him salvation. Starting with this notion of a personal and inward covenant, the theologians extended it to the church and state. They argued that a nation of saints, all of whom were personally in covenant with God, would also be in covenant with Him as body politic. (17)

Thus the New Englanders *as a community* had by a double act of free volition—migrating to North America and submitting to the laws of the

Bible—made themselves into a chosen people in a promised land. In their religious-political tracts they, or at least their scribes, expressed the belief that had forged a covenant that could be enacted in a state. However, by the time of the American Revolution, the notion of a covenant with God was being overlaid by a self-framed contract, sustained through the laws of nature. The "citizenry," or rather their ruling and writing classes, had discovered natural rights—God-given in basis, but "self-evident" laws of nature nevertheless. These were laws that just required writing down by God-fearing rational scholars (and gentlemen) in order to become laws of state. Thus, contrary to the claims of the modernist theories of the nation, here we find two cosmologies, the biblical and the modern rational, coming together, albeit in contradictory and overlaying ways. "Americans had succeeded," Perry Miller says with muted irony, "where the Jews did not, in recovering something of the pristine virtue.... Yet once the machinery of national humiliation proved effective in producing the providential victory of the Americans, were they not bound to the prophecy that by their utilization of the form, they, and they alone, would bring about a reign of national bliss?" (Miller: 103, 105). In other words, the "citizenry" now written into existence by the Declaration of Independence were, at the level of their communion in the abstracted state, set free from God to make their own way in the world. The constitution (in both senses of the word) of the abstract state became the highest expression of that freedom and the republic of "these United States" (plural not singular) was about to be born. At this point, Liah Greenfeld again gets carried away, this time into swooning summation of the civic purity of this beginning: "in a certain, analytic, sense," she says, only partly covering her partisan tracks, "the American nation is an ideal nation: the national element in it is challenged by the fewest counter-influences; it is a purer example of *national* community than any other" (403). The evidence, including her own detailed narrative, suggests otherwise. The United States is born not as nation or nation-state but as a republic in a complex intersection of continuities with the past and discontinuous new beginnings. The projected covenant with God waits until the middle of the nineteenth century to become the cultural evocation of an emerging nation and, during the same period, the contract with men (no women were there for the writing of the Constitution) becomes the political codification of the federating unitary state. The state in effect rejects any such covenant while the nation makes it a contested expression of piety (Foster).

It is indicative of this tension that in the highest written document of state, the Constitution, the Bible is absent, as is the concept of "the nation." Even in the draft Declaration of Independence—written by a secret congress of strangers meeting in the home of a lecturer in scientific obstetrics—God is reduced to "nature's god" (lowercase). Nature's god is embedded within the first couple of paragraphs of the Declaration as it begins by naturalising the break with the British Crown: "... in the course of human events it becomes necessary for one people to dissolve the political bands which have connected them with another, and to assume among the powers of the earth the separate and equal station to which the laws of nature and of nature's god entitle them..." (qtd. in Wills: 374). This accords with Thomas Jefferson's contradictory modernism. He calls upon the Bible but writes, for example, with extraordinary relativism, of the "family God of Abraham, of Isaac and of Jacob, and the local God of Israel" (qtd. in Grosby: 62). Here we are at the end of the eighteenth century and, while the postcolonial republic has been formally signed into existence as the United States, there is a long way to go in establishing a nation-state.

While there is no demarcation point, no calendrical marker at which time we can say that the United States became a nation-state, it is possible to give some symbolic high points in the connecting of the secular-state/sacred-nation. In these the Bible is present, even if as rhetorical evocation rather than as indicative of the hopes for a Bible Commonwealth. Gary Wills, despite the postmodern title of his book *Inventing America*, is brilliantly insightful here in his discussion of the biblical overtones in Lincoln's Gettysburg Address of 1863. The speech begins: "Fourscore and seven years ago, our fathers brought forth..." Why such a stilted style? Why fourscore and seven? To hear the phrase in the context of Victorian America is to hear the biblical overtones, says Wills. There is no reason to immediately start counting back eighty-seven years from 1863 to get 1776. It allows Lincoln, in effect, to get around the issue that the date 1776 is no automatic marker of the beginning of the nation-state. In fact, the thirteen original colonies had instructed their delegates to sign the Declaration of Independence on the basis that it did not imply a unified polity. Even more pointedly Lincoln was talking in the middle of a war of states that would by its end kill over half a million people. Why centre the nation on the phrase "Our fathers brought forth"? President Lincoln is drawing on the biblical references to Our Father and the faith of our fathers. As Wills puts it, "Lincoln is talking about generation on the spot. The nation is rightly called new because it is brought forth maieutically, by midwifery; it is not only new but newborn. The suggested image is, throughout, of a *hieros gamos*, a marriage of a male heaven ('our fathers') and a female earth ('this continent'). And it is a miraculous conception, a virgin birth" (xv).

At the very time of Lincoln's calling upon the language of redemption to connect a nation-at-war-with-itself, the Bible had ceased to be substantially more than a legitimating *signifier* of the state-nation. Though, as I argued earlier, the bureaucratic state and the religions-of-the-word grew up together, by the nineteenth century this had fundamentally changed. The state and the sacred had ceased to be symbiotic. Individuals continued to have faith, but the state-nation as a polity-community of liberal individuals was assuming a more urgent calling: that of the kingdom of God. In the middle of that century as Congress voted to put the phrase "In God We Trust" on the nation's currency and to recognise officially Thanksgiving Day as one of the nation's holy days, the Bible had become a book to wave around at public meetings, cite passages from, and swear upon, but not a book of instruction to guide the practices of the increasingly abstract state. In short, while the Word continued to be relevant to the nation, it became less and less important to the state. This development would reduce the Bible to a thing of national evocation as the nation and state were drawn together at the end of the nineteenth century.

Carrying through the theme of the Declaration of Independence, I want to finish this essay with a contemporary example of an Independence Day speech, this time in a film about aliens attacking the earth. In *Independence Day* (1996), Bill Pullman, President of the United States, speaks of the Fourth of July becoming the rallying point for all mankind. The President stands to address the assembled:

> Good morning. In less than an hour, aircraft from here will join with others from around the world. And you will be launching the largest aerial battle in the history of mankind. "Mankind"— that word should have new meaning for all of us. We can't be consumed by petty differences any more. We will be united in our common interest. Perhaps it's faith. Today is the fourth of July, and you will once more fight for our freedom. Not from tyranny, oppression or persecution, but from alienation. We're fighting for our right to live, to exist. And should we win the day, the fourth of July will no longer be known as an American holiday, but as the day when the whole world declared in one voice: "we will not go quietly into the night, we will not vanish without a fight, we are going to survive." Today we celebrate *our* independence day! (Emphasis added)

The ambiguity of those tiny little words, "we" and "our," are the key to understanding the passage. It is striking how comfortably Hollywood translates fighting for transnational peace back into the heritage of one nation-state: *pax Americana*. We all know that the Fourth of July is not just another American holiday. It signifies the formation of the modern American nation. However, by the time we get to the last line, "Today we celebrate our independence day," the ambiguous appellation "our" has linked modern nationalism and postmodern cosmopolitanism in a comfortable pastiche that challenges nothing. It draws upon the spirit of *Pax Christi* but surrounds it with postmodern irony: "perhaps it's faith." However, if the Bible is absent from the political faith-statement itself, it still lingers on around the edges. Just before the speech, one of the pilots who is about to fly into space to combat the aliens gets married under the sign of the Christian cross and "in the sight of God," and just after the speech the other pilot hands his father a copy of the Jewish Bible covered by a skullcap.

If you read between the lines of the set speeches in this and similar films, the speakers still assume that the United States sits at the helm of world politics, but supposedly no longer as the modern *homogenising* nation-state against the evil empire. It is now projected as, on the one hand, a postnational representative of a set of self-evident universalistic values and, on the other, as *the* exemplary open-textured nation and state. We are back, full circle, to the introduction to this essay. In the post-Reagan years, from Clinton to Bush or Gore, the exponents of this kind of "postnationalism" move in two directions at once. They call on whatever is at hand to give spiritual and embodied depth to their vision of a world made peaceful for the market, and they underwrite the technological means of conducting human relations at a distance, from communicating with others to conducting undeclared and systematic acts of abstract violence. The undeclared wars over Iraq and Kosovo, for example—that is, put in less euphemistic terms, the waves of bombing from a great height as a way of resolving problems of great complexity—are an outcome of this process, but not simply as acts of wilful domination. They are also about fearing the consequences of their own soldiers dying and coming home in the body bags. This is one of the contradictions of the present: our capacity to live with the systematic destruction of nameless people in places far away, and a heightened sensitivity to the death of a single person if we know their name and can see the image of their face.

Throughout the essay, I have being arguing about the dialectic of continuity and discontinuity. Read though the flickering screen of the globalising and postmodernising nation-state with all its contradictions, it is hard to see any continuities-of-form here. The continuities at most appear as surface content, and even then only as points of reference, a Jewish Bible, a Christian cross, a Stone of Destiny, a slab of engraved marble. However, the postmodern/late-modern nation has all the ontological vulnerabilities of the prior dominant forms of polity—from traditional kingdom and absolutist state to the classical modern nation-state. Despite unprecedented technical power, it still has to legitimise itself, at one level, through basic categories of human existence such as embodiment, placement, and the temporal transcendence—the transcendence of the community-polity despite the assured mortality of all who live within it. And it will continue to do so, for good and evil, so long as we remain embodied persons living with others. This is why its politicians and its people continue, if in changing ways, to draw on writings about faith, existence, and transcendence. It is also why the newest "evil empire" of Islam is another sodality of the Book, why Catholics and Protestants are struggling to sustain the Easter Friday agreement, and why the Palestinians continue to die throwing stones at armoured vehicles.

WORKS CONSULTED

Anderson, Benedict
1991   *Imagined Communities: Reflections on the Origins and Spread of Nationalism.* 2d ed. London: Verso.

Barrow, Harold T.
1947   *Guarding the Crown Jewels.* Croydon: Uplift Books.

Bendix, Reinhard
1978   *Kings or People: Power and the Mandate to Rule.* Berkeley and Los Angeles: University of California Press.

Bouman, C. A.
1957   *Sacring and Crowning: The Development of the Latin Ritual for Anointing Kings and the Coronation of an Emperor before the Eleventh Century.* Groningen: Wolters.

Breeze, David, and Graeme Munro
1997   *The Stone of Destiny: Symbol of Nationhood.* Edinburgh: Historic Scotland.

Clarke, Grahame
1986   *Symbols of Excellence: Precious Metals As Expressions of Status.* Cambridge: Cambridge University Press.

Coulton, G. G.
1935   "Nationalism in the Middle Ages." *Cambridge Historical Journal* 5:15–40.

Evans, Joan
1922   *Magical Jewels of the Middle Ages and Renaissance, Particularly in England.* London: Oxford University Press.

Foster, Gaines M.
1996   "A Christian Nation: Signs of a Covenant." Pp. 120–38 in *Bonds of Affection: Americans Define Their Patriotism.* Ed. John Bodnar. Princeton: Princeton University Press.

Gellner, Ernest
1983   *Nations and Nationalism.* Oxford: Blackwell.

Gerber, Pat
1997   *Stone of Destiny.* Edinburgh: Canongate.

Giddens, Anthony
1985   *The Nation-State and Violence.* Cambridge: Polity.

Godelier, Maurice
1999   *The Enigma of the Gift.* Cambridge: Polity.

Goody, Jack
1986   *The Logic of Writing and the Organization of Society.* Cambridge: Cambridge University Press.

Greenfeld, Liah
    1992   *Nationalism: Five Roads to Modernity.* Cambridge, Mass.: Harvard University Press.

Grosby, Steven
    1993   "The Nation of the United States and the Vision of Israel." Pp. 49–79 in *Nationality, Patriotism and Nationism in Liberal Democratic Societies.* Ed. Roger Michener. St. Paul: Professors World Peace Academy.

Hastings, Adrian
    1997   *The Construction of Nationhood: Ethnicity, Religion and Nationalism.* Cambridge: Cambridge University Press.

Hay, Ian
    1931   *Their Name Liveth: The Book of the Scottish National War Memorial.* Edinburgh: Trustees of the Scottish National War Memorial. (Repr. 1985)

Hobsbawm, Eric
    1990   *Nations and Nationalism Since 1780.* Cambridge: Cambridge University Press.

James, Paul
    1996   *Nation Formation: Towards a Theory of Abstract Community.* London: Sage.

Manzo, Kathryn A.
    1996   *Creating Boundaries: The Politics of Race and Nation.* Boulder: Lynne Rienner.

Miller, Perry
    1967   *Nature's Nation.* Cambridge, Mass.: Harvard University Press.

Nairn, Tom
    1981   *The Break-up of Britain.* 2d ed. London: Verso.

Perkins, Jocelyn
    1937   *The Crowning of the Sovereign of Great Britain and the Dominions Overseas.* London: Methuen.

Schulze, Hagen
    1996   *States, Nations and Nationalism: From the Middle Ages to the Present.* Cambridge: Blackwell.

Smith, Edwin W.
    1926   *The Golden Stool: Some Aspects of the Conflict of Cultures in Modern Africa.* London: Holborn.

Staff of the Royal Commission
    1999   *Kilmartin: Prehistoric and Early Historic Monuments.* An inventory of the Monuments Extracted from Argyll, vol. 6. Edinburgh: Royal Commission on the Ancient and Historical Monuments of Scotland.

Taylor, Arthur
    1820   *The Glory of Regality: An Historical Treatise on the Anointing and Crowning of the Kings and Queens of England.* London: Taylor.

Weiner, Annette B.
    1992   *Inalienable Possessions: The Paradox Keeping-While-Giving.* Berkeley and Los Angeles: University of California Press.

Wills, Gary
    1979   *Inventing America: Jefferson's Declaration of Independence.* New York: Vintage.

Response

A Real Presence, Subsumed by Others: The Bible in Colonial and Postcolonial Contexts

Gerald West
University of Natal

In the Beginning: The Bible and the BaTlhaping

> The bible being on the table gave occasion to explain the nature and use of a book, particularly of that book—how it informed us of God, who made all things; and of the beginning of all things, which seemed to astonish her, and many a look was directed towards the bible. (Campbell: 199)

In the beginning the Bible was there. In this, the first protracted encounter between Christian missionaries and the Thlaping people of southern Africa, the Bible is palpably present. Stating this may seem rather mundane; of course the Bible is present in the missionary enterprise! We would be surprised if it were not. True, but given its foundational presence, it does disappear remarkably quickly from the analytical gaze of postcolonial criticism in its various historical, anthropological, political, and literary guises.

This collection of essays goes some way to remedying this postcolonial remissness. While I would not want to lean too heavily on the adjective "foundational" above, there are grounds for using a formulation like this in discussing the role and presence of the Bible in early missionary encounters in southern Africa. First, it is there in the beginning, along with the guns, beads, ox wagons, ploughs, watches, mirrors, telescopes, letters, tobacco, and other items brought by the missionaries. Second, there are signs that the Bible is perceived by indigenous peoples, at least in southern Africa, as an object of power more like the gun than, say, a utilitarian object like the candle. Third, even in these preliterate days the Bible begins to be appropriated via a range of interpretative moves yet to be documented and analysed, laying a hermeneutical foundation for successive generations of African interpreters in a context in which what we have done and what we do with the Bible really does matter. I will elaborate each of these points briefly below by way of introduction, and they will frame my responses to the essays in this volume.

Among the "goods of strange power" (Comaroff and Comaroff, 1991:182) associated with the arrival of whites in their land was the Bible.

What the missionaries failed to notice—among their many misrecognitions—was "that the attraction of whites to the Tlhaping flowed from the mystical qualities attributed to them and their things in a hinterland where raids were endemic and where guns, beads, and tobacco had become prime valuables" (179). Present among them, though not in the same league as these other items, the Bible did come to be seen as another object of "strange power." The Bible's coming to power and the nature of this power among the Tlhaping cannot be elaborated here; I simply note its presence among other "goods of strange power" precisely because it is not singled and signalled out by Jean and John Comaroff.

While their work does take note of the Bible in the "long conversation," a recurring metaphor of the Comaroffs', between the Non-Conformists and the Southern Tswana, the Bible tends to be subsumed and assumed under terms such as "Christianity," "the message," "the Word," and the like (see also Landau, 1995). Clearly, the Bible is part of the missionary/colonial package in that it is integral to most if not all forms of Christianity and colonial activity, particularly the Non-Conformist forms that were propagated amongst the Tlhaping. While there may be good reasons for treating the Bible separately, at least heuristically, and I will say more of this later, this has not usually been the case. So, firstly, this volume of *Semeia* makes an important contribution by giving a place to the Bible in the colonial/postcolonial landscape.

As I have indicated, objects in the encounter between the Tlhaping and missionaries were charged with power. Indeed, in the earliest encounters "[t]he Tlhaping seem to have related to the Europeans as objects, touching and bearing in on them, enjoying a closeness never again permitted by the etiquette of the mission, with its deference to racial separation and the spatial discreteness of person and property" (Comaroff and Comaroff, 1991:182). But not all objects were charged with the same power. Tobacco, along with beads and knives, was a prized object of exchange and trade (183–84), besides being an object of consumption, but held no particular power in and of itself.

Guns, like tobacco, were greatly desired by the Tlhaping, but were much more difficult to extract from missionaries and traders because of their scarcity and a reluctance to arm local peoples (unless of course this suited colonial objectives).[1] Though an object of "strange power," the power

---

[1] The importance of guns is evident in the account of William Burchell, a traveller who stayed among the Tlhaping for a brief period prior to Campbell's visit. In fact, the whole of Burchell's visit is dominated by Mothibi's determination to get a gun from Burchell, and despite being bested, Burchell tells this story with a real feel for the intricacies and urgency of the acquisition. Finally, Mothibi succeeds, outmanoeuvring Burchell and obtaining a gun (376–405).

of this "most condensed source of European power" (Comaroff and Comaroff, 1991:201) is easily understood. Besides the obvious killing power of the gun, possessing a gun signalled some contact or alliance with missionary/colonial forces, which association was in itself a powerful protection against attack from neighbouring groups, including other indigenous peoples and white (mainly boer) settlers (Burchell: 376–405).

Mirrors, watches, and telescopes are more problematic with respect to determining their power. Missionaries clearly believed that these goods demonstrated the superiority of their culture and civilisation, and so they were constantly exhibiting such items to the Tlhaping. In his first formal meeting with Chief Mothibi, the missionary John Campbell gave the Tlhaping ruler a copper comb, a silver headband, and a chain, "all of which he placed on the royal person, so that the culminating gift, the looking glass, might reveal to him his transformed visage" (Comaroff and Comaroff, 1991:183). Clocks, watches, and telescopes were similarly, in the minds of the missionaries, "devices capable to working transformations, although, being more costly, they were seldom given [as gifts] at the start" (185). Common to all of these items was glass, a commodity "taken to be the window into a new way of seeing and being" (185); in enlightenment self-conceptions, "seeing is believing" (186). Telescopes and pocket compasses were indispensable instruments with which to survey and civilise the uncharted and chaotic African landscape, and mirrors both literally and metaphorically showed the heathen "their own likeness in all its imperfection" (186). But quite what the Tlhaping made of these items is less clear from the missionary record. Missionaries and other travellers assumed that the "childlike" Africans were drawn to shiny objects, though some did recognise that utility was more connected with beauty for Africans than it was for Europeans (184). So, while these objects obviously had some power and hold over the missionaries who brought them, the Tlhaping do not seem particularly intrigued by them, being more interested in objects that had a more pragmatic value, objects such as candles and metalworking tools.

But what of the Bible? What power does it wield? We catch glimpses of Tlhaping apprehensions of the Bible in the missionary record, which by reading against the grain might provide some sense of the Bible's form of power. Here I offer only one such glimpse. Some days after arriving in Dithakong, Chief Mothibi's city, John Campbell and his company are impatiently still awaiting the arrival of Chief Mothibi, who is away on tribal business. Campbell's major preoccupation during this time is seeking permission to "instruct the people." The local leadership consistently insists that he wait for Mothibi's return, and when Campbell and his men indicate an interest in using the time until Mothibi's return "to visit a large village about a day and a half's journey higher up the country," they receive a visit, that evening, after a busy day full of formative transactions, including

Campbell's showing "a person his own face in the looking glass," from Mmahutu, "the queen," Mothibi's senior wife (Campbell: 200, 207). She entered their tent and said that she "was averse" to their "going any where till Mateebe came," and that at the very least they should leave part of their wagons and party behind. Using this as a lever, the missionaries claim that they would would never have thought of leaving Dithakong "even for a day before Mateebe's return" had they "been permitted to instruct the people; but that having nothing to do," they wished to visit that village and hunt. However, they are persuaded not to leave, and once this matter is settled, the missionaries "endeavoured to convey some information" (199).

What follows is a remarkable exchange, signifying as it does a range of possible appropriations of the Bible:

> We explained to her the nature of a letter, by means of which a person could convey his thoughts to a friend at a distance. Mr. A. shewed her one he had received from his wife, by which he knew every thing that had happened at Klaar Water for two days after he left it. This information highly entertained her, especially when told that A. Kok, who brought it, knew nothing of what it contained, which we explained by telling her the use of sealing wax. The bible being on the table gave occasion to explain the nature and use of a book, particularly of that book—how it informed us of God, who made all things; and of the beginning of all things, which seemed to astonish her, and many a look was directed towards the bible. (Campbell: 199)

Returning to a theme they have already raised while attempting to instruct the local leadership, the reliability of text over against oral transmission from father to son, the missionaries draw Mmahutu's attention to the power of the letter as text in at least two respects. First, text can re-present "every thing" that happened in a place in a person's absence. Second, text can be made to hide its message from the bearer and reveal its contents only to the intended receiver. Turning from the letter to a quite different genre of text (from the perspective of the missionaries), the Bible, but a text nevertheless, the missionaries use the interest generated in their exposition of the letter to return to their preoccupation with the contents of the Bible, particularly the matter of origins.

Mmahutu is astonished, but what she is astonished at may not be what the missionaries imagine. Clearly, from her perspective texts have power, with some appearing to have more power than others, hence "many a look" at the Bible. Text can reveal and text can hide; text can be manipulated by the people who transact with it. Clearly too, text contains knowledge/ power; its contents, for those who have the power to make it speak, has to do with matters of importance to a community. This becomes clearer in a letter written by Campbell to a friend, Mr. David Langton, some days later

(27 July) in which he elaborates on this episode. Immediately following the final sentence in the quotation above, the following is added: "Mr Reads eye caught a verse very suitable to our situation in the page that was lying open, viz. Math. 4-16."[2] If this text was read, and the literary context suggests it would have been, Mmahutu would have heard this: "The people which sat in darkness saw great light; and to them which sat in the region and shadow of death light is sprung up." This then makes some sense of Mmahutu's questions, recorded in the next paragraph of the journal entry: "'Will people who are dead, rise up again?' 'Is God under the earth, or where is he?'" (Campbell: 199). But only some sense, for her questions do not seem to deal directly with the passage read. The passage clearly makes sense to the missionaries, being made to bear the full weight of English missionary images of Africa (see Comaroff and Comaroff, 1991:86–125). However, such allusions are probably absent from Mmahutu's hearing of this sentence from the Bible. Whatever she hears, and it may be the word "death," prompts here to bring her own questions to the text/missionaries, disturbed as she and others have become by talk of people rising from the dead, worrying especially that their slain enemies might arise (Moffat: 403–5; Comaroff and Comaroff, 1997:342).

Already we see emerging evidence from this very early encounter of a recognition that the Bible is power/knowledge, that as power/knowledge it can be manipulated by those who control it, that it is beginning to be prised from the hands of the missionaries by indigenous questions, and, most significantly, that the bearer (in this case the missionaries!), like the bearer of the letter, might not know the power/knowledge it contains. I pause here, allowing this thought to linger and do its subversive work.

There is no pause in Campbell's narrative, though. Having "answered her [Mmahutu's] questions," though we are given no hint of how her questions were answered, and having heard and accepted her concerns that they not leave the city until Mothibi's return, the missionaries show her (and her companions) a watch, "which both astonished and terrified them." Commenting on this reaction to the watch, Campbell says, "On observing the work in motion, they concluded that it must be alive, and on offering to put it to their ears, to hear it sound, they held up their hands to drive it away as if it had been a serpent" (200). Their interpreter also comments on this encounter with the watch, in the vernacular, saying "something to them which made them laugh immoderately." But what he actually said was probably hidden from the hearing of the missionaries and so from us, for

---

[2] J. Campbell, Klaar Water, 27 July 1813 (CWM. Africa. South Africa. Incoming correspondence. Box 5-2-D).

when translated, the missionaries "found he had said, that before he went to Klaar Water, he was as ignorant as they were, but there he had been taught many good things, which they also would be taught if Mateebe permitted missionaries to settle among them" (ibid.). How this could have caused Mmahutu and her companions to "laugh immoderately" is difficult to imagine! But the missionaries did not bother to probe any further, for they had heard what they wanted to hear.

The multiple layers of language and translation clearly offered fertile ground not only for accidental misunderstandings but calculated misunderstandings, as the theoretical work of the Comaroffs (see especially 1991:13–39) and James Scott on hegemony, ideology, and resistance amply demonstrate (see also West: 39–49). Language in these early encounters was an obvious site for "infrapolitical" exchanges, "a politics of disguise and anonymity that takes place in public view but is designed to have a double meaning or to shield the identity [and/or ideology] of the actors" (Scott: 19). Here we find, unlike the missionaries, "a tactical choice born of a prudent awareness of the balance of power" (183), in which what was said was intended to communicate one thing to those in the know and another to outsiders (184). Such misunderstandings are a very early, "foundational" (201), form of infrapolitics, a form that was soon to be joined by a host of others as the contours of the colonisation became ever clearer. Misunderstanding and misconceptions, as elementary forms of infrapolitics, are aptly appropriated by the Comaroffs as major metaphors of the "long conversation," "a dialogue at once poetic and pragmatic" (1991:171), a dialogue with "each party using his own language and comprehending very little of what was said by the other; and talking probably on subjects widely different" (Burchell: 433).

Here, then, is "a discernible Tswana commentary ... spoken less in narrative form than in the symbolism of gesture, action, and reaction, and in the expressive play of language itself" (Comaroff and Comaroff, 1991:171). Quite what this commentary (on commentary) says is difficult to determine, but perhaps the reaction to the watch (the first layer of commentary) is not unrelated to the reaction to the Bible, given their proximity in the missionaries' tent (and narrative). Here, perhaps, are two "devices capable of working transformations" (185), "indispensable tools" in navigating, charting, incorporating, and so transforming that which was other (186).[3] Juxtaposed in text and tent, the Bible and watch comment on each other, each occupying a particular place in the missionaries' scheme of things, but just how they are commented on by Mmahutu and her translator must remain somewhat obscure, deliberately so

---

[3] I add the Bible to the Comaroffs' inventory of devices such as looking glass, clocks, telescopes, and compasses (1991:185–86).

for the missionaries, but also, perhaps, somewhat inchoate and incipient for the indigenous commentators themselves as they observed for all they were worth in an attempt perhaps to find a place for these "goods of strange power"—including the Bible—in their rapidly changing world.

Clearly the Bible is a very real presence, as much an object of strange power as any of the other objects being negotiated and transacted in this prelude to the colonial encounter. Indeed, the Bible is in some ways more strange in its power than the other objects we have briefly reflected on. This is recognised by an "old man" who is deeply troubled by Campbell's stated intention to send teachers among them. Confronting Campbell, he stated that "he did not need instruction from any one, for the dice [*bola*] which hung from his neck informed him of every thing which happened at a distance; and added, if they were to attend to instructions, they would have no time to hunt or to do any thing" (Campbell: 193). This fascinating exchange suggests a profound grasp by this "old man," possibly an *ngaka* (doctor/diviner/healer), given that he is wearing a "dice," one of the elements among the bones, shells, and other materials making up the *ditaola* used in divining,[4] of the dangerousness of nonindigenous instruction. The context of the discussion, and the centrality of the Bible in the discussion, almost certainly centrally positioned in the space where this meeting takes place, makes it likely that he assumes that the missionaries' book(s) are their equivalent of his "dice [*bola*]." My conjecture finds some support from Robert Moffat's account of an incident concerning which he writes, "My books puzzled them. They asked if they were my 'Bola,' prognosticating dice" (Moffat: 384; see Comaroff and Comaroff, 1997:345).

Whether his aversion to "instruction" is an aversion to both the source (the Book) and the interpreter of the source (the missionaries) is not clear, but is a question that sits at the centre of my essay. We must not assume that this *ngaka* shares the assumption of the missionaries that the Book and its instruction are one and the same thing. His concern that "if they were to attend to instructions, they would have no time to hunt or to do any thing" may reflect the first signs of resistance to the time schedules and modes of production of established mission station, church, and school routines to the south, whose "notions of time, work, and self-discipline were drawn from the natural lineaments of the industrial capitalist world" (Comaroff and Comaroff, 1991:179; 1997),[5] in which case the focus of his

---

[4] I am grateful to Mogapi Motsomaesi and Mantso "Smadz" Matsepe for elucidating and helping me to interpret elements of this encounter. For a more detailed discussion of the "bones" used by Tswana diviners and of Tswana divination, see Schapera and Comaroff: 57–58.

[5] Their entire second volume might be described as a detailed study of such routines and regimes.

aversion is the instruction regime rather than the source of power/knowledge itself, the Book.

This *ngaka*, like Mmahutu, must not be encumbered with missionary or Western scholarly baggage, for which the Bible is an integral and inseparable part of Christianity. In a long conversation characterised by misrecognitions, we must not imagine the Tlhaping saw what we are accustomed to seeing. As we have seen, and as we are reminded by Jean and John Comaroff, the missionary "had his Bible with him at the very first encounter, for while tinsel might catch the African's attention, his real gift was to be the word" (1991:192). True, but as the Comaroffs also note, "none of these objects was introduced into a void, and while they brought novel values into the Tswana world, they also acquired meanings different from those intended by their donors" (184).

While we have no indigenous detail on how the Tlhaping apprehended the Bible, my brief exegesis of these missionary texts indicates markers of interest. This was not the case with the Word of God! The *ngaka*, Mmahutu, Mothibi, and most of his people graciously welcomed travellers in their midst, but they consistently refused to be manipulated by the devices and desires of the missionaries "to instruct them." They were not interested in the Word of God. It would be many years before missionaries were allowed to come to Dithakong and many more before they were allowed "to instruct." In these very earliest encounters with the Bible, the Tlhaping appear to have made a distinction between this Book and the instruction of the missionaries; there are signs that the Bible (and other books) generated some interest, while it is absolutely clear from the missionary record that the proclamation of the Word was of no interest, at least not initially. As the contours of the colonial landscaped changed, so too did the Tlhaping's interests.

The Lens of Biblical Scholarship

Though not a common move, separating the reception of the Bible from the reception of missionary and colonial Christianity seems to be a reasonable move to make, and others beside me have made it, most notably Vincent Wimbush. In a series of articles Wimbush argues quite convincingly that the reception of the Bible among African slaves in America can and should be treated separately from the reception of Christianity (Wimbush, 1991; 1993). I have discussed Wimbush's work at some length elsewhere (82–86); here I allude to his work in order to observe that it is somewhat ironic that it is biblical scholars who insist on this kind of separation—the separation of the reception of the Bible from the reception of Christianity. As I observed above, other kinds of scholarly commentators on the colonial encounter tend not to distinguish between the Bible's place in indigenous people's transactions with the missionary/colonial enterprise and the place of Christianity. The Bible is subsumed and assumed by Christianity.

My argument here is similar, but with a twist of perspective, to that put forward by Paul Landau, when he argues that historians of religion have too readily subsumed indigenous practices into religious categories that make sense to European researchers generally and missionary Christianity in particular. Scholars of the postcolonial, often having thoroughly mastered the master's categories and concepts, cannot perhaps be expected to make distinctions that are not made in the master narrative. For as James Barr reminds us, the Bible is analytically, in the strict philosophical sense, bound up with being Christian (52). But why should the Tlhaping perceive the order of things as we do? My argument is that they did not (and do not).[6]

And this is why I applaud the conception of this collection of essays. In this volume we have the beginnings, perhaps, of a concerted attempt to treat the Bible's presence in the missionary/colonial/postcolonial milieu with analytical precision and from the indigenous perspective. That it has taken biblical scholars to formulate and propose the question that has generated this project is no accident. Biblical scholars, despite our historical alliance with Christianity, have developed a countertradition in which the Bible is treated in and of itself. This countertradition, ironically but appropriately, now turns and questions history, asking new questions of other (usually marginalised) interlocutors. But biblical scholars are not equipped to take up this task on their own, and this recognition too is incorporated into the design of this volume. We need to form alliances with those with other interests and resources. In particular, and in this respect the volume falls short of its promise, we need to hear the voices of those excluded not only from the missionary/colonial record but also from our present scholarly circles, the voices of those in colonial and postcolonial contexts who encounter the Bible as an object of strange and ambiguous power.

Signposts Noted

There are signs among the essays of what might be called a historical anthropology of the Bible within colonialism/postcolonialism. I am not sure that the term "historical anthropology" is the appropriate one, but by it I intend to acknowledge and conjure up the richly textured historical anthropology of mission among the Tswana, of whom the Tlhaping are one part, provided by Jean and John Comaroff and extensively cited above. This is

---

[6] The present place of the Bible among the Tlhaping cannot be discussed here, but there are signs that my bracket is not misplaced.

just the kind of account we need of the Bible, whatever we call it. And, as I have said, there are signs of this in the volume.

Roland Boer's essay delineates some of the elements of what he calls "explorer hermeneutics," and in so doing provides a preliminary mapping of the contours of the Bible's presence among and its permeation of early explorers of Australia, men (mostly) whose accounts in turn were to construct and constitute "Australia." Significantly, like many of the explorers and missionaries who were the vanguards of empire everywhere, they were not particularly trained in biblical studies. I say significantly, because given the astute and unrelenting scrutiny of travellers by indigenous people, how these travellers used the Bible may be profoundly important in our understanding of indigenous apprehensions of the Bible—the focus of my interests and the lens with which I am reviewing these essays. Boer provides, then, a considerable comparative resource in his account of explorer hermeneutics, enabling those of us in other contexts to trace lines of connection between early explorers, missionaries, and colonial agents from common source countries, and the forms of biblical interpretation that shaped them and which they embodied.

Of course, indigenous peoples did not only imitate their visitors' use of Bible; they also forged their own strategies and techniques for dealing with this object of strange power. While local appropriations are not the concern of Boer's essay, he is sensitive to the ways in which his explorers' own appropriation of the Bible is refashioned by the foreign landscape—quite literally. So, for example, Boer notes the repeated, almost obsessive, focus on water by the explorers. Their new context demands new appropriations of the Bible, and in this respect they foreshadow in their own practice that of those they have come to civilise and convert. Furthermore and further afield, attention to such similarities (despite massive differences) may give us insight crosscontextually into the remarkable interest in the Psalms, to take up Boer's example, as a resource for dealing with adversity found among these explorers in "Australia" and Yoruba Christians in Nigeria (Adamo, 1999; 2000).

The explorer emphasis on favourable and unfavourable comparisons between aboriginal culture and the Old Testament (as the explorers would have referred to it) is another marker of explorer hermeneutics that Boer draws attention to; here too indigenous appropriators of the Bible were to imitate these travellers' interpretative techniques, but to reverse their values where necessary, to assert their own dignity and cultural heritage and to deconstruct colonial Christianity (Ukpong).

Finally, Boer's emphasis on the colonial gaze, magnified as I have indicated by telescopes and directed by mirrors and compasses, deserves the attention it receives from his essay. Controlling as this gaze is, we must not forget that people like the Tlhaping and aboriginal "Australians" had their own mechanisms and methods of observation, and though power relations were to become damagingly skewed, in early encounters indigenous peoples often controlled the landscape. What they made of the Bible while in control, and what they made of it as they began to lose control, of their terrain is a question that requires more study.

Penny van Toorn's excellent essay provides a nuanced "against-the-grain" reading of missionary manuscripts, and in so doing exemplifies the kind of historical anthropology of the Bible I am advocating. Picking up the encounter after Boer's explorers, van Toorn documents the way in which the Bible and other related texts are "displaced, dismembered, torn away" from their "usual anchor points in English culture" (46). Again, the Psalms are accorded a special place in indigenous hands, as both textual and tactile forms. The Bible is manipulated first as material object and only later as verbal text. Her careful analysis of Aboriginal appropriations of "one of the white man's sacred instruments" (ibid.) resonates strongly with similar appropriations among the Tlhaping and other indigenous communities, like the Yoruba mentioned above, where the Bible is appropriated in various ways long before it becomes text.

A significant difference in this case is that the indigenous people were not given access to the Bible in their own languages; in most of Africa, translation into the vernacular was a priority. This difference calls for closer attention, and van Toorn's essay offers the kind of thick description that will bear the weight of comparison with other contexts, enabling us to understand the different trajectories the Bible takes when translated into local vernaculars and when not. The linkage many make between vernacular translations of the Bible and the rise of local nationalisms (see below) is but one concern that such comparisons would contribute to.

The agency of Aboriginals is strongly reflected in van Toorn's essay, a resounding reminder that power is not monolithic and that resistance to domination is as present in colonial transactions as the Bible, and the forms it takes just as complex. A particular strength of van Toorn's essay is that she tracks their agency in its historically diverse forms, from their appropriation and transformation of the Bible as a ritual object to their transactions with the Bible as text at the Wybalenna settlement on Flinders Island.

Besides the complexity of power relations, van Toorn's account of these early Aboriginal transactions with the Bible as text enumerates the many components that constitute such early encounters. For example, that for long periods of time only particular portions of the Bible are translated (in this case, Genesis 1–4); that the translations are often in only one of the vernacular languages (in this case, the language of the Ben Lomond people); that particular sectors of indigenous communities are targeted or select themselves as mediators between missionaries and their communities (in this case, teenage boys); that missionary control and surveillance of many of these components, though considerable, is not hegemonic (in this case, both Thomas Brune and Walter George Arthur manipulated the missionaries for their own ends); and that these early mediations of the Bible exhibit foundational neo-indigenous interpretative techniques (in this case, designating Psalm 23 as a protection psalm and using traditional oral strategies of interpretation to conjure [Smith] with the Bible in sermons).

Using the work of Mikhail Bakhtin and V. N. Vološinov to good effect, and not simply as an end in itself, van Toorn adds to the kind of work produced by the Comaroffs, providing a historical anthropology of mission and colonisation in the Tasmanian context, but one in which the Bible has not been subsumed.

Moving on, again somewhat historically, to those later periods when the Bible is now thoroughly enmeshed in colonial/postcolonial contexts, the question of the Bible's place in the rise of nationalisms has, as Amardeep Singh reminds us, "not been discussed sufficiently in postcolonial criticism to date" (134). Singh's interest is not really in the Bible, but in the role of religion more broadly, but his essay nevertheless probes "the mutual dependence of scriptural and secular images of the 'promised land' in [particular] diasporic nationalisms" (133). The diverse ways in which Scripture, a term Singh uses, is co-opted within literary works, carefully catalogued by Singh in James Joyce's *Ulysses*, serves as a powerful example of the Bible's indirect presence in the public realm. Paul James concurs, documenting how biblically derived iconography "crosses the divide from traditional polity to modern nation-state" (174); indeed, says James, "Evocation of the Bible has always played a role in nation formation and continues to do so even in these late-modern and postsacred times" (173). James's own contribution to the extensive literature on nation formation is to show how "nation formation involves *both* deep continuities and radical discontinuities with traditional (sacredly conceived) ways of life" (174). An important strand in both James's and Singh's analysis, footnoted in Singh's but elaborated in James's essay, is the recognition that vernacular translations of the Bible "marked a turning point in the process of nation formation" (176). In this respect, both Singh and James align their work with the trajectory established by early missionary Bible translation, a process which, according to Lamin Sanneh and Kwame Bediako is foundational for both the revitalisation of indigenous cultures initially demonised by missionaries and the rise of the nation-state.

Though they pick up the trajectory further on in its flight path, their work is an important contribution to our understanding of the place not only of the Bible as sacred object and symbolic content but also as printed word, "the central and most ambiguous early 'commodity' of print capitalism," in the words of James (ibid.).

Sanjay Seth's essay, while not focussing on the Bible independently of its location within missionary and colonial Christianity, provides a valuable account of the exchanges and slippages that took place as peoples in south India transacted with Christianity as artefact. Unlike in much of Africa (Sanneh), in India it was not the Old Testament but education that was seen as a *praeparatio evangelica,* and this despite the efforts of the Serampur missionaries in translating the Bible into Indian languages. How much this had to do with missionary/colonial strategy and how much with local culture and religion is a suggestive question that may enhance our understanding of the local ingredients that shape the Bible's receptions and appropriations.

After her useful introduction to how certain biblical images—Eden, exile, and the promised land—have constituted and permeated white settlement in Australia, Dorothy Jones analyses how a modern Australian author reengages these same images in her account of the lives of a family of post-World War II European migrants settled in Australia. As Jones notes, and as her essay demonstrates, these images "haunt" the Australian imagination and continue to shape Australian perceptions of the world. It is not enough to document and understand early encounters with the Bible as a historical curiosity; the Bible's presence has had and continues to have effects in postcolonial contexts. John Docker concurs, and the effect he is most disturbed by is the Bible's contribution to monotheism. Docker boldly offers postcolonial and contemporary cultural theory a far longer time frame for its "frame stories," stories that he finds "not only too determinedly secular but also blindly and contentedly recent-minded" (150). Monotheism, Docker contends, in both its Old Testament/Hebrew Bible and New Testament forms, represented by particular and predominant appropriations of Moses and Jesus respectively, is the fertile ground in which visions of prohibition, repudiation, separation, conquest, and colonisation grow. By taking us further back than we are wont to go in order to understand the Bible's presence in and complicity with colonisation, Docker destabilises the frames we are familiar with. In so doing, he makes a useful contribution to the kind of project I am calling for.

I conclude by coming back to my beginning, via the essay by Anna Johnston, who analyses the arrival of the Bible among Polynesian communities. She tracks the Bible, "a multifactorial signifier" (14), reading the records of the London Missionary Society against the grain, gesturing "at the ways in which Polynesians and others may have appropriated the Bible" (15). In so doing her essay is a remarkable rendering of the sort of historical anthropology of the Bible I am interested in. Her case study concentrates on the arrival of the Bible as text, and she emphasises the importance of the very early presence of the printing press and translation of the Bible into Polynesian languages. This careful account of the complexities of the translation process, of what historically happens after the Bible as *bola* (so to speak), is a considerable contribution to bringing the Bible as subsumed or even vanishing mediator into focus.

Johnston's close attention to the transaction that is translation adds weight to the work of others already mentioned on the importance of vernacular translation and corroborates those who argue that through the translation process the missionaries grip on the Bible is loosened (Bediako; Maluleke, 2000).

I found Johnston's analysis of the Bible's significance in the ideology of the London Missionary Society particularly insightful. As I have already argued, if we are to understand what indigenous peoples made of the Bible, we must try to understand how the Bible was presented by those who brought it. While I have argued against equating the Bible's reception by indigenous peoples with its place among those who presented it to them, the ways in which missionaries used the Bible, both publically and more privately, would have been closely observed for their potential for appropriation.

But having made this point, I want to reiterate my major concern, namely, that we do not assume that the others who encountered it in colonial contexts apprehended the Bible as those who b(r)ought it. Johnston, it seems to me, shares my concern, asking as she does in her conclusion the question "that has haunted this essay: How was the Bible ... received by indigenous people, despite (or because of) its overt imperialist overtones?" (36). Her own work provides the kind of thick description we need if we are to track the traces of this subsumed mediator. She draws in her final sentence on the anecdote told throughout Africa (and I have used the version familiar to me rather than hers), that "When the white man came to our country he had the Bible and we (blacks) had the land. The white man said to us 'let us pray.' After the prayer, the white man had the land and we had the Bible." While this is true, the question that remains, according to the South African Black theologian Tinyiko Maluleke, is: What does it mean to say that black people "have" the Bible? (1998:134) This question haunts Maluleke and many others; the usefulness of the essays in this volume is that they go some way to providing an answer.

WORKS CONSULTED

Adamo, David T(uesday)
    1999   "African Cultural Hermeneutics." Pp. 66–90 in *Vernacular Hermeneutics*. Ed. R. S. Sugirtharajah. Sheffield: Sheffield Academic Press.

    2000   "The Use of Psalms in African Indigenous Churches in Nigeria." Pp. 336–49 in *The Bible in Africa: Transactions, Trajectories and Trends*. Ed. Gerald O. West and Musa Dube. Leiden: Brill.

Barr, James
1980   *The Scope and Authority of the Bible.* London: SCM.

Bediako, Kwame
1995   *Christianity in Africa: The Renewal of a Non-Western Religion.* Edinburgh: Edinburgh University Press; Maryknoll, N.Y.: Orbis.

Burchell, William J.
1824   *Travels in the Interior of Southern Africa.* Vol. 2. London: Longman, Hurst, Rees, Orme, Brown & Green. (Repr. with a new introduction by A. Gordon-Brown. Cape Town: Struik, 1967.)

Campbell, John
1815   *Travels in South Africa: Undertaken at the Request of the Missionary Society.* 3d corrected ed. London: Black, Parry & Co. (Repr. Cape Town: Struik, 1974.)

Comaroff, Jean, and John L. Comaroff
1991   *Of Revelation and Revolution.* Vol. 1: *Christianity, Colonialism and Consciousness in South Africa.* Chicago: University of Chicago Press.

Comaroff, John L., and Jean Comaroff
1997   *Of Revelation and Revolution.* Vol. 2: *The Dialectics of Modernity on a South African Frontier.* Chicago: University of Chicago Press.

Landau, Paul (Stuart)
1995   *The Realm of the Word: Language, Gender, and Christianity in a Southern African Kingdom.* Portsmouth: Heinemann.

1999   "'Religion' and Christian Conversion in African History: A New Model." *Journal of Religious History* 23:8–30.

Maluleke, Tinyiko S.
1998   "African Traditional Religions in Christian Mission and Christian Scholarship: Reopening a Debate That Never Started." *Religion and Theology* 5:121–37.

2000   "The Bible among African Christians: A Missiological Perspective." Pp. 87–112 in *To Cast Fire upon the Earth: Bible and Mission Collaborating in Today's Multicultural Global Context.* Ed. T. Okure. Pietermaritzburg, South Africa: Cluster Publications.

Moffat, Robert
1842   *Missionary Labours and Scenes in Southern Africa.* London: John Snow. (Repr. New York: Johnson Reprint Corporation, 1969.)

Sanneh, Lamin
1989   *Translating the Message: The Missionary Impact on Culture.* Maryknoll, N.Y.: Orbis.

Schapera, I., and John L. Comaroff
1991   *The Tswana.* Rev. ed. London and New York: Kegan Paul International. (Orig. 1953)

Scott, James C.
   1990   *Domination and the Arts of Resistance: Hidden Transcipts.* New Haven and London: Yale University Press.

Smith, Theophus H.
   1994   *Conjuring Culture: Biblical Formations of Black America.* Oxford and New York: Oxford University Press.

Ukpong, Justin
   2000   "Developments in Biblical Interpretation in Africa: Historical and Hermeneutical Directions." *Journal of Theology for Southern Africa* 108:3–18.

West, Gerald O.
   1999   *The Academy of the Poor: Towards a Dialogical Reading of the Bible.* Sheffield: Sheffield Academic Press.

Wimbush, Vincent L.
   1991   "The Bible and African Americans: An Outline of an Interpretative History." Pp. 81–97 in *Stony the Road We Trod: African American Biblical Interpretation.* Ed. Cain Hope Felder. Minneapolis: Fortress.

   1993   "Reading Texts through Worlds, Worlds through Texts." *Semeia* 62:129–40.

Future Issues of *Semeia*

Titles are descriptive rather than final, and the order given here is not necessarily definitive.

Levinas and Biblical Studies
    Tamara Eskenazi, *Hebrew Union College*
    Gary A. Phillips, *University of the South*

"Yet with a Steady Beat":
U. S. Afrocentric Biblical Interpretation
    Randall C. Bailey, *Interdenominational Theological Center*

Northrop Frye and the Afterlife of the Word
    James M. Kee, *College of the Holy Cross*
    Adele Reinhartz, *Board Editor*

The Bible in Asian America
    Tat-siong Benny Liew, *Chicago Theological Seminary*
    Gale A. Yee, *Board Editor*

Semeia: An Experimental Journal for Biblical Criticism (ISSN 0095-571X) is published quarterly by the Society of Biblical Literature, 825 Houston Mill Road, Atlanta, GA 30329. Periodical postage paid at Atlanta, GA and at additional mailing offices. POSTMASTER: Send address changes to The Society of Biblical Literature, P.O. Box 2243, Williston, VT 05495-2243.

www.ingramcontent.com/pod-product-compliance
Lightning Source LLC
Chambersburg PA
CBHW031312150426
43191CB00005B/197